SOIL FERTILITY HANDBOOK

Publication 611

MINISTRY OF AGRICULTURE, FOOD AND RURAL AFFAIRS

Need technical and business information?

**Contact the Agricultural Information Contact Centre at
1-877-424-1300 or *ag.info.omafra@ontario.ca***

**Looking for field crop production
information on the Internet?**

www.ontario.ca/crops

It's one-stop shopping for factsheets, articles and photos
regarding the production and maintenance of field crops.

Ordering Information

For information, or to obtain copies of this or any other ministry publication, please:
Call 1-888-4-OMAFRA (1-888-422-2372) from within Ontario, 519-826-3700
from outside the province or OMAFRA's TTY line at 519-826-7402 for the hearing
impaired.

E-mail your request to *products.omafra@ontario.ca*, or visit OMAFRA's website at
www.omafra.gov.on.ca.

A complete listing of all OMAFRA products and services, and order forms, is
available on the website. Orders can be faxed to 519-826-3633 or mailed to
ServiceOntario, 1 Stone Road West, Guelph, ON N1G 4Y2.

Published by the Ministry of Agriculture, Food and Rural Affairs
© Queen's Printer for Ontario 2006
Toronto, Canada
ISBN 1-4249-2335-2 (Print)
01-07-5M

Aussi disponible en français.

Editor
Keith Reid, OMAFRA

Co-editors
Tom Bruulsema, International Plant Nutrition Institute; Dale Cowan, OABA; Christoph Kessel, OMAFRA; Dale Peters, OABA; Anne Verhallen, OMAFRA

Contributing Authors
OMAFRA — Doug Aspinall, Christine Brown, Barb Lovell, Michael Payne, Keith Reid, Maribeth Fitts, Anne Verhallen, Christoph Kessel, Donna Speranzini

University of Guelph — K.J. Janovicek, John Lauzon, Ivan O'Halloran, Laura Van Eerd

Tom Bruulsema, International Plant Nutrition Institute; Jean Cheval, Sylvite Sales; Dale Cowan, Agri-food Labs; Craig Drury, AAFC; Wayne Izumi, Stoller Chemical; Mark Janiec, Terratech Environmental; Tom Oloya, AAFC; Dale Peters, Stratford Agri-Analysis; Gary Roberts, Stratford Agri-Analysis; John Rowsell, NLARS (University of Guelph); Tony Vyn, University of Guelph; Jerry Winnicki, Clark Agri-Service Inc.; Laura Young-Neubrand, Cargill Limited

Acknowledgements
The authors would like to thank the following for their efforts in reviewing this publication and making suggestions for improvement: Jim Brimner, Stratford Agri Analysis; Ian McDonald, Adam Hayes, OMAFRA; Greg Patterson, A&L Canada Labs; Burns Stephens, Norfolk Co-op; Ed Tomecek. Photo credits: Janice LeBoeuf, Keith Reid and Elaine Roddy, OMAFRA.

The authors gratefully acknowledge the Canadian National Atmospheric Chemistry (NAtChem) Database and its data contributing agencies/ organizations for the provision of the 1990–1994 and 1996–2000 mean wet deposition maps used in this publication. The agencies/organizations responsible for data contributions to the NAtChem Database include Environment Canada, the provinces of Ontario, Québec, New Brunswick, Nova Scotia and Newfoundland, the United States Environmental Protection Agency and the United States National Atmospheric Deposition Program/ National Trends Network.

TABLE OF CONTENTS

TABLES AND FIGURES

1 SAMPLING

Sampling soil

Farmers sample soil to:
- determine fertilizer and lime requirements
- diagnose problem areas
- monitor soil fertility levels

Sample collection

Soil can be sampled at any convenient time but it is done primarily in the fall after harvest. This leaves enough time to get the analysis back from the laboratory and make plans for next season. For consistency, it's a good idea to sample soils at about the same time each year and following the same crops in the rotation.

Sampling every three years is enough for most soils. You may need to sample sandy soils more frequently, as nutrient levels may change rapidly. This also applies with crops that remove large quantities of potassium such as tomatoes, silage corn and alfalfa. You can plan to sample one third of your fields each year so that the whole farm is done once every three years. Where a particular fertility problem occurs, you should sample the area more frequently. Sample the good areas of the field separately from the poor areas.

You can choose to take a composite sample or several point samples. Composite samples represent the fertility of an entire field at lower cost. The number of samples required to characterize a field depends on the topography and variability of soils within the field, the type of farm and the number and type of crops grown.

Taking samples

For standard Ontario fertility soil tests, soil cores are pulled from a depth of 15 cm, as this will reflect the fertility level of the soil where the bulk of most crop root systems are. Samples taken from a more shallow depth will over estimate the nutrient levels while deeper samples may under estimate them.

In fields containing more than one soil type, sample each type individually. Sample problem areas separately. Avoid sampling in:
- areas close to gravel or paved roads, since road dust will influence the soil test values
- dead furrows, on highly eroded knolls, or where organic waste or lime has been piled, since samples will not be representative of the field

If you are interested specifically in any of these areas, take a separate sample.

Use stainless steel

Use a commercial soil probe or auger that is stainless steel rather than galvanized. Pails should be clean and made of plastic or non-

> **Note:** It is impossible to split a sample of moist soil into two identical sub-samples without special equipment. Much of the variation in results between samples sent to different labs occurs because the samples really are different.

galvanized metal, especially if you are sampling for micronutrients. This will avoid contamination of the sample. Labs prefer to work with a full sample box, so collect enough soil to get a composite sample that will fill the box. See Figure 1-1.

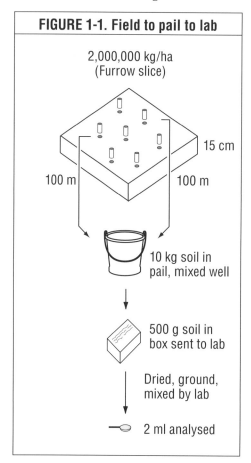

FIGURE 1-1. Field to pail to lab

2,000,000 kg/ha
(Furrow slice)

15 cm

100 m   100 m

10 kg soil in pail, mixed well

500 g soil in box sent to lab

Dried, ground, mixed by lab

2 ml analysed

Mix

Mix cores together thoroughly in the pail, crushing clods and removing stones and crop residue. Fill the sample box or bag with a representative sample from the soil. Careful sampling and mixing is essential to ensure the accuracy of the composite sample.

Keeping records

Label all soil samples for the lab. Number them in such a way that you can later relate the analysis to a particular field. Keep a record for yourself of the samples you have taken and where they were taken on the farm. See Figure 1-3.

Also, keep records on the crops grown in each field, fertilizer applied, weather conditions and final yields. Put this information together with the soil sample analyses. These records will help you detect trends from year to year, make management decisions and pinpoint trouble spots.

A number of software systems are available to assist in organizing crop production information and most crop consultants offer record keeping as part of their service. With the massive increase in the amount of data generated by combine yield monitors and intensive soil sampling, computerized record keeping is essential.

Exception – sampling for nitrate

Soil nitrate is not included in a regular soil test. The nitrogen recommendations included on most soil test reports are based on your crop plans.

Timing of nitrate samples is critical, as soil nitrate levels will vary throughout the year because of leaching and microbial tie-up. You can take samples at planting time for corn or barley or before side-dressing corn. The sample at planting time is slightly more accurate in the absence of manure or legumes but the sample at side-dressing will detect more of the nitrate from organic sources. The choice of sampling before planting or side-dressing depends on your time rather than on differences in accuracy.

Nitrate samples must be taken to a greater depth, usually 30 cm. There is calibration for both 30 and 60 cm sampling depths. Select the depth and remain consistent across the field. Sampling pattern across a field and mixing procedure are the same as any other soil sample.

You must handle the soils with care. They should be stored at temperatures below 4°C until they are extracted. Soil storage at 4°C for periods ranging from one to seven days was compared to either freezing or air-drying the soil samples before extraction, in a recent study involving 66 soils from Ontario (Oloya et al. 2007). When analyzed one day after sampling, about 70% of the inorganic nitrogen was in the nitrate form (NO_3-N) and the remaining 30% was ammonium (NH_4-N). As the soils were stored moist at 4°C for longer periods, ammonium was slowly converted to nitrate through the nitrification process. See Fig 1-2. This conversion would have been even greater if the soils were stored at room temperature. Freezing was found to increase soil ammonium levels by 22% and air-drying increased soil ammonium levels by 37%. Soil nitrate levels were also increased but to a lesser extent. Hence freezing or air-drying is not recommended, especially when the ammonium data are considered. Instead, it is recommended the soils be stored at 4°C and extracted field moist within four days of sampling.

Note: Do not freeze or air-dry the sample if it is going to be analyzed for ammonium content.

FIGURE 1-2. Impact of sample handling on soil mineral N content

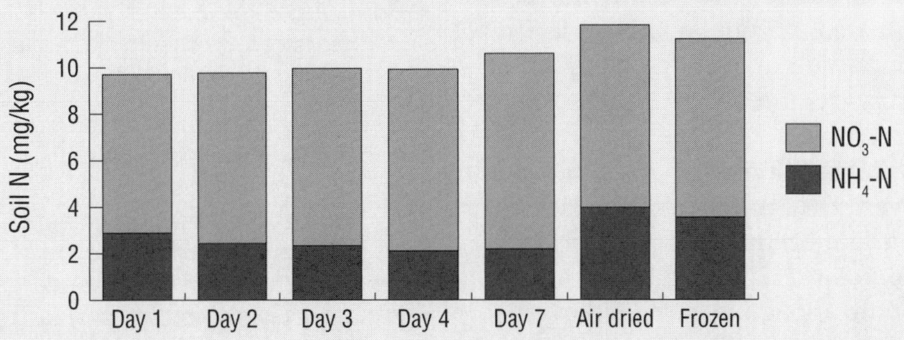

Oloya, T.O., Drury, C.F. and K. Reid. 2007.

FIGURE 1-3. Example field crop records

DATE/TIME	FIELD NAME/#	OPERATION	DETAILS

Example Codes: PL=plant, SP= spray, SC=scouting, SA=sampling, TI=Tillage, HV=harvest, M=manure application, FE=fertilizer application, VI=visual inspection

Soil variability

Soil varies across wide areas of the landscape and also within the space of a few centimetres. This variability can be important for crop growth, sampling strategies and fertilizer application. Significant variation can exist within the rooting zone of a plant. However, this may have no effect on its growth since the roots proliferate in the zones of optimum fertility.

Large or rapid variations in soil fertility over a bigger area can affect crop growth, but it may not be practical to manage this. In an area of 18 m by 30 m, nutrient content may vary greatly but it is smaller than the area covered by one pass of the spreader. In other words, it is smaller than the minimum management area. In general, this variation is important in deciding the number of cores required for a representative sample.

While soil type has an influence on variation, the over-riding factor is management, particularly the amount and type of fertilizer and manure applied to each field over the years. It is difficult to predict what nutrients might be limiting yield in a particular field without a soil test.

The goal of a soil sampling program is to predict the most profitable rate of fertilizer for the field or part of a field. To design a good program, you must know the potential for economic return to management, the probable variability within each field and the resources available.

What causes soil to vary?

Variability stems from soil forming factors (parent material, topography, biological activity, climate and time) as well as from tillage and fertilization, and crop residues.

Tillage-induced variation is created when the mouldboard plough and other implements pull soil off the tops of knolls and deposit it downslope. This creates areas on the knolls of low organic matter, low fertility and generally higher pH.

Several years of applying fertilizer and manure unevenly may also create variability in soil fertility. The consolidation of small fields into larger ones makes the variation greater. When crop residues are left unevenly distributed, they also contribute to variable soil fertility.

Sampling strategies

Composite samples

The most common strategy is to take one composite sample from each field. See Figure 1-4. Usually, the maximum field size for a composite sample is 10 ha. The number of cores in each composite sample should be at least 20, no matter how small the area, to average out small-scale variations. This strategy is appropriate where the value of the crop is low or there is low potential for return to variable fertilization, where there is little variation in soil fertility or where the entire field is high enough in fertility that no response to fertilizer is expected.

In the case of very low soil test levels from a field, it is generally safe to assume that the entire field will respond to fertilization. If the test levels of the composite sample are very high, it is likely that, while there will be considerable variation, the whole field will be high enough so that even the lowest-testing areas will not likely respond to added fertilizer.

Sub-samples

In fields with soil tests in the medium to high range, there is more potential for response to variable rate fertilizer application. The challenge is to find an inexpensive way to identify the areas that are responsive.

The most common method of sub-sampling fields is to take uniformly spaced samples from within the field and use geo-statistical software to predict the values between the samples. This approach assumes that the samples adequately describe the average value at the point where they were taken and that the samples are taken close enough together to produce an accurate picture of the pattern of variability. A growing practice is sampling by management unit. This involves taking a composite sample from areas of the field that can be managed separately.

Crop value, not the amount of variability, has been the driving force in dictating sampling intensity. A 1 ha grid has become quite common in Ontario, with some high value crops sampled more intensively. We don't yet know what the most appropriate sampling intensity is in all situations.

Georeferencing

Georeferencing, or systematic soil sampling, uses global positioning system (GPS) technology and geographic information system (GIS) techniques to collect soil sample data and present it in map form. See Figure 1-5.

This technique has been called grid sampling. The most common spacing between sample sites has been 1 ha. Although this data may

---

Note: For a more complete discussion of the development of Ontario's soils, see the OMAFRA/Agriculture and Agri-Food Canada booklet, *Best Management Practices – Soil Management*.

not fully represent all the detail in a given field, management zones may become evident when the data is combined with other data such as yield maps or topographic maps.

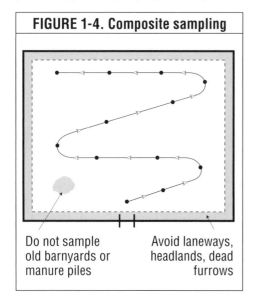

FIGURE 1-4. Composite sampling

Do not sample old barnyards or manure piles

Avoid laneways, headlands, dead furrows

A common practice is to create a field boundary with GPS and mapping software. A grid pattern is superimposed on the map to serve as a guide for sample collection. Each sample point is logged. The evenly spaced sample points allow a degree of statistical validity.

After lab analysis, the nutrient values from each sample are merged with the map data, using GIS software. Comparing the information from a 1 ha sampling scheme to that of composite sampling on a 40 ha field would give 40 sample values versus a typical composite plan of four. Having 10 times more data represented in map form heightens the awareness of the spatial variability of nutrients, which may affect management decisions.

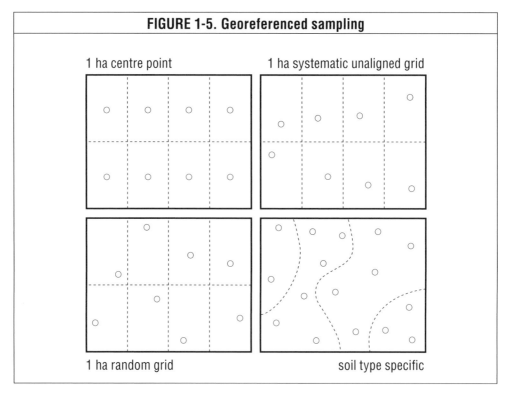

FIGURE 1-5. Georeferenced sampling

1 ha centre point

1 ha systematic unaligned grid

1 ha random grid

soil type specific

Special sampling conditions

No-till

Fertilizer recommendations are based on the nutrient content of the top 15 cm of soil. Therefore, sampling depth for nutrients is the same in reduced tillage systems as in conventional tillage. Nutrient stratification is sometimes suggested under no-tillage systems. Consult Chapter 6 page 125 for further information.

The exception to this is soil pH. Where nitrogen is surface-applied in a no-till system, a shallow layer of acidic soil may develop. A separate, shallow sample (5 cm) can be taken to check for this. Note: Adjust for the shallow depth of sample when using the liming recommendations in Chapter 4 page 92.

Zone-till, strip-till, ridge-till, and injected manure

Fields with zone-till, strip-till, ridge-till and banded fertilizer or injected manure pose extra challenges because nutrient additions are concentrated in parts of the field. The best strategy for sampling under these conditions is to take twice as many soil cores as indicated above. This will increase the randomization of the sampling, helping to ensure a better sample.

Sampling for problem diagnosis

Nutrient deficiencies may be suspected as a cause of reduced crop growth in specific areas within the field. These areas should be sampled separately, along with a sample from the field area with normal growth. Be sure to take at least 8–10 cores for each composite sample, to ensure the sample is representative of the area.

For further information on problem diagnosis using soil samples, see page 12.

Sampling plant tissue

Farmers sample plant tissue for:
- perennial tree fruit and grape crops, to determine fertilizer recommendations
- annual crops, to diagnose fertility problems, particularly micronutrient deficiencies

Tree fruit and grapes

Take tissue samples from fruit trees between July 15 and 31. Take samples of grape petioles between September 1 and 15. These dates correspond to standard nutrient levels of mature leaves, against which your tissue samples will be compared in the lab.

Sample each variety and block of fruit trees separately. Collect at least 100 leaves for each sample. The best way to get a representative sample is to take five leaves each from 20 trees. Do not combine healthy and unhealthy leaves. See Figure 1-6.

To sample grape vines, select only the stems (petioles) of mature leaves. Keep varieties and blocks of different ages separate. Ideally, collect stems from a number of different rows in a block. Collect at least 100 stems for each sample. For Vinifera and French hybrid varieties, collect 150 petioles.

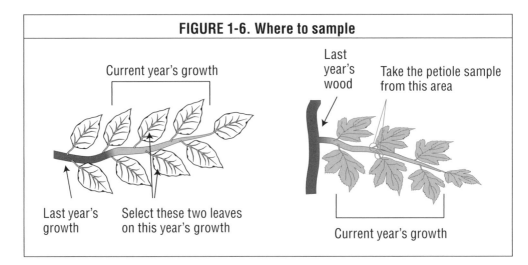

FIGURE 1-6. Where to sample

Current year's growth

Last year's growth

Select these two leaves on this year's growth

Last year's wood

Take the petiole sample from this area

Current year's growth

Field grown crops

Take samples from at least 50 plants collected randomly from across the field. Keep in mind the lab needs at least a 250 g fresh weight sample.

Use the chart in Table 1-1. *Recommended timing and plant part for tissue sampling*, to find the right time to sample, as you want your samples to be comparable to the standard values. More detailed sampling times are available for many of the vegetable crops. Consult a current edition of OMAFRA Publication 363 *Vegetable Production Recommendations*.

The most common errors in collecting plant tissue samples are:
- not collecting enough material
- collecting chlorotic or dead tissue or insect damaged leaves
- collecting plant tissue contaminated with soil
- shipping the sample in plastic bags

Do not sample tissue to which foliar fertilizers have been applied.

Sampling outside recommended times

You may have to sample outside the recommended times to diagnose problems in the field. In this case, the nutrient contents will not correspond to the values at the standard times. You will have to compare healthy and affected areas. For further information on problem diagnosis using tissue samples, see page 12.

Shipping

Put leaf or petiole samples into paper bags, not plastic or they will sweat and rot. Label each bag so that you will be able to relate the analysis to the specific block in the orchard.

Keeping records

Keep records of each block sampled, including variety and year. Keep the analysis of each block with the records of fertilizer applied, weather conditions and final yields. This will help determine trends in fertility levels.

TABLE 1-1. Recommended timing and plant parts for tissue sampling		
	Timing	Plant part
Corn	3–5 leaf stage	whole plant (zinc and phosphorus only)
	silking	middle third of ear leaf
Soybeans	first flowering	top fully developed leaf (3 leaflets + stem)
Cereals	at heading	top 2 leaves
Forages	late bud	entire above ground portion
Edible beans	first flowering	top fully developed leaf (3 leaflets + stem)
Potatoes	early, mid or late season	petiole of 4th leaf from tip
Tomatoes	early bloom	petiole of 4th leaf from tip
Broccoli, cauliflower	start of head formation	midrib of young, mature leaf
Cabbages	at heading	midrib of wrapper leaf
Carrots	mid-growth	petiole of young, mature leaf
Celery	mid-growth	petiole of newest elongated leaf
Lettuce	at heading	midrib of wrapper leaf
Onions	minimum 3 times per season	tallest leaf
Spinach	mid-growth	petiole of young, mature leaf
Sugar beets	12 weeks	youngest mature leaf
Tree fruits	last two weeks of July	fully expanded leaves from mid-point of current year's growth
Blueberries	mid August	fully expanded mature leaves, including petioles
Grapes	September 1–15	petioles (leaf stalks) from leaf opposite bunch
Raspberries	recently matured	fully expanded leaves
Strawberries	late June for fruiting, mid August for non fruiting plantings	fully expanded recently matured leaflets only (discard petiole)
Tobacco	at topping	10th leaf from top

Sampling manure

Farmers sample manure to:
- determine, in advance, the amount and kind of nutrients to be applied
- help determine requirements for additional nutrients

Sampling liquid manure

For liquid manure, take a sample each time the storage is emptied until a trend becomes evident. Manure applied from a storage emptied in spring will be different from the manure applied from the same storage emptied in late summer.

Agitate the storage completely. In a plastic pail collect samples from various depths of the storage as it is being emptied. Mix 10 to 20 of these samples thoroughly and transfer a portion to a plastic jar. The jar should only be half full to avoid gas build-up and explosion. Seal it tightly and put it in a plastic bag that is securely tied. Store the sample in a cool place until shipping.

Sampling solid manure

For solid manure, take a sample every time the storage is emptied until a trend becomes evident. Then you can sample every few years or when you make a major change in manure source or in management. These can include changes to ration, bedding or storage methods.

Solid manure is more difficult to sample randomly. On clean cement or plywood, take samples (a forkful) of manure from various loads leaving the pile or from various parts of the pile. Chop the manure with a shovel or fork and mix the samples together as thoroughly as possible. Divide the manure into 4 portions and discard 3.

Continue mixing and dividing the manure until you can fill a plastic jar or shipping container — about half a litre.

Place the tightly covered sample in a plastic bag and store it in a cool place until shipping.

> Ship manure samples early in the week so that they reach the lab before the weekend.

Manure varies from farm to farm

Several factors affect the quantity of nutrients in manure. Some classes of livestock have higher manure nutrient contents. For example, poultry manure usually has a higher value for all nutrients than dairy manure. Within the poultry category, broiler manure is usually higher in nutrient value, especially phosphorus and potassium, than manure from laying hens.

The nutrient content of manure usually reflects the type of ration being fed to the livestock. Thus, manure from young animals being fed a concentrated ration has a higher nutrient content than livestock fed a lower quality feed. Properly balanced rations give optimum performance with the least throughput into the manure.

The amount and type of bedding affects the concentration of nutrients in the manure (dilution) and may influence the nitrogen available for a crop. Wood chips or wood shavings have a higher carbon-to-nitrogen ratio (500:1) than grain straw (80:1). The higher the carbon-to-nitrogen ratio, the more nitrogen can be tied up while the carbon compounds are being broken down, affecting the amount of nitrogen available.

Added liquids from any source dilute the nutrient content of the manure. A dairy manure with added milkhouse washwater and yard runoff needs a much higher application rate for similar nutrients than, for example, hog manure from a barn with wet-dry feeders.

Losses from storage can have a large impact on the nutrient content of manure. Runoff from a solid manure pile can carry away a significant portion of the nitrogen and potassium, while most of the phosphorus remains bound in solid forms. This is not only an environmental risk but a waste of resources.

Sampling to diagnose deficiencies and toxicities in the field

Explaining trouble spots within a crop requires an open mind and examination of all the information available. When scouting a field for problems check:

- soil for differences in structure, texture, horizons, compaction and the standard soil fertility analysis
- plants for growth stages, varieties, planting dates, planting depths, tissue colours for deficiencies and disease, root development
- for pests like weeds, insects, disease and pest control effects

Then do an overview of the crops in the area. Look at a circle of at least one concession to see if the problem is specific to one field or general.

Do an overview of the entire field before moving to the specific site. Compare the good to the poor if you can. Look for patterns that can help identify the causes of poor growth, such as:

- **strips or rectangular patterns**. These suggest application problems, particularly if they are repeated across the field.
- **vector driven diseases**. Barley yellow dwarf, for instance, can be distributed by insects or sometimes floats in on the prevailing wind leaving a pattern much the same as snow drifting across a field. If the area in the shadowed side of trees is unaffected, that's an indication of something being vector-driven.
- **the impact of wheel tracks**. These can be positive or negative. Normally, wheel tracks cause compaction and poor growth. Generally, areas can be measured and compared to the wheel spacing from weight bearing wheels on farm equipment. However, on occasion, slight packing from wheel traffic may improve seed to soil contact resulting in earlier emergence, particularly on very loose soils.

Patterns can be difficult to see if they appear and disappear. Sometimes the problems are not severe but if soil or weather conditions within a field change just a little, the problem may manifest itself. For example, soybean cyst nematode may not show symptoms in a field for years although the populations are gradually building. It may finally give rise to typical symptoms in sections of the field where there is another stress such as compaction.

Look at crop production records for general trends in yield or quality. Whether a problem manifests in all crops in the rotation, or only one, can provide hints about the cause of the problem.

Collecting soil samples for problem diagnosis

Where soil fertility is suspected as the cause of reduced crop growth or yield in part of the field, it is important to sample these areas individually to confirm your diagnosis. Sample nearby good areas to compare with the problem areas. Nutrient deficiencies in plants may either be due to inadequate concentration of nutrients in the soil or inability of the plant to access the nutrients due to restricted root volumes. Any problem diagnosis should consider both these factors.

Keep a detailed record of the location of problem spots. Continue sampling problem areas every year to every other year until the fertility levels are adequate.

Collecting tissue samples for problem diagnosis

Tissue samples can be valuable for the confirmation of nutrient deficiencies in plants, particularly for micronutrients. Follow proper sampling technique, as described earlier, and be sure to collect a large enough volume of plant tissue that the analysis can be completed. Sample both normal growth and affected areas. Do not sample dead plants but those from border areas. See Figure 1-7. Take soil samples from the same areas to check pH and nutrient status.

You may have to sample outside the recommended times to get a diagnosis. In this case, the nutrient contents will not correspond to the values at the standard times. You will have to compare healthy and affected areas. Critical values for tissue concentration may be misleading in any case, because the concentration of nutrients in unhealthy plants may be high simply because there is not enough tissue to dilute the nutrients.

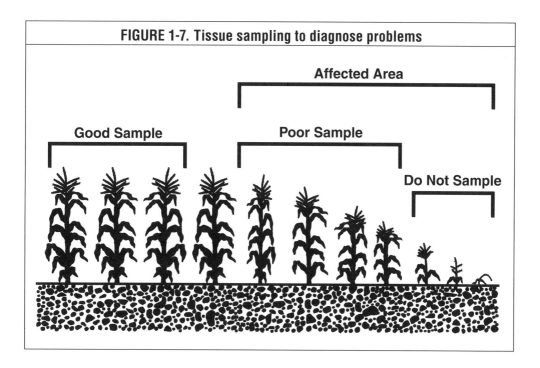

FIGURE 1-7. Tissue sampling to diagnose problems

Affected Area

Good Sample

Poor Sample

Do Not Sample

References

Oloya, T.O., Drury, C.F. and K. Reid. 2007. *Effect of soil storage on soil extractable ammonium and nitrate levels.* Canadian Journal of Soil Science (in review).

Potash & Phosphate Institute, 2003. *Soil Fertility Manual.* PPI/PPIC, Norcross, GA 30092-2837 USA.

Rehm, George W., Antonio Mallarino, Keith Reid, Dave Franzen, John Lamb, 2002. *Soil Sampling for Variable Rate Fertilizer and Lime Application.* NCR-13 Committee, available from University of Minnesota (*www.extension.umn. edu/distribution/cropsystems/DC7647.html*).

2 SOIL, PLANT TISSUE AND MANURE ANALYSIS

Profitable crop production depends on applying enough nutrients to each field to meet the requirements of the crop while taking full advantage of the elements already present in the soil. Since soils vary widely in their fertility levels, so does the amount of nutrients required. Soil and plant analysis are tools used to predict the optimum fertilizer rates for a specific crop in a specific field.

Soil analyses

Handling and preparation

When samples arrive, lab employees:
- check submission forms and samples to make sure they match
- make sure client names, sample IDs and requests are clear
- attach ID to the samples and submission forms
- prepare samples for the drying oven by opening the boxes or bags and placing them on drying racks
- put samples in an oven at 35°C (95°F) until dry (1–5 days). (Nitrate samples should be analyzed without drying)
- grind dry samples to pass 2 mm sieve, removing stones and crop residue
- move samples to the lab where sub-samples are analyzed

What's reported in a soil test

There are variations between labs and between analytical packages within labs as to exactly what is included in a soil test. There is even more variation in how the report is structured, so you may need to read the headings carefully to find the relevant information. Some analyses however, are common to almost every soil test report.

Soil pH is included in almost all soil tests. Although it is not a nutrient, soil acidity or alkalinity has a great influence on the availability of nutrients and on the growth of crops. The buffer pH will also be reported for acid soils to determine the lime requirement.

The main nutrient analyses reported are phosphorus, potassium and magnesium. These represent the nutrients, aside from nitrogen, most commonly applied as fertilizer. Some labs include an analysis for calcium. Nitrate nitrogen analysis is performed on a separate soil sample taken to a greater depth.

Micronutrient tests are not performed as frequently but are becoming more popular. Zinc and manganese have tests that are well calibrated with crop requirements and these are performed almost routinely. Other micronutrients (copper, iron, boron) are not well calibrated but some reports include them. Sulphur tests are rarely done

Soil tests help	Plant tissue tests help
determine fertilizer requirements	determine fertilizer requirements for perennial fruit crops
determine soil pH and lime requirements	diagnose nutrient deficiencies
diagnose crop production problems	diagnose nutrient toxicities
determine suitability for biosolids application	validate fertilizer programs
determine suitability for specific herbicides	

in Ontario, although they are common in western Canada.

More labs are routinely analyzing for organic matter. It is often used as an indicator of soil quality and also tied to herbicide recommendations. Soils where excess salts are suspected can be analyzed for electrical conductivity. Table 2-1. *Information found on a soil test report*, shows more detail on what is included in a typical soil test report.

How the numbers are reported

Soil test results are expressed in many ways, particularly if you deal with labs from outside Ontario. Most Ontario labs express results as milligrams per litre of soil (mg/L), that is, the weight of nutrient extracted from a volume of soil. This is close in value to the weight-by-weight measure of milligrams per kilogram of soil (mg/kg), which is equivalent to parts per million (ppm).

Some labs, particularly in the United States, express soil test results as pounds per acre of available nutrient, which is confusing since the soil test results don't reflect a physical quantity. An acre-furrow slice weighs about 2 million pounds. The results can be converted back to parts per million by dividing by 2. For example, if a soil test phosphorus is 120 lb/ac, divide by 2 to get 60 ppm. Quebec results are expressed as kg/ha.

(kg/ha × 0.455 = ppm)

It is also important to know the extractants that have been used to perform the soil test.

TABLE 2-1. Information found on a Soil Test Report

General Information

Sample Number	This is provided by the grower so he/she can relate the sample results to a particular field.
Lab Number	This is assigned by the lab, to track the sample through the various analytical steps.

Analytical Values

Soil pH	Every report should include soil pH, measured in a soil-water paste.
Buffer pH	Buffer pH is only measured on acid soils (normally where soil pH < 6.0).
Phosphorus	Ontario accredited soil tests must include the results from the sodium bicarbonate extraction (Olsen method). Some labs will also include results from Mehlich or Bray extractions. The method, and the units, should always be shown.
Potassium, Magnesium (Calcium, Sodium)	The cations are measured in an ammonium acetate extract, with the results reported as mg/litre of soil. Calcium and sodium are sometimes also reported.
Nitrate-N	This is not part of a regular soil test, since the interpretation of results is only valid for a deeper sample taken at planting or pre-side-dress time.
Sulphur	This optional test has not been calibrated. It should be used on deeper samples, similar to nitrate.
Micronutrients	Mn and Zn are the only micronutrients with an Ontario accredited test. The other micronutrients may have reported values but Ontario research has not shown reliable correlation to plant availability.
Organic Matter	This is an optional test. Note carefully whether the result is for organic matter or organic carbon.
Conductivity	This optional test indicates the presence of excessive salts in the soil.

Ratings for soil test values are based on the soil test result and the crop to be grown.

Derived Values

Zinc and Manganese Index	These are calculated from the analytical result and the soil pH.
Cation Exchange Capacity and Base Saturation %	These numbers are calculated from the soil pH and analytical results for K, Mg, and Ca. They may be skewed in high pH soils by the presence of free lime. Ontario fertilizer recommendations are not affected by CEC or Base Saturation.

Nutrient Recommendations

Fertilizer and Lime Recommendations	These will only be printed if information about the crop to be grown has been provided. The analytical results can be used to determine nutrient requirements for specific crops from tables in the appropriate production recommendations.
Adjustments to Fertilizer Recommendations	Adjustments for manure application or for a previous legume crop will be included in the fertilizer recommendations, if the information is provided.
Notes and Warnings	Some reports will include additional information based on the crop and soil test data.

Extractants

Analyzing soils to determine fertilizer requirements is complicated because we try to estimate how much nutrient is available from a specific soil to a wide variety of crop plants throughout the entire growing season. This would be simple if all the nutrients were wholly available for plant uptake or if there were only one method by which plants took up nutrients. However, soil is an extremely complex medium with a wide variety of physical, chemical and biological interactions occurring simultaneously. The interactions at the soil-root interface are even more complex and less well understood.

An example of this complexity is phosphorus. The most common chemical form of phosphorus in the soil is phosphate. In neutral to alkaline soils phosphate will combine with calcium. In neutral to acid soils it will bind to iron or aluminum. Phosphate also reacts with various clay minerals or organic compounds to form complex combinations and it may be present in the organic fraction of the soil or the soil biomass. All these forms are available to a greater or lesser degree to plants through a variety of processes, which we try to measure with a single, rapid chemical test.

Every chemical analysis has two steps. The compound being analyzed is converted to a form that can be measured. Then this material is analyzed. Because we estimate only the available portion of the nutrient in the soil, the first step differs from a normal chemical analysis. First, the soil is treated with an extractant to remove a portion of the nutrient that is related to the amount available to plants. This extract is then analyzed to determine the amount of nutrient that was extracted.

Choosing an extractant

To be useful in predicting crop needs, an extractant must provide the best possible estimate of the amount of additional nutrient needed for optimum crop yields. This is complicated to measure so the assessment of extractants is more commonly made by measuring how well the extractant estimates the nutrients available to plants in the range of soils tested in the lab or in a region. The extractant must also be relatively inexpensive and easy to use, involve as few toxic or corrosive chemicals as possible and use procedures that are reproducible from lab to lab.

No extractant pulls out exactly the fraction available to plants. Each has strengths and weaknesses specific to various soils. The choice of an extractant should be governed by how appropriate it is to the soils in question and to the availability of data relating it to crop response. See Chapter 6 for more details.

First was water

The first extractant used for soil testing was water. This removed only the portion of nutrient present in the soil solution. While this fraction is immediately available to plants, it is only a tiny part of the total available nutrient in the soil. It is not well related to the total nutrient supply, since soils vary tremendously in the nutrient reserve they hold.

Researchers had noted that plant roots excrete weak acids from their surfaces so the next step was to experiment with acid solutions. From there, the range and variety of extractants has proliferated as researchers seek better and more appropriate extractants for a wide range of soil conditions. These extractants are often named for the scientist who developed it or the main ingredient in the extracting solution.

Regionally specific

The choice of an extractant is specific to each region, since the most appropriate extractant will depend to a large extent on the soils of that region.

The first step in determining an appropriate extractant or soil test method is to collect samples of a wide range of soils from across the region and then to grow plants in each soil. These plants are harvested, weighed and analyzed to find the amount of nutrient taken up by the plants from the different soils. Different extractants are used to remove the nutrients from the soils and the extracts are analyzed. The final step compares the results of the extractions with the amount taken up by the plants, which is the measure of the nutrient supplying capacity of the soil. The extractant chosen for a region is normally the one with the highest correlation (agreement) to the plant uptake.

Soil test extractants for phosphorus can be broadly divided into acidic and alkaline solutions. The acidic solutions (Bray and Mehlich) are generally used in areas where the soils are predominantly acid. In alkaline soils, these extractants underestimate the amount of available phosphorus because the acid is partly neutralized by the free lime in the soil. See Table 2-2.

The alkaline extractants (sodium bicarbonate, ammonium bicarbonate) give more consistent results over a wide range of soil pH.

TABLE 2-2. Correlation of extractable P with P uptake in controlled greenhouse conditions				
Extractant	All soils (88 soils) correlation (r^2)*	pH>7.0 (46 soils)	pH 6.1–7.0 (30 soils)	pH<6.1 (12 soils)
Sodium bicarbonate	0.74	0.79	0.64	0.87
Ammonium bicarbonate	0.73	0.71	0.63	0.95
Bray-Kurtz P1	0.54	0.52	0.33	0.73
Bray-Kurtz P2	0.65	0.60	0.40	0.90
Mehlich III	0.66	0.57	0.40	0.93

* An r^2 of 1.00 is complete agreement.

Source: T.E. Bates, "Prediction of phosphorus availability from 88 Ontario soils using five phosphorus soil tests," Communication in Soil Science Plant Analysis 21 (1990): 1009-1023.

Potassium, calcium and magnesium are extracted using another similar cation, usually ammonium, to remove them from the cation exchange complex. Micronutrients may be extracted using a chelating agent or weak acid to remove them from the soil.

Following the choice of extractant, field trials are carried out to determine the optimum fertilizer application for each soil test level with different crops. These calibrations are unique to the extractant and are expensive. Inevitably, there is resistance to changing the soil test extractant unless an alternative method has a large advantage.

Extractant results are not interchangeable

Different extractants will often give widely different values from the same soil. The amount of phosphorus extracted by a sodium bicarbonate solution, for example, may be one half or less of that extracted by a Bray P1 extractant. In the proper conditions, however, both could provide an index of phosphorus availability to crops. Problems arise if someone uses the numbers from one test with fertilizer recommendation tables developed for a different test.

The results from different extractants are not related perfectly to one another. So, while there is a trend that as the soil test level for one extractant increases, the others increase as well, there are exceptions. Even where the extractants increase consistently, the relationship between extractants is often different at low soil test values than at high soil test values. For this reason, you should avoid converting values from one extractant to another. Be sure you know which extractant is being used and use those results with fertilizer recommendation tables developed for that extractant.

Quality control

As with any chemical process, quality control must be used to ensure that results from each lab are accurate. This is accomplished in Ontario through an accreditation program administered by the Ontario Ministry of Agriculture, Food and Rural Affairs. The details of this program will keep changing over time but the basic principles will remain the same.

Goals of a lab accreditation program

The goals of a lab accreditation program are to:

- provide a correct analytical result for each soil sample submitted to the accredited labs, within reasonable expectations for each analytical procedure
- provide consistent results from any of the accredited labs
- encourage the use of appropriate soil test extractants for which there is a body of fertilizer response calibration data for Ontario soils
- promote the use of accredited labs, which perform the standard analyses and perform them correctly

- promote the use of fertilizer recommendations based on Ontario research
- keep the system open enough to permit the addition of labs that meet the criteria

The basis of any quality control program is the procedures followed in the lab. Each lab has one or two standard soils that are included in each analytical run to ensure the analytical results don't drift. Standard solutions must also be prepared carefully and used to calibrate the instruments and to check their calibration periodically. Careful records are necessary to track the performance of the lab over time and to use for troubleshooting.

An external check sample program is an extra check on the system. This allows comparison between labs and should catch any problems that have been overlooked by the lab's internal quality control.

History of soil test accreditation in Ontario

In 1989 it was proposed that, instead of a single OMAFRA-recognized lab for soils, feed, plant tissue and greenhouse media analysis, all labs that could show proficiency in analyses for these substrates would be recognized. As a result, 33 labs showed interest in the accreditation program.

OMAFRA personnel visited each lab and provided the Ontario Soil Management Research and Service Committee methods for soil analyses. Also, staff took a list of analytical equipment and lab tracking and quality control methods. The labs also analyzed a number of soil samples in triplicate and had to meet standards for analytical accuracy.

To be accredited, a lab had to perform well in the areas of pH, buffer pH, phosphorus, magnesium and potassium. Optional accreditation could be obtained for zinc and manganese indices.

Three labs were accredited in 1989. In 1991, a new accreditation exercise was completed with five sets of soil, each set randomized separately. In 2005, Ontario had six accredited soil labs.

In 1998, Ontario joined the North American Proficiency Testing Program. While this means that some of the program samples will come from areas with soils that are not representative of Ontario soil, this is more efficient and allows for greater harmonization of labs. Sample exchanges are conducted four times per year, with five soils per exchange that the labs analyze three times over three days. Labs must maintain acceptable accuracy in all the accredited methods to retain their accredited status.

New labs can be accredited provided they demonstrate acceptable accuracy on the NAPT exchange samples, as well as a series of independent samples with known values.

Soil test methods accredited in Ontario

Tested For	Testing method
Soil pH	Saturated paste
Lime requirement	SMP buffer pH
Phosphorus	Sodium bicarbonate (Olsen)
Potassium, magnesium	Ammonium acetate
Zinc index	DTPA, modified by soil pH
Manganese index	Phosphoric acid, modified by soil pH
Soil nitrate	Potassium chloride extraction

Soil pH

Soil pH is the measurement of the hydrogen ion activity or concentration in the soil solution. This activity affects the availability of most nutrients and controls or affects most biological processes.

The hydrogen ion concentration is measured with a pH electrode. The heart of the electrode is a glass bulb that is only porous to hydrogen ions. As the positive ions move into the electrode, a current is set up that is measured with what is essentially a voltage meter. The voltage reading of several standards is read and a graph set up. The voltage readings of the samples are then compared to the graph and given pH values.

There is some debate about what soil-to-water ratio is best for measuring pH. Usually, soil pH is measured using de-ionized water to form a saturated paste or a 1:1 or 1:2 soil-to-water ratio. Saturated paste is the accredited method in Ontario and liming recommendations are based on this method. The measured pH tends to increase as the amount of water added to the soil increases. The difference will be greatest in the soils with the lowest buffering capacity, i.e. coarse sands.

Other methods employ calcium chloride solutions to prepare the paste or slurry, reducing the amount of interference from high salt levels. This method tends to give a lower pH reading than a slurry with pure water.

The saturated paste is prepared by adding just enough water to the soil sample to completely saturate the soil without leaving any free water. Properly preparing a saturated paste is time consuming and difficult, but it provides a closer approximation of the pH at the root-soil interface than the more dilute slurries. The high soil-to-water ratio of the paste is abrasive on the pH electrodes, causing a higher rate of failure under automated conditions.

Buffer pH

Shoemaker, McLean and Pratt method (SMP)

The measurement of soil pH is used to indicate whether a field requires lime. Depending on the crop, soils

The little p in pH

In math, "p" is used to denote the negative log of...

In this case, it is the negative log of hydrogen ion (H) concentration in the solution.

Pure water contains some molecules that have broken apart into individual ions, either hydrogen (H^+) or hydroxyl (OH^-).

$$water\ (H_2O) = H^+ + OH^-$$

In pure water, there is an equal amount of hydrogen and hydroxyl ions, and the pH is neutral. If you were to count the number of H^+ ions in pure water, you would find

1/10,000,000 moles of H^+ ions
per litre of water

In scientific notation, this is 10^{-7} H^+ ions, and the negative log of this number is the positive value of the little number on top, or 7. As the concentration of hydrogen ions increases, the value of the pH decreases and the solution becomes more acidic.

Since this is a logarithmic scale, a pH of 6 is 10 times more acid than a pH of 7.

A pH of 5 is 10 times more acid than a pH of 6.

with a pH less than 6.1 need lime and a buffer pH is done to determine how much lime is required.

The buffering capacity of the soil is its ability to resist changes in pH. In an acid soil, this ability to resist change is due to the reserve acidity. Reserve acidity is due to hydrogen, aluminum and other cations that are held on the cation exchange complex. The greater the reserve acidity, the more lime is required to bring the pH into optimal range.

Reserve acidity is measured by adding a buffer solution (SMP) to the soil sample and reading the pH of the soil and buffer mixture after a half hour. This buffer resists change in pH and starts out at a pH of 7.5, but the soil acidity reduces the pH of the buffer in proportion to the amount of reserve acidity in the soil. If the pH of this mixture is low, the soil has a high reserve acidity and requires a large amount of lime to neutralize it.

The lime requirement is calculated according to formulas in Table 2-3.

TABLE 2-3. Calculating lime requirements

pH to which soil is limed	Equation
7.0	lime (t/ha)* = 334.5 - 90.79 pH_B ** + 6.19 pH_B^2
6.5	lime (t/ha) = 291.6 - 80.99 pH_B + 5.64 pH_B^2
6.0	lime (t/ha) = 255.4 - 73.15 pH_B + 5.26 pH_B^2
5.5	lime (t/ha) = 37.7 - 5.75 pH_B

* Lime requirement is calculated at tonnes per ha of lime with an agricultural index of 75. (See chapter 4, page 91 for more details.)
** pH_B = buffer pH

TABLE 2-4. Interpreting soil conductivity readings in field soils		
Conductivity "salt" reading millisiemens/cm	Rating	Plant response
0–0.25	L	suitable for most if recommended amounts of fertilizer used
0.26–0.45	M	suitable for most if recommended amounts of fertilizer used
0.46–0.70	H	may reduce emergence and cause slight to severe damage to salt-sensitive plants
0.71–1.00	E	may prevent emergence and cause slight to severe damage to most plants
>1.00	E	expected to cause severe damage to most plants

Soluble salts

Soluble salts in soils can result from excessive applications or spills of fertilizers and manures, runoff of salts applied to roads and chemical spills. There can also be high salt levels in areas affected by brine seeps or spills from recent or historical oil and gas exploration. High concentrations of soluble salts in or near a fertilizer band can restrict plant growth severely without seriously affecting the salt concentrations in the rest of the soil. Soluble salts also interfere with the uptake of water by plants. A given amount of salt in a soil provides a higher salt concentration in soil water, if the amount of water is small. Plant growth is most affected by soluble salts in periods of low moisture supply (drought) and low water holding capacity (sands and gravels).

Soluble salts can be measured in the lab by measuring the electrical conductivity of a soil-water slurry. The higher the concentration of water soluble salts, the higher the conductivity. Table 2-4. *Interpreting soil conductivity readings in field soils,* provides an interpretation of soil conductivity reading for Ontario field soils in a 2:1 water-to-soil ratio. This slurry is prepared by mixing air-dried soil with twice the volume of water and using a conductivity meter to measure the conductivity of the resulting liquid layer.

For greenhouse soils, the OMAFRA-accredited soil test uses a larger soil sample and measures conductivity on a saturation extract. For greenhouse crops using this method, conductivity readings up to 3.5 milliSiemens/cm are acceptable.

It is difficult to identify excess salts in a starter fertilizer band because of the limited volume of soil affected and because the excess salts can dissipate quickly into the surrounding soils with rainfall.

Testing for nitrate nitrogen

Nitrate nitrogen content of the soil at planting time can be used to fine-tune nitrogen fertilizer applications for corn and spring barley. Extensive calibration work has not been carried out in Ontario for other nitrogen-using crops such as wheat, canola or most horticultural crops. Work has been done with potatoes and tomatoes but results did not lead to definite recommendations.

Routine nitrogen analysis is not done on soil samples because nitrate contents vary greatly from week to week; nitrate nitrogen samples are taken to a greater depth than standard soil tests; and samples must be handled carefully to prevent changes in the soil nitrate content.

Some users request analysis for ammonium nitrogen as well as nitrate, even though it is not used for recommendations. The same extraction method is used, although a different analytical procedure is used on the extract. If the sample is to be analyzed for ammonium, it should be refrigerated and analysed within four days. Drying the sample will invalidate the ammonium nitrogen test.

Methods

Nitrate nitrogen is present in the soil almost exclusively within the soil solution and is extracted easily. The standard method is to use potassium chloride solution.

A sample of the soil is mixed with the potassium chloride solution at a ratio of 1 part soil to 5 parts extracting solution, shaken for half an hour and then filtered. The extract is analyzed using an auto-analyzer, which measures the intensity of colour produced after mixing the extract with specific chemicals.

Comments

- The standard method produces highly reproducible results and is relatively straightforward.
- Fertilizer recommendations are calibrated for samples taken at planting time. Samples taken at pre-side-dress time for corn (early June) will contain about 1.3 times as much nitrate nitrogen as planting time samples.
- Interpretation of the soil nitrate test is complicated by the variability of soil nitrate contents within the field.
- Soil nitrate content may underestimate the amount of available nitrogen where organic sources of nitrogen have been applied (eg. livestock manure, sewage sludge, legume ploughdown) and have not had a chance to mineralize. Research is underway to develop soil tests for the easily mineralizable portions of soil and added organic matter.

Phosphorus

In testing for phosphorus, the major difference in the methods is usually the type of treatment the sample undergoes to extract the phosphorus from the soil. The three common methods for extracting available phosphorus are Olsen (sodium bicarbonate), Bray P1 and Mehlich III. See Table 2-5. *Phosphorus extractants.*

Whatever extractant is used, the next step is to determine the concentration of phosphorus in the extract. Several analytical methods can be used, some of which are related to a specific extractant. The most common involves adding molybdenum as a colour reagent. It will form a blue colour when combined with phosphorus. The greater the amount of phosphorus, the more intense the colour.

The Olsen extractant is very alkaline so it tends to react differently with the colour complex than the Bray or Mehlich. As well, the Bray or Mehlich extracts tend to have higher phosphorus concentrations than the Olsen so the standards used in the analysis are different.

Sodium bicarbonate method (Olsen)

The sodium bicarbonate method (also called the Olsen method) is the one recommended for use in Ontario.

This extracting solution has a pH of 8.5 and so is best with soil pHs that range from 6.0 to 8.0. The calcium phosphates in the soil and some of the organic phosphates are dissolved by the sodium bicarbonate. The sodium bicarbonate method will predict the relative available phosphorus in a wide range of soil types.

Comments

- The sodium bicarbonate method requires a longer shaking time than the Mehlich or Bray (a half hour, as opposed to five minutes).
- The sodium bicarbonate method is very sensitive to temperature, pH and shaking times, so uniform conditions

are required throughout the analysis to ensure consistent results. Olsen found the extractable phosphorus can increase almost 0.5 ppm for a 1°C increase in temperature of the extracting solution between 20°C and 30°C.

Bray P1

The Bray extraction solution contains hydrochloric acid and ammonium fluoride, which form an acidic solution. This tends to simulate an acid soil environment. This test is better for acidic than for alkaline soils.

The Bray extractant tends to extract more phosphorus than the sodium bicarbonate method. At high pH values though, the acid nature of the extracting solution may dissolve the calcium phosphates, over-estimating the available phosphorus. However, the free lime in the soil may also neutralize the acid nature of the extracting solution making it less effective. These two situations indicate that the Bray P1 extraction provides unpredictable results under alkaline conditions.

A modified Bray P2 (strong Bray) extractant was used in Ontario during the 1960s, which used a more concentrated acid to overcome the neutralizing effect of alkaline soils. It was replaced by the sodium bicarbonate extractant, which was more consistent over the range of soils in Ontario.

TABLE 2-5. Phosphorus extractants			
Method	Extracting solution	Solution pH	Where used
Sodium bicarbonate	0.5 M $NaHCO_3$ solution,1 part soil to 20 parts solution, shaken for 30 min.	8.5	Ontario, Iowa, most western states
Bray P1 (weak Bray)	0.025 M HCl + 0.03 M NH_4F, 1 part soil to 10 parts solution, shaken for 5 min.	2.5	Michigan, Ohio, Indiana, Illinois, eastern states
Bray P2 (strong Bray)	0.1 M HCl + 0.03 M NH^4F, 1 part soil to 10 parts solution, shaken for 5 min.	2.5	early 1960s in Ontario before sodium bicarbonate
Mehlich III	0.2 M CH_3COOH + 0.25 M NH_4NO_3 + 0.015 M NH_4F + 0.013 M HNO_3 + 0.001 M EDTA, 1 part soil to 10 parts solution.	2.5	Quebec, Maritime provinces, Pennsylvania, south-eastern states

Mehlich III

The Mehlich III is a multi-element extracting solution composed of acetic acid, ammonium fluoride, ammonium nitrate and the chelating agent ethylene diamine tetra-acetic acid (EDTA). It combines chemicals from Bray P1, ammonium acetate and DTPA extracting solutions.

Mehlich III extracts phosphorus with acetic acid and ammonium fluoride. It extracts potassium, magnesium, sodium and calcium with ammonium nitrate and nitric acid and extracts zinc, manganese, iron and copper with EDTA.

This method is often used because of the savings in analysis time. When used with an ICP machine capable of running simultaneous elements, this method is appealing for the labs. The value measured using an ICP may be different from the value measured by a colour reaction, although the reasons for this are not clear. These should be considered to be two separate tests, with different inter-pretations for making fertilizer recommendations.

Because of its acidic nature, the Mehlich III solution is best suited to acidic soils and is routinely used in Quebec and the Maritimes. The relatively high acid concentration in this extractant means it will perform adequately in slightly alkaline soils, although it will provide inconsistent results in soils with high carbonate (free lime) contents.

Potassium, calcium, magnesium, sodium

Potassium, magnesium, calcium and sodium all possess a positive charge (that is, they are cations). They can all be extracted by the same solution, since the mechanism is to flood the soil with another cation to displace them from the exchange complex.

Potassium and magnesium are the cations that most often limit crop production and they are measured routinely in Ontario. Potassium is absorbed by the plant in larger quantities than any other element except nitrogen.

Calcium supply is generally adequate if the soil pH is suitable for crop growth so not all labs measure it. Calcium contents are often high enough that extra dilutions are required to bring the extract within the operating range of the lab equipment, adding extra time and inconvenience.

Sodium is not an essential nutrient for crop production and is analyzed only where environmental contamination is suspected.

Complicating the measurement of calcium and magnesium is the presence of free lime in calcareous soils. This free lime is partly dissolved by the ammonium acetate solution and causes extra calcium and magnesium to show up in the extract. The amount of lime dissolved will depend on the pH of the extracting solution and the ratio of soil-to-extracting solution, so it is important for labs to follow analytical procedures exactly.

Ammonium acetate

The most common cation used for extracting soil cations is ammonium from ammonium acetate.

The availability of potassium is influenced by the drying temperature of the soil. Temperatures higher than 35°C tend to cause the potassium to be bound up on the exchange sites. This is the reason that at least 2 days of lab time is spent drying. Speeding up the process would either leave water in the soil, affecting the final concentration of the nutrients, or overheat the soil,

making the readings for potassium inaccurate.

After extraction, the cations in the ammonium acetate solution are measured.

Mehlich III

The Mehlich III extractant can be used for potassium and other cations as well as phosphorus. The ammonium ions from ammonium nitrate and ammonium fluoride behave the same as the ammonium from ammonium acetate, displacing the cations from the exchange sites. The concentration of the cations are then measured in the extract.

The Mehlich III method extracts comparable amounts of potassium from the soil as the ammonium acetate method.

Micronutrients

Measurements of micronutrients in the soil are generally less reliable than the measurement of macronutrients and soil pH. This stems from the extremely small quantities.

The concentrations in the extracting solutions may be near the detection limit of the equipment and there is potential for contamination of the sample from sampling tubes, pails or dust. Add to this the effects of soil pH, organic matter, clay content and mineralogy on both the extractions and the plant availability of micronutrients and it is easy to see why the micronutrient tests are difficult to correlate with plant uptake.

In Ontario, tests have been accredited for zinc and manganese.

The other micronutrients are not well enough correlated to be used for fertilizer recommendations. Tissue analysis should be the primary tool in diagnosing deficiencies of these elements. The soil test can be useful, however, as a secondary tool.

Most of the micronutrients are chemically active and would form insoluble compounds with an extracting agent, making them difficult to measure. Chemists get around this by using chelates or weak acids to extract micronutrients. Chelates are organic compounds that "complex" the metal ions, binding to the ion at more than one point and wrapping themselves around the ion. This keeps the ions in the solution and allows them to be separated from the soil for measurement.

The most common chelating agents are diethylene triamine penta-acetic acid (DTPA) and ethylene diamine tetra-acetic acid (EDTA). While both behave similarly, they have slightly different affinities for different metal ions.

By varying the pH, chelating agents can be adjusted to extract specific nutrients. DTPA is adjusted to a pH of 7.3 for most soil extractions. Triethanolamine is added to the extracting solution to buffer it against pH changes during the extraction. Calcium chloride is also added to prevent the calcium carbonate in calcareous soils from dissolving.

Zinc

DTPA extraction

For this extraction, the soil is mixed with a 0.005 M DTPA solution at a ratio of 1 part soil to 2 parts solution and shaken for 1 hour. The zinc in the soil is complexed by the DTPA and held in the solution.

Following extraction and filtering, the zinc content in the extract is measured.

Comments

- The DTPA extraction process does not reach equilibrium so it is necessary to maintain strict procedures with regard to shake time, speed and filtering for the tests to be consistent.
- The high soil-to-solution ratio (1:2) makes it difficult to filter out adequate sample sizes. Filtration may take several hours to overnight.
- The long shake and filtration time makes DTPA extraction one of the most time consuming processes in the lab.
- This analysis is susceptible to contamination during the soil sampling process. In the field, be sure to use only plastic or stainless steel equipment. The use of galvanized or iron implements will contaminate the sample with zinc or iron.

Zinc availability index

The availability of zinc is influenced more by soil pH than by the amount of nutrient in the soil. Soil tests in Ontario for zinc report an availability index instead of, or in addition to, the nutrient analysis.

Formula to calculate the zinc index

Zinc index = 203 + 4.5 (DTPA extractable zinc in mg/L soil) − 50.7 (soil pH) + 3.33 (soil pH)^2

Interpreting the index

greater than 200	suspect contamination of the sample or field
25 to 200	adequate for most field crops
15 to 25	adequate for most field crops but bordering on deficiency for corn
less than 15	likely deficient for corn

Mehlich III extraction

The EDTA in the Mehlich extractant behaves much like DTPA. However, there has not been as much work done with the Mehlich extractant in Ontario, so its results should be used with caution.

Manganese

Phosphoric acid extraction

In Ontario a weak phosphoric acid solution is used as an extracting solution with a 1:10 soil-to-water ratio. Other areas may use the DTPA extractant, but the phosphoric acid method has given more consistent results in Ontario.

Comments

- Manganese is extracted from the soil much more quickly by phosphoric acid than by EDTA.
- The ratio of soil-to-extracting solution is much lower than with DTPA so the samples filter rapidly.

Manganese availability index

The availability of manganese is influenced much more by soil pH than by the amount of nutrient in the soil. Soil tests in Ontario for this nutrient report an availability index instead of, or in addition to, the nutrient analysis.

Formula to calculate the manganese index

Mn index = 498 + 0.248 (phosphoric acid extractable Mn in mg/L soil) − 137 (soil pH) + 9.64 (soil pH)^2

Interpreting the index

greater than 30	adequate for field crops
15 to 30	adequate for most field crops but approaching deficiency for cereals or soybeans
less than 15	likely insufficient for cereals or soybeans

Iron and copper

Neither iron nor copper has a soil test that correlates well with plant uptake or fertilizer response in Ontario. Copper deficiency has been observed on muck soils but is rare on mineral soils. There are no confirmed cases of iron deficiency in Ontario.

Plant analysis is a much more reliable indicator of availability of these nutrients.

Boron

There is no accredited test for boron in Ontario. To give a rough indication of availability, boron can be determined by extracting with hot water using barium chloride to flocculate the soil. Boron in the extracting solution can be read using a colour-forming reaction or ICP.

Because levels of boron are often less than 1 ppm, it is much more difficult to get an accurate measurement than it is for other soil nutrients. As well, the borate ion is mobile in the soil so that concentrations fluctuate, depending on leaching and mineralization.

Plant tissue analysis is a much more sensitive indicator of boron availability than a soil test.

Sulphur

Soil test labs in Ontario do not routinely analyze for sulphur. Irregular supplies, due to leaching and mineralization, make it difficult to correlate soil test values to plant uptake. It is likely that sulphur test results will be more meaningful from a 30 cm sample rather than a 15 cm sample. In any case, rain and snow supply enough sulphur for most crops in southern Ontario. See Figure 3-12, page 68. There are no fertilizer calibrations for Ontario conditions.

Labs will do sulphur analyses on request. The most common technique is to extract sulphur from the soil using a calcium phosphate solution. The amount of sulphate in the extract is measured by adding barium to form barium sulphate crystals and measuring the turbidity of the resulting suspension or by reducing the sulphate to sulfide and measuring it through a colour-forming reaction. Other labs may analyze sulphur in a Mehlich III extract using an ICP.

Organic matter

Soil organic matter content is not used to adjust fertilizer recommendations in Ontario but it plays an important role in soil fertility.

Organic matter adds greatly to the cation exchange capacity of a soil, enhancing its ability to hold nutrients available for plant uptake. Through microbial action, many nutrients also cycle through organic and mineral forms, so that organic matter is a reservoir of slowly available nutrients. Adequate organic matter is essential for soil tilth and water holding capacity. The level of organic matter is also important for the activity of several herbicides.

Soil organic matter determination has taken on new importance with the need to understand the dynamics of soil carbon in relation to greenhouse gas emissions or sequestration. Soil management can influence the net movement of carbon into or out of the soil and this can create opportunities for farmers to participate in carbon credit programs. Evaluation of the effectiveness of these programs will require precise measurements of changes in soil organic matter content.

There are two approaches to measuring soil organic matter. The first is to measure the amount of organic carbon in the soil, using either wet chemistry or a combustion analyzer and to multiply this weight by a factor to convert it to organic matter. The second approach is direct measurement of the weight of organic matter lost from the soil when it is burned (loss on ignition or LOI). Organic carbon measurements are more precise than LOI, particularly on soils with low organic matter contents, but they require either aggressive chemicals to dissolve the organic compounds or specialized equipment.

The measurements of organic matter and organic carbon are fairly well correlated but the carbon content of organic matter can vary depending on the source and age of the material. This will lead to slightly different measurements, depending on the method used.

In Ontario, the loss on ignition method has been determined to be sufficiently precise for farm soils. However, most scientific research uses the increased precision of organic carbon determinations. Soil organic matter content is about 1.8 to 2.0 times the organic carbon content.

Loss on ignition (LOI)

LOI is a direct measure of soil organic matter content. Samples are placed in a muffle furnace overnight at 425°C and the weights before and after ashing are compared. Higher temperatures must be avoided because any carbonates present in the soil will break down, increasing the measured organic matter content. Pre-drying the samples at 120°C will reduce the variability of this test.

Determining organic carbon

Modified Walkley Black

The Walkley Black method operates on the principle that potassium dichromate oxidizes soil carbon. The potassium dichromate changes colour depending on the amount it is reduced and this colour change can be related to the amount of organic carbon present. The final solution is read on a spectrophotometer and compared to a chart.

Comments
- The Walkley Black method measures organic carbon rather than organic matter. The conversion factor itself may be a source of error. Also, some organic compounds are not completely oxidized by the dichromate, which results in low test values.
- This method cannot be used with soils containing over 7.5% organic matter.

- The reagents used in this analysis are toxic and must be disposed of as hazardous waste.

Combustion furnace

This furnace burns the sample at a temperature of more than 900°C and measures the concentration of carbon dioxide released—the total carbon. The results are fast and accurate but the equipment is expensive.

Then, another sample is ashed overnight in a muffle furnace to remove the organic carbon. The inorganic carbon (carbonates) in the residue is measured. Organic carbon is the difference between the total carbon and the inorganic carbon.

Soil texture

Texture estimation

Soil texture is not measured in most soil samples but is estimated by hand. Soil texture is recorded on most soil reports as a letter. The four categories are C – Coarse, for sand or sandy loam; M – Medium, for loam; F – Fine, for clay or clay loam; and O – Organic.

These are used only to give the client a rough idea of the texture. It is sometimes a useful check that the samples are from the right fields.

Texture measurement

Dispersing the soil in a detergent solution and measuring the amount of soil settling out over time can measure soil texture. This method is based on the fact that large particles will settle out faster than finer ones. Between half a minute and one minute after agitation, all the sand will have settled. Between 6 hours and 24 hours after, all the silt will have settled out, leaving the clay in suspension. The technique uses a pipette or hydrometer to measure the concentration of soil in suspension at these times.

The technician uses a pipette to sample the solution. The solution from the pipette is dried in an oven and the amount of soil in the pipette is determined by weight. The technician can also use a special hydrometer to measure the density of the suspension. As the soil settles out of suspension the density decreases and the hydrometer sits lower in the water. The pipette method is more accurate than the hydrometer method but more expensive and time consuming.

Ordinarily organic matter does not significantly affect the texture measurement. An amount for organic matter can be deducted from the silt or clay fraction, or, before determining texture, the organic matter can be removed by chemical means. Once the proportion of sand, silt and clay has been determined, the texture class is determined as shown in Figure 2-1.

FIGURE 2-1. Soil texture triangle

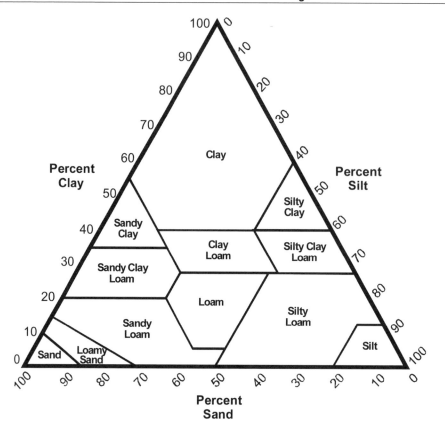

Shows relationship between the class name of a soil and its particle size distribution. The points corresponding to the percentages of silt and clay in the soil are located on the silt and clay lines respectively. Lines are then projected inward, parallel in the first case to the clay side of the triangle and in the second case to the sand side. The name of the compartment in which the two lines intersect is the class name of the soil.

Particle sizes of the soil fractions

Sand 0.05–2 mm

Silt 0.002–0.05 mm

Clay <0.002 mm

Particles larger than 2mm (gravel and stones) are not included in determining soil texture.

Cation exchange capacity and per cent base saturation

Cation exchange capacity (CEC) and per cent base saturation are not used for fertilizer recommendations in Ontario. In calibration trials where these factors have been considered, the accuracy of fertilizer recommendations has not been improved and has sometimes been decreased.

Many soil test reports do, however, include these determinations. They are useful as a general indication of soil fertility and can point towards some potential production problems. Understanding how these numbers are derived can help keep them in perspective.

Cation exchange capacity

Cation exchange capacity (CEC) is a relative reflection of the total ability of the soil to hold cation nutrients —its potential fertility. For a full discussion, see Chapter 3, page 41.

Cation exchange sites are the major source of available cations for

Formula for estimating cation exchange capacity

bCEC value = (Ca value ÷ 200) + (K value ÷ 390) + (Mg value ÷ 120)

(bCEC = cation exchange capacity occupied by bases)

where each of the Ca, K, and Mg values (mg/kg of soil) is obtained from the ammonium acetate extraction. This equation converts them to the centimole per kilogram value.

A factor is also added for the H+ content of the soil:

if the pH is between 6.0 and 7.0, then CEC value = bCEC value + 1.2

if the pH is greater than 7.0, then CEC value = bCEC value.

if the pH is less than 6.0, then

CEC value = bCEC value + $\{1.2 \times [70 - (pH_B \times 10)]\}$.

$(pH_B = $ buffer pH)

This formula, developed in Michigan, takes into account the pH of the soil and the electrical charge of each cation. It does not take into account the presence of other cations such as aluminum or the amount of calcium or magnesium dissolved from free carbonates in the soil.

Another quick method of estimating CEC is to use the per cent clay and organic matter. Multiply the per cent clay by 0.5 and the per cent organic matter by 2. The sum of these figures estimates the cation exchange capacity of the soil.

plant uptake. CEC may be measured directly or estimated by adding the total cations measured in a soil test.

TABLE 2-6. Per cent base saturation equations
% Ca saturation = (ppm Ca ÷ 200 ÷ CEC value) × 100
% K saturation = (ppm K ÷ 390 ÷ CEC value) × 100
% Mg saturation = (ppm Mg ÷ 120 ÷ CEC value) × 100

Estimating CEC

The cation exchange capacity is often estimated from the nutrients extracted by ammonium acetate. This estimation assumes only the nutrients occupying the cation exchange sites are extracted, which is not always the case. The presence of calcium carbonate (lime) in soils with high pH may distort the values for cation exchange capacity because the ammonium acetate will dissolve some of this calcium as well.

CEC measurement

A more accurate indication of the cation exchange capacity can be obtained by measuring it in the lab. The process involves flooding the soil with a particular marker cation, forcing all other cations off the exchange sites. This marker cation is then itself extracted with the ammonium acetate solution. This solution is then analyzed for the quantity of marker cation, which represents the total cation exchange capacity.

Barium is a good marker ion because it is not a common element in the soil and it has a strong enough affinity for the exchange sites to force the other cations off.

Per cent base saturation

The per cent base saturation is the ratio of basic cations to the cation exchange capacity expressed as a per cent. See Table 2-6. The term is often used loosely and sometimes refers to each individual cation or to the sum of all the basic cations.

Care must be taken when calculating and interpreting the values for per cent base saturation because the values depend on the how the CEC is obtained. For example, a potassium saturation value derived from a CEC estimate in a calcareous soil will be misleading because of the artificially high values for calcium and magnesium.

As a rule, per cent base saturation should increase with increasing pH and soil fertility.

Lab equipment

Auto analyzer

This machine automates the repetitive tasks of chemical analysis. The concentration of most elements in a soil or plant extract can be measured by reacting them with specific compounds to produce a coloured reaction product. The intensity of the colour is related to the concentration of the nutrient element.

In the auto analyzer, small samples of extracts, separated from each other by air bubbles, are drawn into fine plastic tubing. Other chemicals are introduced into the tube in proper proportions and mixed. The mixture might be heated or cooled or passed over a catalyst. The end product is passed through a photocell to measure the intensity of colour produced. A specific analysis track is necessary for each nutrient being tested, although they can often be set up in parallel, so that one set of samples can undergo two or more analyses.

These machines are commonly used in the analysis of nitrate, ammonium and phosphorus.

The auto analyzer is much faster than manual analysis but must be carefully calibrated with a range of stock solutions for accurate correlation to actual concentrations. Constant quality control is necessary.

Atomic absorption

This equipment uses a flame to break the extract down into its elements and then passes a beam of light through the flame to measure the absorption of light by those atoms. Each element absorbs light of a specific wavelength so that a light source is used with a wavelength specific for the element being tested. The concentration of the element is proportional to the amount of light absorbed. The flame temperature is important to ensure the compounds are broken down into atoms.

Because the atoms that make up the air also absorb light, this method cannot be used for elements with absorption wavelengths in the range of the elements found in air. This means that atomic absorption spectrometry cannot be used to measure nitrogen, phosphorus, sulphur or boron. This method can be used for several micronutrient (Fe, Mn, Zn, Cu, etc) and alkaline earth (K, Ca, Mg) elements.

Emission spectrometry

At very high temperatures and in strong electrical fields, atoms can become excited and emit light. Each element emits light at specific frequencies, which can be measured by a photocell. The intensity of light emission indicates the amount of each element present.

Inductively coupled plasma spectrometer (ICP) or direct coupled plasma spectrometer (DCP) rapidly measure the concentration of elements in a solution. A tiny sample of soil or plant extract is passed through a torch that produces high temperatures and simultaneously through a strong magnetic field to excite the atoms. When the excited atoms return to their stable state, they emit light waves at specific wavelengths. The intensity of the emission indicates the amount of each element present.

This instrument produces accurate measurements of total elements present in the extracting solution over a relatively wide range of concentrations but it must be carefully calibrated with stock solutions for each element.

In Ontario with the bicarbonate extractant, ICP analysis is not used due to mechanical difficulties with the solution itself.

Organic materials

Handling and preparation

Plant tissue

Plant tissue samples may be sent to the lab in fresh condition or air dried if they cannot be shipped immediately. Samples should never be dried in an oven, since high temperatures can affect the analysis.

It is critical to avoid contamination from soil, dust or fertilizer. Ship the samples in paper bags, never plastic, to avoid condensation and mould.

At the lab, the samples are identified, logged and dried. The dry samples are ground to a particle size of 1 mm or less and stored in airtight containers until analysis.

Manure

At the lab, liquid manure samples are analyzed as they are received. Containers are mixed by inverting them several times before sampling.

Part of the solid manure sample is tested for nitrogen. The balance is dried in an oven at 100°C overnight, and then ground to pass a 1 mm screen and stored in an airtight container until analysis. Moisture content of the manure is determined in the drying process.

Nitrogen

Combustion method

This method determines total nitrogen (ammoniacal, protein and nitrate sources) in organic materials. Samples are ignited in a furnace and the gases collected. Oxygen, carbon dioxide and moisture are removed and the nitrogen gases determined by thermal conductivity.

In general, nitrogen determination by combustion results in slightly higher values than the conventional Kjeldahl method because the Kjeldahl method accounts only for the protein and ammoniacal sources of nitrogen.

Comments
- Uniformity of particle size and fineness is essential. A particle size of 1mm diameter or less is recommended.
- Frequent calibration and maintenance of reagents in the instrument are crucial.

Kjeldahl method

This is the standard method for nitrogen determination but it is not commonly done because of the time and toxic materials needed. The basis of this method is the digestion of the sample in concentrated acids with catalysts to convert organic nitrogen to ammonium and then measuring the amount of ammonium in the digest.

Ammonium nitrogen

Ammonium nitrogen in liquid manure can be measured using an ammonium specific electrode. In either solid or liquid organic materials, the ammonium nitrogen can be measured by steam distillation, or by extracting the ammonium with a KCl solution and measuring the concentration in the extract.

Ammonium nitrogen can be lost during sample drying so the determination should be made on fresh samples or the sample should be acidified before drying to retain the ammonium.

Available nitrogen from manure or biosolids can be more accurately determined if both the ammonium and organic nitrogen are known, rather than just total nitrogen. Organic nitrogen is assumed to be the total nitrogen content minus the ammonium nitrogen.

Calcium, phosphorus, potassium, magnesium, manganese, copper, iron, boron

The concentration of these elements is determined after oxidizing (ashing) the plant tissue and then dissolving the ash in acid. The samples are burned at 550°C for two hours. The acid digests are then analyzed for their nutrient contents. Some elements, such as phosphorus, potassium, boron and copper, tend to volatilize at elevated temperatures. Care must be taken to avoid ashing at greater than 500°C for a long period.

Regulated metals in biosolids

There are currently 11 metals that cannot exceed specified limits in a non-agricultural source material if it is going to be land applied. These are arsenic, cadmium, cobalt, chromium, copper, mercury, molybdenum, nickel, lead, selenium and zinc. Dissolving the organic material in a strong acid and then analyzing the concentration of these elements in the digest determine these metals. Mercury is determined using a slightly different procedure to prevent the release of toxic mercury vapour.

Seven of the regulated metals are also essential nutrients for either plants or animals. The concentrations determined in this procedure are useful indicators of the potential for build-up of these elements to harmful levels in the soil but are not always good indicators of availability for uptake by plants.

Other resources

Basic references

Black, Charles A. 1993. *Soil Fertility Evaluation and Control.* Lewis Publishers.

Havlin, J. L, J. D. Beaton, S. L. Tisdale and W. L. Nelson, 2005. *Soil Fertility and Fertilizers: An Introduction to Nutrient Management.* 7th ed. Pearson Education Inc., Upper Saddle River, New Jersey 07458.

For more detail

Brown, J.R., ed. 1987. *Soil Testing: Sampling, Correlation, Calibration, and Interpretation.* SSSA Special Publication Number 21.

Carter, Martin L., ed. 1993. *Soil Sampling and Methods of Analysis. Canadian Society of Soil Science.*

Kalra, Y.P. and D. G. Maynard, 1991. *Methods Manual for Forest Soil and Plant Analysis.* Forestry Canada, Northwest Region, Northern Forestry Centre, Edmonton, Alberta. Information Report NOR-X-319.

Miller, Robert O. and Kotuby-Amacher, Janice. 1996. *Western States Laboratory Proficiency Testing Program Soil and Plant Analytical Methods, Version 3.00.* Utah State University.

North Central Region - 13. 1988. *Recommended Chemical Soil Test Procedures for the North Central Region.* North Dakota State University Bulletin #499.

Northeast Coordinating Committee on Soil Testing. 1995. *Recommended Soil Testing Procedures for the Northeastern United States.* 2nd ed. University of Delaware Bulletin #493.

Page, A.L. ed. 1982. *Methods of Soil Analysis.* American Society of Agronomy.

3 NUTRIENTS

Since crop production removes nutrients from land, applying them back in some form is essential to the sustainability of agriculture. Nutrients are applied to replace nutrients removed by harvest, boost yield, enhance nutrition and increase quality and utility of crops.

Specific markets for crops demand quality, consistency and continuity of specified characteristics. Crop production has and continues to reach new levels of sophistication in a quest to meet consumer demands for choices of variety, nutrition and health benefits. Understanding the role of nutrients in attaining these attributes is of utmost importance.

Nutrients reside in the soil in numerous forms, have many pathways of transport to the roots and have specific roles in plants.

Nutrient forms

Nutrients are held in the soil matrix in many forms:
- dissolved in the soil solution
- held to soil surfaces
- tied to, or contained within, organic matter
- held as insoluble compounds
- fixed within clays

Dissolved in soil solution

For many nutrients only a small proportion is in soil solution at any time. Even nutrient absorption by direct interception can only take place through a film of water.

The importance of these dissolved nutrients is far greater than their quantity. Only a tiny fraction of the total nutrient in the soil is in solution at any time. Most of the nutrient remains in the soil in other forms of varying availability. As nutrients are removed from the soil solution by crop uptake, they are replenished from these other forms.

Held to soil surfaces

Most nutrients within the soil solution are present as ions and have either a positive or negative electrical charge. An ion with a negative charge is an anion and a nutrient possessing a positive charge is a cation. Soil particles, especially clay particles, also possess negative electrical charges. Opposite charges attract, therefore soil particles attract and hold nutrients in the soil.

The dominant charge on soil particles, by a huge margin, is negative. This means that most of the ions held in the soil this way are positively charged or cations. The number of cations that can be held is equivalent to the amount of negative charge. This amount is called the cation exchange capacity (CEC).

Cation exchange capacity is a measure of the ability of the soil to hold positively charged nutrients. It is expressed as centimoles per

TABLE 3-1. Typical CECs of clay minerals	
Clay Mineral	Cation Exchange Capacity (cmol/kg)
Smectite (includes Montmorillonite and Vermiculite)	10–150
Illite	15–40
Kaolinite	3–15

kilogram (cmol/kg). These units have replaced milliequivalents per 100 grams but the numeric values remain the same, i.e. 15 centimoles per kilogram = 15 milliequivalents per 100 grams.

The magnitude of the CEC depends on the texture of the soil, the types of minerals present and the amount of organic matter. As the texture gets finer, the amount of surface area in each gram of soil

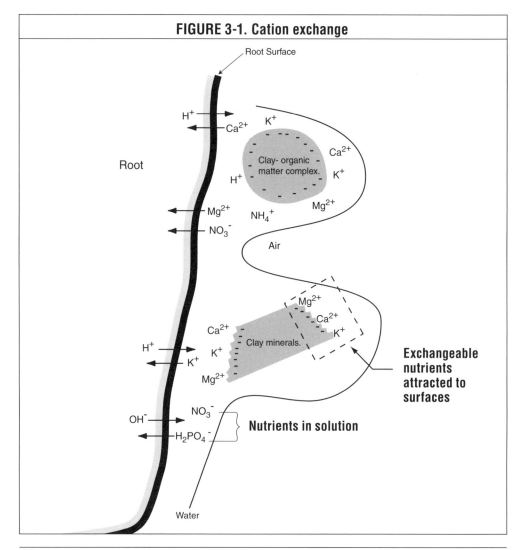

FIGURE 3-1. Cation exchange

increases, creating more places where the negative charges can occur and the CEC increases.

The types of minerals in the clay fraction of the soil are different than the minerals in the coarser fractions. Instead of being round or angular, the clay minerals are flat plates with negative charges concentrated around the broken edges of the plates. The amount of negative charge varies with the type of clay mineral. See Table 3-1.

The clay minerals in Ontario and surrounding regions are predominantly illite and smectite. The kaolinite clays are dominant in the strongly weathered soils of the southern states but uncommon in Ontario.

Organic matter also carries a large negative charge.

Cations

Cations in the soil solution and adsorbed to soil surfaces come from the weathering of soil minerals, the breakdown of organic matter and additions of mineral and organic fertilizers.

Cations are positively charged elements such as calcium (Ca^{2+}), magnesium (Mg^{2+}), hydrogen (H^+) and potassium (K^+). The cations held on the organic matter and clay surfaces act as a reserve of nutrients, continually re-supplying the soil solution.

Cation exchange

Too often, cation exchange capacity is presented as a static number. In fact it represents an active equilib-rium between ions in solution, on the soil surfaces and in other forms in the soil.

The cations are attracted to the soil surfaces, with the strongest attraction and the highest concentration near the surfaces and less attraction farther away. Cations constantly move back and forth between the solution and the soil surfaces but the average movement to and fro is in balance. The system is in equilibrium.

If something changes the system, the balance of movement will shift. If nutrients are removed from the soil solution by plant uptake, there will be a net movement off the soil surfaces to regain the equilibrium between solution and soil.

Absorb: take in or make part of itself.

Adsorb: cause a gas, liquid or dissolved substance to adhere in a thin layer to the surface of a solid.

Tied to organic matter

Organic matter in the soil consists of crop residues, microbial matter, humus and organic materials in various states of decomposition. Plant nutrients are held within this organic matter and adsorbed to the surfaces.

In addition to its role in nutrient cycling, organic matter plays an important role in the water holding capacity of the soil and in maintaining soil structure. Organic matter exists as discrete particles but most exists in an intimate relationship with clay and other soil particles to form aggregates. The organic matter breakdown facilitated by soil microbes provides the glue to hold soil aggregates together.

Nutrients from crop residues and manures are released to the soil solution in mineral form through decomposition by soil organisms. These same organisms can absorb nutrients from the soil solution if they need them for their own growth and development. This frequently occurs with nitrogen when organic materials high in carbon are added to the soil. The microbes have an ample food source but need nitrogen for the proteins and amino acids in their bodies so nitrogen is absorbed from the soil and held unavailable within the microbes until some of the carbon compounds are digested. See Organic Nutrient Sources, page 97.

Because microbial action mediates the release of nutrients from organic materials, it is affected by the weather. Too cold, too wet or too dry can delay the release of nutrients, which can affect crop production. It is not unusual to see symptoms of nitrogen deficiency on corn or cereals following legumes or manure if the spring weather is cooler than normal.

Breakdown of organic matter plays an important role in micronutrient supply.

Manganese deficiency can show up in cool, dry springs and boron deficiency is common when soil conditions are dry.

The cation exchange capacity of organic matter is greater than clay. Weak organic acids on the outside of the humus particles are the source of negative charges on organic matter. These sites are affected by pH and in acid soils the hydrogen binds so tightly that these sites are not available for nutrient exchange. This means that the CEC of organic matter is lower in acid soils than in alkaline.

Held as insoluble compounds

Several nutrients react strongly with other minerals in the soil forming insoluble or slightly soluble compounds. The best example is phosphorus.

Phosphate binds with iron or aluminum in acid soils or with calcium or magnesium in alkaline soils to form insoluble compounds. Phosphate also reacts with iron and aluminum oxides in the soil,

TABLE 3-2. Typical CECs of soil textures and organic matter	
Material	CEC (centimoles per kilogram)
Sandy soil	2–10
Loam soil	7–25
Clay soil	20–40
Organic matter (humus)	200–400
Muck >20% OM	25–100

forming compounds that are only slightly soluble.

Fixed within clays

Illite clays have spaces between the layers that match closely to the size of a potassium ion. When potassium is added to these soils the ions can move into these spaces and the clay layers collapse around them, a bit like eggs in an egg carton, trapping the potassium within the clay mineral. Ammonium is also subject to being trapped like potassium.

Nutrients fixed in this manner are slowly available to plants. They are not directly exchangeable but are released gradually as the clay minerals are weathered or dispersed by extreme drying, wetting, freezing and thawing.

Nutrient transport to roots

For ions to be absorbed into the plant, they must be in the soil solution and in close proximity to the root surface. This happens by root interception, mass flow and diffusion. See Figure 3-2.

Root interception

Nutrient ions are absorbed by direct contact with the root and any associated mycorrhizae. Because this form of absorption is based on direct contact, the amount of nutrients available equals the amount of nutrients in the volume of soil in contact with the roots. See Figure 3-3.

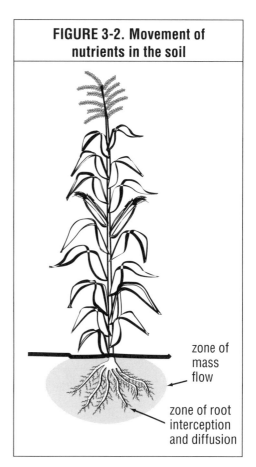

FIGURE 3-2. Movement of nutrients in the soil

zone of mass flow

zone of root interception and diffusion

Roots of most crops occupy 1% or less of soil volume. However, as roots grow they take the easiest route through soil pores and planes of weakness between soil clods. Some pores such as worm burrows are nutrient enriched. The worms smear the burrow wall with their faeces, which are high in available nutrients. As a result, roots can contact directly a maximum of 3% of available immobile nutrients.

Root structure varies from species to species. Root length directly affects the volume of soil the root has contact with. Some plant species also have root hairs or other structures that can aid in nutrient uptake.

Root hairs increase the depletion zone or the soil volume that the root draws nutrients from, as shown in Figure 3-4. For example, onions have virtually no root hairs while canola has some of the longest root hairs. Canola can thus access 20 to 30 times the soil volume that onions can.

Phosphorus and potassium uptake is strongly tied in many plant species to root hairs. In soils low in extractable phosphorus, root hairs can account for 90% of total uptake. Root hairs are more efficient at absorbing phosphorus than the main root because of the smaller diameter of the root hair. This helps to maintain higher diffusion rates of phosphorus.

Root hair formation is affected by the concentration and availability of nutrients such as phosphorus and nitrate. Soils in which phosphorus is readily available generally exhibit root structures with few and short root hairs. Root hair density and length increases greatly in soils low in phosphorus.

Other aspects of root growth, like root exudates and symbiotic relationships such as the one with mycorrhizae (see box page 47) can increase the depletion zone or the volume of soil available to pull nutrients from.

Root exudates such as the mucilage that covers root surfaces, particularly the tip, can help increase uptake. This gelatinous material is secreted by the cells at the root tip and the epidermis. It helps to lubricate, prevents the root from drying out and assists with ion uptake. Mucilage is particularly important in dry soils as it improves the soil-root contact and plays a role in the uptake of phosphorus and micronutrients.

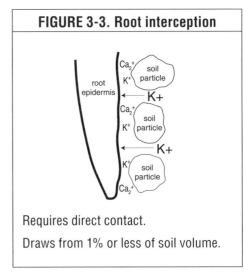

FIGURE 3-3. Root interception

Requires direct contact.

Draws from 1% or less of soil volume.

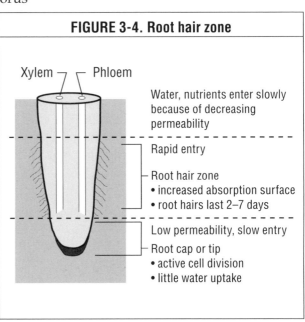

FIGURE 3-4. Root hair zone

Xylem — Phloem

Water, nutrients enter slowly because of decreasing permeability

Rapid entry

Root hair zone
• increased absorption surface
• root hairs last 2–7 days

Low permeability, slow entry

Root cap or tip
• active cell division
• little water uptake

Vesicular arbuscular mycorrhizae (VAM)

The term *mycorrhiza* comes from myco or fungi and rhizae or root. This refers to a symbiotic relationship between fungi and the roots of some plants where the hyphal threads (a root-like structure in fungi) act as an extension of the plant root system.

This can enhance root interception of nutrients as it increases the soil volume that nutrients can be pulled from. Some calculations suggest an increase of up to 10 times that of uninfected roots.

The benefit of this symbiotic relationship is seen most in soils that are low in fertility, particularly in phosphorus. Plants with *mycorrhiza* have an uptake rate of phosphorus per unit of root length that is two to three times higher.

Most agronomic crops, with the exception of canola and other Brassica species, have *vesicular arbuscular mycorrhiza*. It is thought that *mycorrhiza* have a larger potential in undisturbed soils such as no-till or potentially with longer term perennial crops such as trees. Research in this area continues.

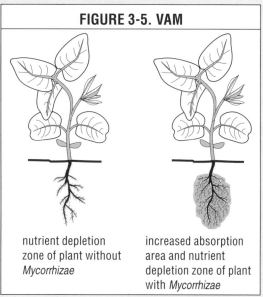

FIGURE 3-5. VAM

nutrient depletion zone of plant without *Mycorrhizae*

increased absorption area and nutrient depletion zone of plant with *Mycorrhizae*

Mass flow

A plant draws water from the soil, carrying plant nutrients and other materials in solution. See Figure 3-6. Some mass flow is also caused by water losses from evaporation and water movement through capillary action.

The water use of the plant and the nutrient concentration in soil water determine the amount of nutrients that reach the plant. This is the prime mode of transport for nutrients in solution such as nitrate, sulphate, chloride, boron, calcium and magnesium.

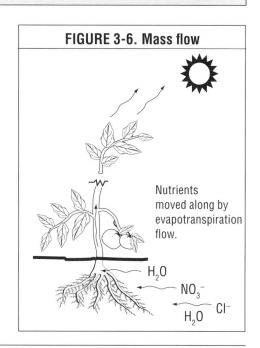

FIGURE 3-6. Mass flow

Nutrients moved along by evapotranspiration flow.

H_2O

NO_3^-

Cl^-

H_2O

Mass flow plays a larger role in fertility when the plant is actively growing, as there is a greater transpiration flow. Less nutrient movement occurs at low temperatures because of a decreased transpiration rate, less plant growth and less evaporation at the soil surface.

Diffusion

Diffusion refers to the movement of ions from areas of high concentration to areas of low concentration.

Plant roots absorb nutrients from the surrounding soil solution, decreasing the concentration of the nutrient at the root surface. The concentration in the soil solution is higher. This creates a nutrient gradient that causes ions to diffuse towards the area of lower concentration, as shown in Figure 3-7. The process is influenced by plant need, soil moisture, soil texture and the nutrient content of the soil.

Diffusion is slow under most soil conditions and occurs only over tiny distances. It is the key mode of transport for phosphorus and potassium. Research suggests that in the time that nitrogen travels 1 cm, phosphorus travels 0.02 cm and potassium 0.2 cm.

The surface area of the root system determines the uptake rate of nutrients dependent on diffusion.

Plant uptake of nutrients

Generally, when we refer to nutrient uptake we are talking about the uptake and transport of nutrients through the root system. Plants can also absorb nutrients through the stomata and cuticle of leaves and fruit but roots are the primary path for nutrient absorption.

Plants take up ions through passive and active mechanisms. Ions move passively (no energy expenditure) to a barrier through which ions are actively (requires energy from plant) transported to the plant organs that will metabolize the nutrient. This movement of ions occurs through plant cells and the liquid film lining the spaces between cells.

Cations (+ ions) are exchanged along the negatively charged sur-

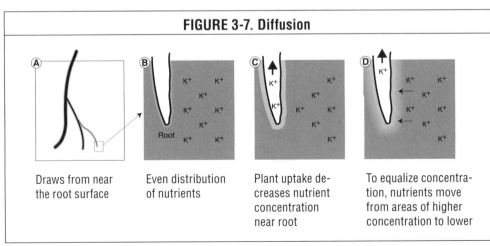

FIGURE 3-7. Diffusion

| A Draws from near the root surface | B Even distribution of nutrients | C Plant uptake decreases nutrient concentration near root | D To equalize concentration, nutrients move from areas of higher concentration to lower |

faces of root cells. Root cells release positive hydrogen ions (H⁺) to maintain electrical neutrality. As a result, the soil solution pH declines near the plant root.

Most nutrient ions reach the leaf cells through the xylem. See Figure 3-8. However, nutrients can penetrate the leaves through the stomata and leaf cuticle to reach the free space between cells in the leaf and become available for absorption. Ions in rainwater, in irrigation water or from foliar applications of fertilizer can follow this path.

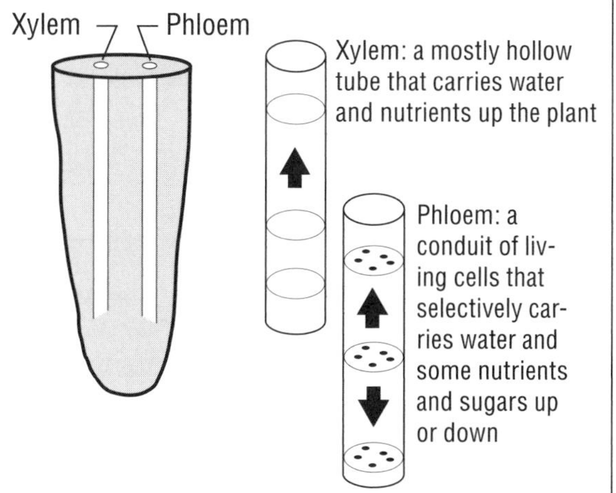

Nutrient ions move from the plant roots to shoots and other plant parts as part of the water flows through the plant. The rate of water

absorption and transpiration help determine how effectively the ions move through the plant. Some nutrient ions are quite mobile within the plant and will move through the phloem to areas of new growth

FIGURE 3-8. Xylem and phloem

Xylem — Phloem

Xylem: a mostly hollow tube that carries water and nutrients up the plant

Phloem: a conduit of living cells that selectively carries water and some nutrients and sugars up or down

TABLE 3-3. Relative significance of the ways ions move from soil to corn roots				
Nutrient	Amount required for 150 bu/ac corn	Percentage supplied by		
		root interception	mass flow	diffusion
nitrogen	170	1	99	0
phosphorus	35	3	6	94
potassium	175	2	20	78
calcium	35	171	429	0
magnesium	40	38	250	0
sulphur	20	5	95	0
copper	0.1	10	400	0
zinc	0.3	33	33	33
boron	0.2	10	350	0
iron	1.9	11	53	37
manganese	0.3	33	133	0
molybdenum	0.01	10	200	0

This example applies to a fertile silt loam soil near neutral pH. Proportions differ for different soil conditions.

Source: Stanley A. Barber, *Soil nutrient bioavailability.* (New York: John Wiley & Sons, 1984).

TABLE 3-4. Form and mobility of nutrients in soil and plants

	Mobility in soil	Plant available forms in soil	Mobility in plant
Macronutrients			
nitrogen	med–high	ammonium ion NH_4^+, nitrate ion NO_3^-	high
phosphorus	low	phosphate ion $H_2PO_4^-$, HPO_4^{2-}	high
potassium	low–med	potassium ion K^+	high
Secondary Nutrients			
calcium	low	calcium ion Ca^{2+}	low
magnesium	low	magnesium ion Mg^{2+}	high
sulphur	medium	sulphate ion SO_4^{2-}	low–med
Micronutrients			
boron	high	boric acid $B(OH)_3^0$, borate ion $H_2BO_3^-$	low–med
copper	low	cupric ion Cu^{2+}	low
iron	low	ferrous ion Fe^{2+}, ferric ion Fe^{3+}	low
manganese	low	manganous ion Mn^{2+}	low
molybdenum	low–med	molybdate ion MoO_4^{2-}	med–high
zinc	low	zinc ion Zn^{2+}, $Zn(OH)_2^0$	low
chlorine	high	chloride ion Cl^-	high

from established growth while others cannot.

Knowledge of the mobility of the various nutrients will aid in diagnosing field problems. Mobile nutrients like nitrogen or potassium move out of older tissues to the growing point, which causes deficiency symptoms to show up on older leaves first. Deficiencies of immobile nutrients, on the other hand, show up on new growth. Noting where the symptoms occur can help identify which nutrients are deficient.

Role of nutrients in plants

The majority of plant tissue is made up of carbon, hydrogen and oxygen, which plants derive from water and carbon dioxide. The remaining essential nutrients are generally combined with these elements to play roles in the plant ranging from structural components or energy transfer to enzyme systems. For convenience, nutrients are divided into primary, secondary and micro nutrients, reflecting the relative quantities required for plant growth and reproduction.

Adequate nutrients are required for optimum crop growth and a deficiency of any of the essential nutrients will reduce yield and/or quality. The specific requirements for nutrients are also related to environmental factors, as is the reduction in growth caused by a deficiency. For example, a deficiency of potassium or chloride may increase the susceptibility of a plant to disease so the response to these nutrients may be higher when disease is present. Determining nutrient requirements for crops is discussed more fully in Chapter 6.

Primary nutrients

A primary nutrient, or macronutrient, is required by plants in large quantities for basic plant growth and development. The six nutrients that fall into this category are carbon, hydrogen, oxygen, nitrogen, phosphorus and potassium.

Plants get carbon, hydrogen and oxygen from the air and water. The remaining macronutrients must be obtained from the soil. Fertilizer, manure, nitrogen fixation or mineral weathering replenish the soil nutrients. Primary nutrients most frequently limit plant growth.

N Nitrogen

Nitrogen present in the soil comes initially from nitrogen in the atmosphere. The air we breathe is 78% N by volume. However, it is largely unavailable to most plants and must be chemically converted from gaseous nitrogen (N_2) to a form that can be used by plants (ammonium or nitrate). Most nitrogen is taken up as nitrate (NO_3^-) by plants and only a small percentage is taken up as ammonium (NH_4^+). The various transformations that nitrogen undergoes, known as the nitrogen cycle, are illustrated in Figure 3-9.

In the soil, most of the nitrogen is present in the organic matter. Soil reserves of organic N can be high and amount to thousands of pounds per acre.

N-Fixation

Nitrogen fixation includes any process that converts gaseous nitrogen (N_2) from the air to ammonium (NH_4^+) or nitrate (NO_3^-).

Industrial fixation uses high temperature and pressure, in the presence of a catalyst, to combine nitrogen gas with the hydrogen from methane to produce ammonia. This is the basis for the production of all other nitrogen fertilizer materials.

Biological fixation – symbiotic and non-symbiotic

Symbiotic fixation involves a host plant and beneficial infecting bacteria. The most common and well known is the *B. japonicium* rhizobia, which infects soybean roots. As well there are a host of other beneficial rhizobia infecting legumes such as alfalfa and clovers. See Table 3-5. The host plant provides carbohydrates to the colonizing bacteria, which in turn fixes atmospheric N in the nodule for transfer to the plant for protein synthesis. This activity is affected by soil N level, pH, plant stress and climate. Symbiotic fixation is slowed by high residual soil N. When the soybean plant needs nitrogen it sends a biological signal from the roots that exude a promoter protein to attract the rhizobia.

Non-symbiotic organisms such as free-living bacteria and azotobacter, azospirillium and actinomycetes also fix nitrogen from the air. Other forms of fixation include lightning, which produces enough heat and electrical energy to combine nitrogen gas with oxygen to form nitrates. The amount of available nitrogen produced this way is small.

> The amount of nitrogen received in precipitation is estimated to be in the range of 2–15 kg/ha, with half, or less, of that value making up the amount fixed by lightning.

Mineralization

Plants cannot take up the nitrogen contained in organic compounds. Mineralization is the microbial breakdown of these materials that releases the mineral forms of nitrogen. The nitrogen is released initially as ammonium, which is rapidly converted to nitrate by nitrifying bacteria. Mineralization and immobilization occur at the same time and the balance between the two is affected by the carbon-to-nitrogen ratio of the organic materials in the soil. Soil pH is also important as higher pH provides a more desirable environment for bacterial proliferation (6.5 to 7.0). However, this also favours a high population of denitrifying bacte-

TABLE 3-5. Rhizobium species associated with specific legume crops

Rhizobium species	Legume crops
Sinorhizobium meliloti	Alfalfa, Sweet Clover, Fenugreek
R. trifolii	Clover (except Kura clover)
R. leguminosarum	Peas, Vetch, Sweetpeas, Lentils
R. phaseoli	Beans
R. lupine	Lupines
Bradyrhizobium japonicum	Soybeans
R. loti	Trefoil

ria so denitrification is much more rapid at high soil pH.

Immobilization

Immobilization occurs when NH_4^+ and NO_3^- are being taken up by soil organisms. Nitrogen becomes part of the body and processes of the soil organisms. If immobilization occurs because of unfavorable C:N ratio, the Nitrogen is consumed by soil bacteria and is unavailable to crops.

Nitrification

This is the process where soil micro-organisms convert NH_4^+ to NO_3^-, the form of nitrogen most readily taken up by plants.

Denitrification

Denitrification is the process where NO_3^- is converted to gaseous forms of nitrous oxides or atmospheric nitrogen. This occurs in areas with low oxygen and poor aeration in

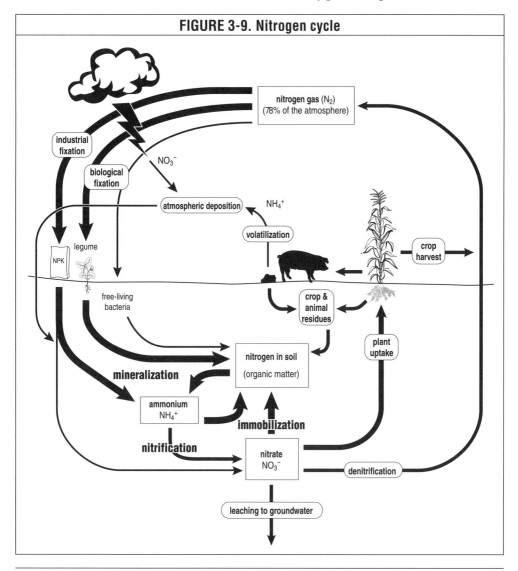

FIGURE 3-9. Nitrogen cycle

the soil (poorly drained or standing water). Loss of nitrogen in saturated soils maybe estimated from Table 3-6., which illustrates the potential loss associated with temperature and soil conditions.

TABLE 3-6: Potential for nitrate-N loss from saturated soils at different temperatures

Soil Temperature	Potential Denitrification Rate (% of NO_3-N in soil)
< 12°C	1 to 2 % per day
12 to 18°C	2 to 3 % per day
> 18°C	4 to 5 % per day
	Source: Hoeft, Robert 2002.

Leaching

Leaching is the downward movement of nitrate nitrogen by excess water. The amount of nitrate loss and depth of movement will depend on soil texture, initial moisture content and the amount of water entering the soil as well as the duration of the event. Leaching is more prevalent in early spring and the fall post-harvest period. Very little leaching occurs during periods of rapid crop growth.

Careful management of irrigation is required to avoid excessive movement of nitrate nitrogen. Figure 3-10 shows the variation in depth where rainfall or irrigation will wet the soil to field capacity in different texture classes. Nitrate and other solutes won't be moved deeper by a single wetting event than the wetting depth for the net infiltration (precipitation or irrigation amount

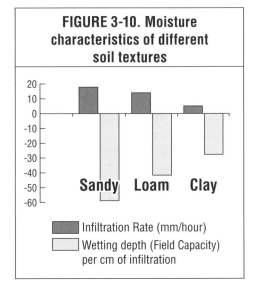

FIGURE 3-10. Moisture characteristics of different soil textures

■ Infiltration Rate (mm/hour)
□ Wetting depth (Field Capacity) per cm of infiltration

minus the amount of runoff and evapotranspiration).

Role of nitrogen

Nitrogen is involved in many plant processes and structures. Compared to other nutrients it is required in large amounts.

Nitrogen is a main component of amino acids, which form proteins within the plant. Enzyme proteins are important in a number of plant processes, particularly growth and yield. Protein is usually highest in the harvested part of the plant; hence, it often is an important item in the nutritional value of the crop.

Nitrogen has an important role in the production of chlorophyll, which creates the green color in plants. Chlorophyll is responsible for the conversion of sunlight to energy needed by the plant in the process of photosynthesis during the daytime reaction.

Ammonium N tends to depress pH in the rhizosphere. This can

increase the availability of some micronutrients, in particular manganese.

Nitrogen deficiency

Nitrogen deficiency is relatively common in Ontario agriculture because of this element's mobility within the soil. The most common causes of nitrogen deficiency are leaching, poor nodulation in legumes, denitrification caused by waterlogged soils, under-fertilization, or conditions that delay mineralization such as dry soil conditions or cold weather.

Nitrogen is a very mobile nutrient within the plant. As the plant grows and develops, the nutrient can be moved or reallocated to the rapidly growing tissues. Consequently, symptoms will appear on the lower or older leaves first.

Carbon-to-nitrogen ratio

The carbon content in relation to the nitrogen content of an organic material determines mineralization or immobilization. Bacteria need nitrogen to decompose plant or other residues. Breakdown of organic material high in carbon will slow until a favourable amount of nitrogen is present. Soil bacteria will consume available N for breakdown creating a risk of N deficiency in season until a favorable C:N ratio is established.

As a rule of thumb, mineralization occurs if the C:N ratio is less than 25:1. If it is greater than 25:1, immobilization occurs.

Symptoms of nitrogen deficiency in:

- Corn
  - yellowish green colour in whole plant in young plants, spindly stalks
  - V-shaped yellowing forms along the midrib of older leaves, beginning at the tip (see inside front cover)
- Legumes, including soybeans, alfalfa
  - pale green, stunted and spindly plants
  - in later stages leaves turn yellow
  - seen in alfalfa and soybeans on acid soils where nodulation is poor
  - more common in soybeans during early spring as the plants switch from the nitrogen supplies of the seed to the nodules
- Cereals
  - pale green and eventually yellow plants
  - stunted and spindly plants (winter wheat under nitrogen stress maybe predisposed to take all disease or Septoria. When these diseases are present, there may be yield increases from higher than normal N applications)
- Tomatoes, potatoes, peppers
  - in young plants, whole plants pale, light green
  - in older plants, older leaves yellow
- Strawberries
  - pale, off colour plants
  - reduced growth

- Vine crops
  - stunted leaf growth, pale foliage
  - stems slender, hard and fibrous

Nitrogen can affect plant disease

Imbalanced plant nutrition and, particularly an excess of nitrogen, can lead to lush growth, which is softer and less able to withstand disease. Excess nitrogen can also lead to dense plant canopies, which trap humidity within the canopy and create conditions where many fungal diseases can thrive.

Phosphorus

Forms of phosphorus in soil

Phosphorus occurs in soil in three basic forms: Soluble P, Labile P and Non Labile P. Less than 5% of a soil's total phosphorus is available or slowly available to plants at any time. The rest may be held in organic matter or a number of mineral forms.

Soluble P

Monohydrogen phosphate $(HPO_4)^{2-}$ and dihydrogen phosphate $(H_2PO_4)^-$ found in the soil solution are the forms used by plants. The soluble P is also a concern environmentally as it can be lost by movement of surface water overland or through tile. Even though it is a small amount it can have a significant impact on surface water quality. Effective management involves application techniques, rates of P application, soil test levels, cropping and land management practices.

Labile P

Another portion of phosphorus is held by the surfaces of clay particles. As phosphorus is removed from the soil solution by plant uptake, more phosphorus is released from the soil surfaces into solution.

Non Labile P

In the soil, phosphorus reacts with ions such as aluminum, iron and calcium and forms compounds with very low solubility. Some of the phosphorus becomes adsorbed to

---

Primary and secondary forms of phosphate

Plants absorb most of their phosphorus as an anion, either primary $(H_2PO_4^-)$ or secondary (HPO_4^{2-}) orthophosphate.

Studies indicate that plants prefer the primary form by about 10 to 1. But since the two forms interchange quickly in the soil, it's not important.

Soil pH influences the ratio. At pH 7.2, plants take up about equal amounts of primary and secondary. Below this level, they favour the primary.

Other forms of phosphorus may be used but in much smaller quantities than the orthophosphates. Polyphosphates are as effective as orthophosphates as sources of phosphorus for crops. Although plants can take up some polyphosphate directly, most will convert to orthophosphate in the soil.

> ### Turnover of phosphorus in the soil solution
>
> If the soil solution has a phosphorus concentration of 0.01 ppm and the soil contains 30% moisture by volume, then the top 50 cm of this soil contains 0.045 kg/ha of phosphorus.
>
> To meet the crop uptake requirements for a 10,000 kg/ha corn crop, the soil solution would have to be replenished 667 times during the growing season.

clays and is virtually unavailable to plants.

Since phosphorus concentrations are relatively low in the soil solution and the compounds resulting from chemical reactions between it and other elements, like aluminum and iron which have low water solubility, little of the available phosphorus is lost to leaching.

Factors affecting phosphorus availability

pH

At high pH values phosphate reacts with calcium and magnesium compounds, which decreases its water solubility and plant availability.

In acidic soils, phosphate reacts with iron and aluminum to produce insoluble compounds and reduce plant availability.

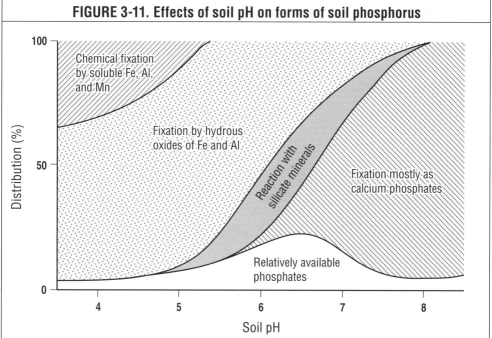

FIGURE 3-11. Effects of soil pH on forms of soil phosphorus

Inorganic fixation of added phosphates at various soil pH values. The proportion of phosphorus remaining available depends on contact with the soil, time for reaction, organic forms and other factors.

Source: N.C. Brady, *The nature and properties of soils*, 10th ed. (MacMillan Publishing Company, 1990).

> **Caution:** Phosphorus deficiency in perennial crops is difficult to correct. Do soil tests before establishment to make sure there is enough phosphorus (orchard, berries, vineyards).

Maximum phosphorus availability occurs at pH 6.0–7.0 See Figure 3-11.

Moisture and temperature

Phosphorus moves primarily by diffusion. As soil moisture levels decrease, the water film surrounding soil particles becomes thinner, making diffusion more difficult.

Organic matter breakdown can be a source of phosphorus. Water and temperature play a role in the release of phosphorus from organic matter through mineralization. As temperature increases, the rate of mineralization increases and more phosphorus is released.

Fertilizer

In any given year, plants will use up to 30% of the phosphorus applied as fertilizer or manure. This depends on the background phosphorus content in the soil, placement of the fertilizer and the crop. The more phosphorus applied as fertilizer or manure, the more is available to plants. The phosphorus not used in the year of application does have a residual value.

Time and placement of fertilizer

Movement of phosphorus by diffusion accounts for only millimetres each year. Banding phosphorus at planting time is more effective than broadcasting, as this decreases the amount of phosphorus that comes into contact with soil and reduces the fixation of phosphorus. The application of phosphorus close to planting time decreases the time between application and use by the plant, which reduces the fixation of phosphorus.

Soil compaction can severely limit root expansion and limit surface area available for nutrient uptake. Starter fertilizers may help to alleviate the negative impact that soil compaction may have on phosphorus uptake.

Clay content of soil

The higher the clay content of a soil, the more phosphorus becomes adsorbed and the less is in solution and available to plants. However, clay soils also have a greater reserve of phosphorus from which to replenish it in the soil solution, as plants take it up.

Crop residues

Tillage systems with large amounts of surface residue can have greater response to starter phosphorus because the residues keep the soil cooler and wetter and the roots are less able to extract phosphorus from the soil. Surface residues keep more water near the soil surface, which allows roots to continue taking up phosphorus from the topsoil later in the season. Organic residues on the soil surface can delay soil fixation reactions with applied phosphorus. Thus, broadcast applications of phosphorus in no-till can be available to the crop, although this application method may not be desirable if there is risk of runoff and water contamination.

Relationship of phosphorus to other nutrients

Nitrogen

As nitrogen increases in the soil solution, the uptake of phosphorus increases. This effect could be caused by a decrease in pH when there is a greater amount of ammonium ions in the soil solution. Also, increased nitrogen increases the rate of translocation of phosphorus from the root to the plant shoot.

Zinc

In soils with a combination of high levels of phosphorus fertilization and low or marginal soil levels of zinc, zinc deficiency symptoms can result.

Role of phosphorus in plants

Like nitrogen, phosphorus is an important factor in many plant metabolic processes, such as:

- photosynthesis and respiration
- energy storage and transfer (ATP)
- protein and carbohydrate metabolism
- cell division and enlargement
- structure of DNA
- component of cell membranes

The effect of the availability and supply of phosphorus on these plant processes is reflected in particular aspects of crop growth.

Roots tend to proliferate in the parts of the soil most enriched by phosphorus. Overall, however, high soil phosphorus levels reduce the total mass of roots. When phosphorus is limiting, the plant adjusts by shifting more of its resources to root production and less to top growth. When phosphorus supplies are adequate, the increased energy and carbohydrate metabolism results in better winter survival of crops such as wheat and alfalfa. Phosphorus hastens maturity of many crops, including corn, cereal grains and tomatoes. The reasons for this are not fully understood but could be related to enhancement of energy transfers or rates of cell division.

Phosphorus does not move great distances in the soil at any time. Under poor growing conditions (e.g. cool, dry or saturated soils), a weather-induced phosphorus deficiency may appear. This type of deficiency tends to be the result of restricted root growth, not necessarily low soil phosphorus content.

Field crops such as corn and cereals usually take up a significant amount of their P when only 20% of the plant growth has occurred. This may be related to a plant's ability to take up P at rates greater than metabolic need when it is readily available and store it internally in cell vacuoles. This stored P may be used to buffer P needs during later growth stages. Phosphorus nutrition is a regulatory factor in seed development at the time of grain fill. As most of the seed needs for P are from sources translocated from the plants leaves and stems.

Phosphorus deficiency

Purpling in plants is associated with phosphorus deficiency but this symptom is unreliable. The production of anthocyanin, which creates the purple colour, is a standard stress response. Many other factors can induce purpling.

Phosphorus deficiency is harder to detect visually than a deficiency of nitrogen or potassium.

Symptoms of phosphorus deficiency in:

- Corn
  - dark green plants
  - may develop a reddish purple colouring on older or lower leaves first (although this can be hybrid specific)
  - purpling progressing up the plant as severity increases
  - early growth often stunted, later stalks may be slender, shortened
  - delayed maturity
- Wheat
  - dark green, slow growing plants
  - delayed maturity
- Legumes, including soybeans, alfalfa
  - retarded growth, spindly, small leaflets, dark green leaves
  - perennial legumes like alfalfa also show poor winter survival
- Tomatoes, peppers, potatoes
  - slow growth, delayed maturity, purple interveinal tissue on underside of leaves
- Cole crops
  - purple leaves and stems
  - stunting and slow growth
- Potatoes
  - Plants are stunted. Leaves are dark green, and their margins roll upward.
  - Early and late blight disease symptoms may worsen with P deficiency
- Strawberries
  - darker green or bluish-green foliage
- Tree fruit
  - reduced shoot growth, flowering and fruit set
  - rarely, dark green to purple leaves

K Potassium

Forms of potassium in soil

Soil minerals are rich in potassium although little is available to plants. Potassium is present in the soil in many forms.

Unavailable potassium

90 to 98% of the soil's potassium is unavailable to plants. It is tied up in minerals such as mica and feldspar that are relatively resistant to weathering. However, with continuous weathering, these minerals do slowly release potassium into the soil.

Slowly available potassium

1 to 10% of total potassium in the soil is slowly available. It's trapped between layers of silica and alumina clays. These clays shrink and swell during dry and wet cycles.

Potassium trapped between the layers of clay is released slowly during the swelling cycle and becomes unavailable during the dry or shrinking cycles.

Available potassium

1 to 2% of the soil's potassium is readily available, held in the soil solution or in an exchangeable form with soil organic matter or clays.

In the soil solution, potassium maintains a dynamic equilibrium. Potassium ions that are taken up by plants are rapidly replaced by exchangeable potassium. Also, the addition of potassium fertilizers increases the potassium in solution dramatically. Adsorption of potassium to clay and organic matter quickly re-establishes the equilibrium.

Factors affecting the availability of potassium

Soil temperature

Potassium moves to the plant root by diffusion. As temperatures increase, the rate of diffusion, root growth and the rate of conversion from slowly available to available potassium increase, making more potassium available.

Root systems

Diffusion can only move potassium small distances. Therefore an extensive root system will contact and be able to use more of the soil's available potassium.

A developing root system benefits uptake of non-mobile nutrients.

Soil aeration

Under conditions of poor aeration (e.g. compaction, water logged soils), the low oxygen levels decrease the uptake of potassium. This effect is more severe for potassium than for nitrogen or phosphorus.

Moisture – dry conditions reduce movement, increase fixation

Lower soil moisture conditions decrease the movement of potassium to the root. Low moisture levels also result in more of the soil potassium becoming fixed between layers of clays.

Clay and organic matter content

Soils that are low in clay and organic matter have fewer exchange sites and therefore retain less potassium. High rainfall on these soils may result in the leaching of potassium ions. This is why sandy soils may need more frequent sampling and possibly more frequent applications.

Relationship of potassium to other nutrients

Magnesium

High potassium levels can reduce the uptake of magnesium. In some cases, this can result in magnesium deficient plants. When large amounts of potassium are applied to low-magnesium soils, magnesium deficiencies may result.

In forages, low magnesium affects the nutrition of animals before it affects the growth of plants.

Dry cow rations

With more intensive forage management and more efficient use of the nutrients in manure, total potassium applications to some forage fields have been rising. When soil potassium levels are high, plants may take up more potassium than is needed for maximum yield.

This luxury consumption by alfalfa and forage grasses can lead to high levels of potassium in the forage part of the ration.

The level of potassium in dry cow forages can be a nutritional and health concern for dairy cows. In the three to four weeks prior to calving, excessive potassium in the diet can increase the incidence of milk fever and retained placentas. As cows consume a diet high in cations their blood pH increases. This interferes with the cows' calcium metabolism. The maximum amount of potassium desired in dry cow diet varies. Generally, the forage potassium should be less than 2.5% on a dry matter basis. Addition of grains or corn silage during the 3 to 4 weeks before calving may help meet the rising energy demands and provide a better dietary ionic balance to reduce milk fever incidence by having a more favorable effect on blood pH.

Lactating cows generally do not have as much of a problem with excessive potassium. The diet of a lactating cow is higher in energy, supplied by grains and corn silage, which are lower in potassium.

Potassium levels in forage vary dramatically. See Table 3-7. Forage analysis can aid in soil fertility management as well as improve livestock feeding. See a livestock nutrition specialist before changing feed rations.

TABLE 3-7. Potassium concentration in some forage samples

	Average %K	High %K	Low %K
Legume haylage	2.5	4.0	1.1
Mixed haylage	2.5	4.1	0.9
Grass haylage	2.3	4.1	0.8
Legume hay	2.2	3.6	0.6
Mixed hay	2.1	3.0	0.5
Grass hay	2.0	3.4	0.4
Corn silage	1.0	1.7	0.3

Data obtained from samples submitted for analysis to Agri-Food Laboratories, Guelph, 2000–2005.

Role of potassium in plants

Plants need potassium in about the same amount as nitrogen. Potassium is unique in that it remains in a soluble form in the cell solution and does not become an integral component of the plant materials. It is involved in many plant processes. Potassium:

- promotes formation of structural components like lignin and cellulose, which play a major role in stalk strength and lodging resistance
- influences the uptake of carbon dioxide, photosynthesis and the regulation of stomatal opening in the leaves
- influences water uptake by roots

- influences starch and sugar content (and cell integrity), enhancing storage quality in potatoes, juice quality in grapes and the peelability and processing characteristics in whole-pack tomatoes
- aids in disease and insect resistance
- reduces the amount of soluble non protein nitrogen in forages

Potassium deficiency

Since potassium is mobile within the plant, deficiency symptoms usually appear first on older leaves, often as a chlorosis (yellowing) or necrosis (browning) of the leaf margins.

The most common causes of potassium deficiency are under-fertilization, rotations that include many whole plant crops, restricted root growth from soil compaction or the early stages of adaptation to reduced tillage systems on heavier soils. Dry weather conditions on sand soils are also a cause.

Symptoms of potassium deficiency in:

- Corn
  - margins in older leaves yellow or brown
  - stunted growth
  - chaffy kernels, abortion of kernels at tip of cobs
  - weaker stalks - lodging, stalk rots
- Alfalfa
  - small white or yellow dots near the leaf margin (see inside front cover)
    - premature decline of alfalfa in mixed stands
    - more winterkill
    - slower re-growth
- Soybeans, dry beans, snap beans
  - yellowing or browning of margins in older leaves (see inside front cover)
  - possibly a downward cupping of leaves
  - reduced nitrogen fixation
  - uneven maturity
- Cereals
  - overall yellowing
  - leaves may be yellowed or bronzed along the outer edges
  - excessive tillering in some cases
- Tomatoes
  - yellowing of leaf margins
  - yellow shoulders on ripe fruit (interferes with whole-pack recovery)
- Grapes
  - edges of leaves bronze
  - leaves cup
- Potatoes
  - leaf scorch
  - decreased yield
- Cucurbits
  - chlorotic leaves
  - fruit development irregular, small at stem end large at blossom end

Secondary nutrients

Calcium, magnesium and sulphur are required in moderate amounts. They are usually classified as secondary elements because they are less likely to limit crop growth. These nutrients are usually present in the soil in adequate amounts.

 Calcium

There are relatively large amounts of calcium in most Ontario soils as they were formed from calcium bearing parent material. The calcium in soil solutions is picked up by plants or enters the exchange complex of the soil and is held by the negatively charged organic matter and clay colloids.

As with any cation, equilibrium exists between the solution phase and the exchangeable. If calcium in the solution phase is taken up by the crop or lost to leaching, the calcium ion (Ca^{2+}) will be released from the exchange sites to replenish the supply and re-establish equilibrium. Conversely, if the Ca^{2+} supply increases in the solution, more calcium will attach to the exchange sites.

The availability of calcium to plants is a function of:
- the total calcium supply
- soil pH because low pH soils are more likely to be low in calcium
- CEC because the ability of the soil to hold cations will determine the amount of calcium that can be released and made available for plants
- soil types, as calcium is lost by leaching in sandy soils

Relationship of calcium to other nutrients

Calcium uptake is depressed by ammonium-based nitrogen, excessive potassium, magnesium, manganese and aluminum. Nitrate nitrogen is a preferred nitrogen source where calcium supply may be marginal or critical for crop quality. When the plant takes up the negatively charged nitrate, it can more easily take up the positively charged cations, including calcium.

Role of calcium in plants

Calcium is absorbed by plants as calcium ions (Ca^{2+}). It usually reaches root surface by mass flow and interception. Calcium is important in the stabilization of the cell wall and is involved in the metabolism and formation of the cell nucleus. Calcium pectate in cell walls provides a physical barrier to disease entry. Increases in marketable yield by reductions of physiological disorders have been attributed to adequate levels of calcium.

Calcium serves a minor role as a catalyst in the activation of a few enzymes and the detoxifying of metabolic acids.

Calcium moves by mass flow caused by the demand for water by transpiration of the plant. As a result, most of the calcium goes to large leaves where there is greater water need often bypassing fruit, which has relatively little transpiration loss. Calcium disorders can develop.

Calcium moves in the xylem transport system, deficiency shows in the new and terminal end growth.

but not greater total yield (Ozgen, Palta and Kleinhenz, 2006).

When calcium deficiency occurs, symptoms are seen in actively growing tissues, as calcium is immobile in the plant once it is fixed in the cell structure.

Calcium disorders

Blossom end rot (BER) is a result of a lack of calcium in the tomato fruit. See inside back cover. Often the soil has enough calcium, but the transpiration stream carries the bulk of the calcium through the plant to the leaves rather than to the fruit. Water stress, whether induced by root pruning, a restricted root system, excess nitrogen fertilization or just a lack of water, makes the plant more prone to this condition.

Trials have shown no advantage to applying calcium containing fertilizers such as calcium nitrate or applying foliar calcium to tomatoes. The problem is one of internal calcium regulation.

Tipburn in lettuce, blackheart in celery and potatoes and bitter pit in apples are a similar expression of calcium deficiency. In many of these cases, foliar application of calcium may have some benefit for specific crops.

Managing calcium in intensively managed crops

There are some areas of sandy, low CEC, poorly buffered soils in Ontario with apparent neutral pH and low calcium. These soils usually suffer from moisture limitations before any apparent calcium deficiency occurs.

These are desirable soils, however, for drip-irrigated crops. These modest levels of calcium may become limiting as water becomes non-limiting in this production system. An application of gypsum, limestone, calcium nitrate or calcium chloride to increase calcium content of the soils is a consideration.

Calcium deficiency

Calcium deficiency is rare in Ontario. When soil pH is in the recommended range, calcium supply is adequate for most crops. A soil test of less than 350 ppm calcium has been cited in literature as being low enough that potatoes responded to added calcium with larger tubers

 **Magnesium**

Magnesium levels vary widely across Ontario, according to the parent material. Like calcium, magnesium is strongly attracted to cation exchange sites but it leaches somewhat more readily than calcium.

Magnesium is present in the soil in solution and exchangeable forms, as well as slowly available forms like dolomitic limestone, clay minerals and feldspar. There are limited areas of soils, particularly in eastern Ontario, where magnesium levels are higher than the calcium level. These soils are characterized by poor structure and poor internal drainage. Applications of calcitic limestone or gypsum may improve productivity of these soils.

Magnesium moves to the root by all three transport methods: mass flow, root interception and diffusion.

Relationship of magnesium to other nutrients

The availability of magnesium is influenced by several other nutrients. Potassium, if present at high levels and exchangeable, can interfere with magnesium uptake. Ammonium can also interfere with the availability of magnesium to plants. This occurs mostly when high rates of ammonium fertilizers are applied to soils low in magnesium.

Some research suggests that magnesium encourages the uptake of phosphorus and mobility in plants. Magnesium is lost from soils by crop uptake, leaching and erosion.

Role of magnesium in plants

Magnesium has several roles in plant growth and development:
- structure of chlorophyll molecules
- protein synthesis
- essential for enzyme activation

Magnesium deficiency

Magnesium deficiency symptoms are frequently found in the lower leaves. This is due to the fact that magnesium is mobile in plants and can be moved to the new growth and reused. On some plants, magnesium shows as a crimson colour and on others as dead tissue between the veins or a pale green colour caused by low chlorophyll content.

Like calcium, magnesium deficiencies are linked to pH problems. Coarse textured, acidic soils are more likely to develop a magnesium deficiency. Coarse soils low in magnesium, which receive manure on a long-term basis, may be prone to induced magnesium deficiency due to the high potassium content of manure, especially ruminant manure.

Grass tetany

Grass tetany or hypomagnesemia is a magnesium imbalance in ruminant livestock as a result of consuming feeds low in magnesium. The low magnesium content of the feed can come from high rates of ammonium or potassium fertilizers being applied to the crop. A high protein content in the feed ration will also depress magnesium uptake within the animal.

Symptoms of magnesium deficiency in:
- Corn
  - initially yellow to white interveinal striping of older leaves, the striped areas eventually die (see inside front cover)
  - older leaves develop reddish to purple colour

- often confused with zinc but striping with magnesium is definite, extends from base to tip in the leaf
- Soybeans
  - pale green between veins on lower leaves during early growth
  - leaf margins curl down, entire leaf yellow except at the base
  - symptoms move to middle leaves, looks like early maturity
- Alfalfa
  - pale green colour in older leaves
  - stunted, low vigour, rusty specks develop into necrotic spots between leaf veins and leaf margins may die back
  - poor nodule development
- Cereals
  - lack of vigour, stunted with reproductive delays
  - large irregular spots uniformly across leaf tips and down leaf margins toward the leaf base on older leaves
  - may appear striped, leaves may develop colours from pale green to yellow, red and brown
- Potatoes
  - chlorosis with green veins and brown spots on young mature leaves (leaf scorch between veins)
  - in severe deficiency leaves will dry off but remain attached, new leaves green
- Tomatoes
  - older leaves affected first

- veins dark green, interveinal areas become yellow, lack of nitrogen intensifies the symptoms
- Celery, carrots
  - marginal necrosis and interveinal chlorosis on older leaves
  - leaves curl up
- Grapes
  - interveinal and marginal leaf necrosis
  - interveinal yellowing or reddening
  - development of brown-green patches

S Sulphur

The reduction in air-borne sulphur emissions and the use of more refined fertilizer products over the past several decades has lead to a decline of sulphur deposition in the Great Lakes Basin. See Figure 3-12. Sulphur is an essential element for plant growth. In the past, assumptions were made that soil sulphur supplies were adequate for crop production in Ontario. Responses to sulphur applications in general field crops has been sporadic and anecdotal.

Determination of sulphur status involves soil testing, plant tissue, observation and crop specific requirements. An Ontario accredited sulphur test is currently unavailable. However, laboratories in Ontario offer a sulphur soil test used in other jurisdictions. The challenge is to interpret the

FIGURE 3-12. Atmospheric sulphur deposition

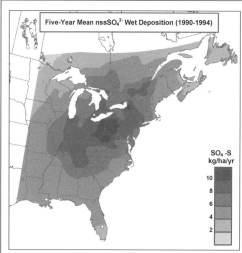

Five-Year Mean nssSO₄²⁻ Wet Deposition (1990-1994)

SO₄-S
kg/ha/yr

10
8
6
4
2

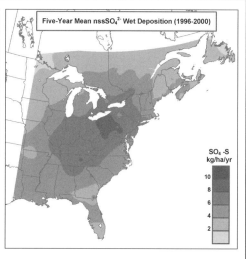

Five-Year Mean nssSO₄²⁻ Wet Deposition (1996-2000)

SO₄-S
kg/ha/yr

10
8
6
4
2

* nssSO₄²⁻ = non sea-salt sulphate sulphur deposition

Source: Ro et al, 2006.

analytical result into a sulphur recommendation as calibration data is currently lacking for Ontario growing conditions. An inherent risk exists in using recommendations from other growing areas. Often plant tissue evaluation, along with sulphur strip trials in fields, is useful in determining sulphur status of a particular cropping system. Crops with a known sulphur requirement such as canola require special attention.

Sulphur occurs in the soil in many forms, both organic and inorganic. The sulphate ion (SO_4^{2-}) is the form of sulphur available to the plant. Most of the sulphur in the soil is in organic matter. The transformation of sulphur from organic and inorganic forms to plant available sulphate involves four main steps:

- mineralization
- immobilization
- oxidation
- reduction

Mineralization is the decomposition of organic matter where the organic sulphur is broken down by bacteria into the plant available sulphate.

Immobilization is the opposite. Bacteria convert sulphate back to organic, unavailable sulphur.

Soil temperatures, pH, or moisture that affects microbial growth will affect the mineralization of organic matter and rate and amount of sulphate available to plants.

Oxidation is the reaction of sulphur with oxygen to form sulphate. This is an important process since some fertilizers are reduced forms of sulphur and this conversion helps make them available to plants.

Reduction is the opposite process. Sulphate is stripped of its oxygen under anaerobic conditions. Soils that are poorly drained are subject to this reaction and can produce sulphide compounds under prolonged waterlogged periods.

Factors affecting sulphur requirements

Carbon-to-sulphur ratios

Sulphur undergoes many of the same mineralization and immobilization reactions as nitrogen in the soil. Adding residues with a wide C:S ratio (>200:1) can result in sulphur immobilization and temporary sulphur deficiencies. This is more common with mature crop residues like straw than with fresh materials like clovers and green manures.

Nitrogen-to-sulphur ratios

The ratio of N:S in plant tissues ranges from 7:1 to 15:1, depending on the species and the stage of growth. Crops that receive high rates of nitrogen when sulphur supply from the soil is low can suffer from induced sulphur deficiency. This has led to a common practice, in western Canada, of applying ½ kg of sulphate sulphur to canola for every 3–4 kg of nitrogen. Ontario growers may have to consider a similar practice for intensively managed canola crops, particularly if atmospheric deposition of sulphur continues to decline.

Role of sulphur in plants

Sulphur is a constituent of two of the 21 amino acids that form proteins. It also:

- helps develop enzymes and vitamins

- is involved in nitrogen fixation in legumes
- aids in seed production
- is needed for chlorophyll formation

Sulphur also adds colour, flavour and distinctive odours to plants such as garlic, onions and cabbage and puts the heat in horseradish

Sulphur deficiency

Symptoms of sulphur deficiency are similar to nitrogen deficiency except sulphur is not mobile, so the entire plant remains light green.

Symptoms of sulphur definciency in:

- Corn
  - in small plants general yellowing of foliage, stunting and delayed maturity
- Legumes including soybeans, alfalfa
  - small, yellowish green leaves at top of plant
  - thin, erect stems, woody and elongated
- Cereals
  - interveinal yellowing of youngest leaves
  - erect tillers
- Potatoes
  - entire plant light green
  - in severe deficiency leaflets curl upward
- Canola
  - newly emerged leaves are yellowish green with dark veins, cupped
  - cupped, purple leaves, few small pods or empty pods
  - sulphur deficiencies can occur at any growth stage

- mild deficiencies give good vegetative growth but pale flowers and pods are under developed
- post-harvest re-growth of stubble
- root rots can cause deficiency symptoms to appear

Micronutrients

Micronutrients are as important as the primary and secondary nutrients. Micronutrients are needed in much smaller quantities by the plant and are often less prevalent in the soil. The need for these nutrients varies with crop, variety, soil conditions and farm management. General responses of various crops to micronutrients are shown in Table 3-8, page 72.

The use of micronutrients has increased over time. The need for micronutrient application may be increasing because of:

- continued high yield cropping that may have depleted soil reserves
- more refined fertilizer materials with fewer impurities such as micronutrients
- specialized agriculture with fewer fields receiving manure
- soil degradation and erosion

 Zinc

Zinc is relatively immobile in the soil, so that leaching does not pose a problem.

Zinc that may become available to plants is present in the soil solution as Zn^{2+}. It is held on the surfaces of clay, organic matter and soil minerals as exchangeable zinc or complexed with organic materials.

Zinc availability is reduced by:
- high pH because at high pH, zinc forms insoluble compounds
- adsorption on the surfaces of clay, organic matter, carbonates and oxide minerals

Zinc is important in early plant growth and in grain and seed formation. It plays a role in chlorophyll and carbohydrate production.

Zinc deficiency

Zinc deficiencies are most often seen on high pH soils, on soils with marginal zinc levels where there have been large applications of phosphorus, on sandy soils or on eroded or leveled soils where the subsoil is exposed. Deficiencies may also occur in organic (muck) soils.

Zinc deficiency is rarely seen on livestock farms as manure generally contains zinc. Liquid swine manure, for example, can contain over 85 grams of zinc per cubic meter, while solid poultry manure may contain over 200 grams per metric ton.

Because zinc is relatively immobile within the plant, deficiency symptoms develop first on young foliage.

Symptoms of zinc deficiency in:

- Corn
  - usually seen in young plants as interveinal chlorosis on new leaves
  - can appear as pale to white bands between the leaf margin and mid-vein in the lower part of the leaf
  - in severe deficiency, new leaves emerge from the whorl completely white (white bud)
- Legumes including soybeans, alfalfa
  - thin, short stems, pale green bronzed foliage with yellow mottling and some necrosis
  - interveinal chlorosis continues to develop and veins appear darker green (unlike manganese deficiency the chlorosis appears more mottled)
- Tree fruit and strawberries
  - chlorosis of young leaves, green halo appears along serrated margins of young immature leaf blades
  - blind bud, little leaf and rosetting (small basal leaves forming on short terminal and lateral shoots of new year's growth)
- Onions
  - stunted growth with twisted yellow striped foliage

Phosphorus toxicity?

Plants deficient in zinc have an impaired ability to regulate the accumulation of phosphorus. This results in phosphorus being taken up by plants in excess amounts. For this reason, tissue analysis will often show high phosphorus in zinc deficient plants.

Mn Manganese

Most of the manganese absorbed by plants is in the form Mn^{2+}. Manganese in the soil exists in four main forms: mineral, organic, exchangeable and dissolved. Soil contains large amounts of manganese but little is available.

The availability of manganese is influenced by:

- pH because as pH values rise, exchangeable manganese declines rapidly (availability is greatest at pH 5.0 to 6.5)
- high organic matter, which decreases the availability of manganese and is of particular concern in vegetable production on muck soils
- excessive water or poor aeration, which causes soluble manganese to increase
- other nutrients such as nitrogen — if the nitrogen fertilizer

has an acidifying effect, this can enhance uptake of manganese

Manganese is involved in photosynthesis and chlorophyll pro-duction. It helps activate enzymes involved in the distribution of growth regulators within the plant.

TABLE 3-8. Response of crops to micronutrient fertilizers					
	Manganese	Boron	Copper	Zinc	Molybdenum
alfalfa	low	high	high	low	med
barley	med	low	med	low	low
clover	med	med	med	low	high
corn	med	low	med	high	low
edible beans	high	low	low	high	med
oats	high	low	high	low	low
rye	low	low	low	low	low
soybeans	high	low	low	med	med
wheat	high	low	high	low	low
asparagus	low	low	low	low	low
broccoli, cauliflower	med	high	med		high
cabbage	med	med	med	low	med
carrots, parsnips	med	med	med	low	low
celery	med	high	med		low
cucumbers	high	low	med		
lettuce	high	med	high	med	high
onions	high	low	high	high	high
peas	high	low	low	low	med
peppers	med	low	low		med
potatoes	high	low	low	med	low
radishes	high	med	med	med	med
red beets	high	high	high	med	high
spinach	high	med	high	high	high
sugar beets	high	med	med	med	med
sweet corn	high	med	med	high	low
tomatoes	med	med	high	med	med
blueberries	low	low	med		

Highly responsive crops often respond to micronutrient fertilizer if the micronutrient concentration in the soil is low. Medium responsive crops are less likely to respond, and low responsive crops do not usually respond even at the lowest soil micronutrient levels.

Source: Michigan State University Publication E-486. *Secondary and Micronutrients for Vegetables and Field Crops*, 1994.

Manganese deficiency

Manganese deficiency is seen most frequently in soybeans on high pH soils, in crops on muck soils and high organic matter mineral soils. Deficiencies can also occur in newly tiled fields. Root rots may cause manganese deficiencies. Reduced root growth from Soybean Cyst Nematodes (SCN) may increase Mn deficiencies. Mn deficiency is implicated in many diseases.

Symptoms of maganese deficiency in:

- Soybeans, white beans
  - chlorotic conditions in younger leaves
  - veins in the leaves will remain dark green while between the veins the tissue will go yellow (see inside back cover)
- Small grains
  - pale yellow, stunting, later tips of small grains turn grey to white (grey speck in oats)
- Red beets, sugar beets
  - russetting, curling and dwarfing of foliage
- Lettuce, celery, onions
  - yellowing of leaves, stunting and delayed maturity

Early season foliar application is more effective as a treatment for manganese deficiencies because soil-applied manganese converts rapidly to unavailable forms.

Soil-applied manganese may be useful in acidic, sandy soils. Banded applications are more available than broadcast.

Note: On Red Delicious apples and some peach cultivars, manganese toxicity can occur on coarse textured soils when pH is below 5.0.

The symptoms known as measles are raised pimples on the bark underlain by dark brown spots. Correction sometimes is possible by the addition of lime to raise the pH.

B Boron

Boron in the soil is present as soil solution boron, adsorbed boron and mineral boron. Boron uptake by plants is related to pH. Availability is best at pHs between 5.0 and 7.0. Availability decreases during periods of drought.

Boron plays an important role in the structural integrity of cell walls, fruit set and seed development, and carbohydrate and protein metabolism.

Note: Crops vary widely in their requirements for and tolerance to boron. The line between deficient and toxic is narrow. Boron toxicity symptoms have occurred in seed and sweet corn and soybeans following red beets that had boron applied.

Use boron with care and with concern for the crop rotation.

Boron deficiency

Boron deficiencies are more likely with:

- dry soil
- soil pH extremes
- low organic matter soils
- exposed or eroded subsoils

Symptoms of boron deficiency vary widely from plant to plant. Boron is not readily translocated through the plant.

Symptoms of boron deficiency in:

- Rutabaga
  - hollow centre, brown watery areas (water core)
- Celery
  - stem cracked with brown stripes (cat scratches), heart blackened
- Cole crops
  - hollow stems, brown curds, deformed buds
- Apples
  - small, flattened or mis-shapen fruit, low seed count, internal corking, cracking and russetting, dead terminal buds, dwarfed stiff cupped and brittle leaves, blossom blast
- Alfalfa
  - yellow-reddish top leaves, shortened internodes, poor seed set, terminal leaves form rosette, death of terminal bud (see inside back cover)
- Sugar beets, red beets, spinach
  - yellowing of leaves, spotting, cracking of root
- Cereals
  - greater infection levels of ergot

Copper

Copper is found in the soil solution, on clay and organic matter exchange sites, as part of soil oxides and in biological residues and living organisms. A large proportion, 20% to 50% in some soils, is held in organically bound forms.

Availability of copper depends on:

- texture because copper levels are lower in sands
- soil pH as copper mobility decreases as pH rises
- soil organic matter — availability is extremely low in organic soils and can also be low in soils with very little organic matter

Some nutrients such as zinc, aluminum, phosphorus and iron, if in high concentrations, depress copper absorption by plants.

Copper plays a role in chlorophyll production, as a catalyst for enzymes, and perhaps in disease suppression.

Copper deficiency

Copper deficiencies are most common in crops grown on organic (muck) soils and sandy high pH well-drained soils.

Symptoms of copper deficiency in:

- Carrots
  - pale root
- Onions
  - tip dieback, curl and subsequent pig-tailing, bulb scales thin, pale yellow

- Cereal grains
  - pig-tail (leaf tip dies and may roll and curl to form pig-tail)
  - retarded stem elongation
  - absence of grain heads
  - grain formed maybe unusually high in protein
- Lettuce
  - leaves lose firmness, yellow bleached stems

In western Canada, copper deficiencies were identified in the early 80s and research has since identified millions of acres in the Prairies that are deficient in this essential nutrient.

Chlorine

Chlorine is generally found in nature as chloride (Cl^-). Chloride is readily soluble, highly mobile and easily taken up by plants. In Ontario soils, leaching keeps chloride at low levels. Higher levels of chloride can be found in the lower slope positions of the field landscape where water accumulates and subsequently results in higher plant tissue levels of chloride.

The availability of chloride is not affected by soil pH. The uptake and accumulation of chloride by plants is depressed by high concentrations of nitrate and sulphate.

Chloride in plants plays an important role in stomatal regulation and water flow. Chloride is also involved in photosynthesis. Research outside Ontario suggests that chloride helps in the suppression of take all and leaf rust and septoria in wheat and barley, as well as stalk rot in corn. The application of potassium as muriate of potash may provide enough chloride to attain these benefits. Demonstration trials in Ontario have suggested a slight yield advantage to chloride applied with nitrogen on winter wheat.

Some tree fruit and cane fruit crops are sensitive to chloride, particularly in the seedling stage. Chlorides are also of concern in tobacco because of their effect on burn quality.

Chlorine vs. chloride

Some concern exists about the effect of chlorine from fertilizers like muriate of potash on soil bacteria. What is in the fertilizers, though, is chloride.

Chlorine and chloride are not the same and cannot be used interchangeably. Their behaviour and reactions in the soil and their effects on plants and micro-organisms are entirely different.

Chlorine (Cl_2) is a corrosive, poisonous gas used to make bleaching agents and disinfectants. When chlorine gas is dissolved in water, it forms a hypochlorite ion, the active ingredient in household bleach. Commercial liquid chlorine (compressed chlorine gas) is used as a water treatment to kill bacteria. Both hypochlorite and chlorine are effective bactericides.

Chloride (Cl^-) on the other hand, is the ionic form of chlorine found in nature. It has a negative charge and is most often associated with sodium (common salt) or other positively charged ions like potassium. It is non-toxic and readily absorbed and used by plants.

Compare the concentrations of chloride and chlorine in water. Sea water, which is teeming with bacterial life, contains chloride levels in the order of 20,000 ppm. Water treatment plants typically aim for chlorine levels of 1.7 ppm to disinfect the water.

Source: Eric Bosveld, The Agromart Group

 Iron

Iron is abundant in most soils but its solubility is very low. The form taken up by plants is the ferrous ion (Fe^{2+}). It plays a number of functions within plants. Iron:
- is a catalyst in the formation of chlorophyll
- is required for plant respiration
- functions in the formation of some proteins

The greatest use of iron is in the turf, nursery and sod industries where applications are used to give a darker green appearance to the foliage.

Iron deficiency

Iron deficiencies are rarely found in Ontario. When blueberries and rhododendrons are grown on soils with higher than recommended pH, iron deficiency can be a problem.

Factors associated with iron deficiency in other parts of the world are:
- imbalance with other metals such as molybdenum, copper or manganese
- excessive phosphorus in the soil
- plant genetics
- low soil organic matter
- combination of high pH (>7.8), high lime, wet cold soils and high bicarbonate levels (lime-induced chlorosis)

Symptoms of iron deficiency in:

- Blueberries, rhododendrons
  - young leaves showing interveinal chlorosis or striping along the entire length of the leaf
  - in severe cases growth may be stunted

These crops perform best in acidic soils because they have a high demand for iron.

Mo Molybdenum

Molybdenum is found in soil as non-exchangeable molybdenum in soil minerals and as exchangeable molybdenum on iron and aluminum oxides in the soil solution and bound organically.

Availability of molybdenum is influenced by:

- soil pH because as pH levels rise molybdate availability increases (liming can improve the availability on acidic soils)
- aluminum and iron oxides, as molybdenum is strongly adsorbed to these, making it less available

Molybdenum is taken up by plants as molybdate (MoO_4^{2-}). Phosphorus enhances its absorption. However, deficiencies are most likely to occur under low soil moisture conditions, as this reduces mass flow and diffusion. There are also significant differences in sensitivity to low levels of molybdenum between plants and even between varieties of plants.

Molybdenum plays an important role in nitrogen metabolism within the plant and nitrogen fixation in legumes. It also plays a role in pollen viability and seed production.

Symptoms of molybdenum deficiency in:

- Legumes
  - poor nodule formation, nitrogen deficiency symptoms
- Cole crops
  - early symptoms similar to nitrogen or sulphur deficiency: pale yellow or light green leaves, stunted plants that may show yellow mottling
  - small necrotic areas of the leaf tissue followed by scorching and upward curling of the upper blade margins (whiptail in cauliflower)

Ni Nickel

Nickel is taken up by plants as Ni^{2+}. High levels in the soil can induce zinc or iron deficiency symptoms caused by competition between these cations. Nickel is an essential nutrient for legumes. It is important in nitrogen transformations as it is a component of the urease enzyme. Deficiency of nickel in agricultural soils is unknown.

Non-essential minerals

Although not essential for all plant growth, non-essential nutrients may be necessary for some plants or as a part of animal development. They also may become a problem if the soil concentrations reach toxic levels, killing or harming the plant or passing the toxin along to the human or animal that eats the plant.

Beneficial minerals

Cobalt

Cobalt (Co) plays a role in forming vitamin B12 and enhances the growth of nitrogen fixing organisms like Rhizobia and algae. Cobalt also plays a role in forming vitamin B12 in ruminants.

Sodium

Sodium (Na) plays a role in osmotic regulation, helping control the flow of water into and out of the plant. In some plants in low potassium soils, sodium may perform some of the functions of potassium.

Sodium can have a toxic effect on plants. The large amount of rainfall and leaching in the spring and fall means that high sodium soils are not common in Ontario. Areas with high sodium levels are usually associated with old oil wells and spilled brine. Plant growth is reduced in these areas because of the toxic effect of excess sodium and the poor structure of sodic soils.

Silicon

Silicon (Si) can make up as much as 40% of un-weathered sandy soils. Grasses contain 10 to 20 times the silicon concentration found in legumes and other broadleaves.

Silicon has been documented to reduce shading within a crop field through improved erect growth, decreased lodging, increased resistance to root parasites and leaf and root diseases, and prevention of some nutrient toxicities.

Vanadium

Vanadium (V) is beneficial at low concentrations to micro-organisms, although there is no evidence it is essential for crop plants. It is thought to perform some functions in nitrogen fixation and may play a role in biological oxidation and reduction reactions.

Selenium

Selenium (Se) is not needed by plants but must be present in the feed for animal health. A deficiency in selenium results in white muscle disease, a form of muscular dystrophy in animals like cattle and sheep. Some areas of North America with semi-arid to arid climates such as California have soils with high selenium content. Much of Ontario, however, is deficient in selenium and it is added to feed or given by injection to maintain animal health. In some cases, it can be spread as a fertilizer but the cost makes this rare in Ontario.

More problems with selenium deficiencies in livestock have been noted after cold, rainy growing conditions than hot, dry conditions. The use of nitrogen fertilizers to increase forage yields has lowered the selenium content of feed. The plant takes up the same amount of selenium but it is spread across a larger plant and more biomass, diluting the selenium.

Undesirable elements

Lead

Lead (Pb), a heavy metal usually associated with industrial wastes, can be taken up by plants. The symptoms of toxicity are similar to iron deficiency in that there is a yellowing of the plant with interveinal chlorosis.

The build-up of lead in human tissues is a serious problem. Lead poisoning usually results from exposure and inadvertent ingestion of household materials like lead-based paint in old houses or breathing in lead-laden dust during construction. For more information on lead poisoning contact your local health unit.

Mercury and cadmium

Mercury (Hg) and cadmium (Cd) are heavy metals that can accumulate in tissues. Generally, this is not a problem with plants but the accumulation in human and animal tissues can have serious effects.

The level of heavy metals in sewage sludge will determine whether it can be applied to agricultural fields and the rate and frequency of application. These metals do not move or get removed except in plant tissues, so they will accumulate in soil.

References

Bennett, W.F., ed. 1993. *Nutrient Deficiencies and Toxicities in Crop Plants.* American Phytopathological Society.

Havlin, J. L, J. D. Beaton, S. L. Tisdale and W. L. Nelson, 2005. *Soil Fertility and Fertilizers: An Introduction to Nutrient Management.* 7th ed. Pearson Education Inc., Upper Saddle River, New Jersey 07458.

Hoeft, Robert 2002, Nitrogen Loss for 2002. *University of Illinois Pest & Crop Bulletin* (5/3/02).

Ozgen, S., J.P. Palta, and M.D. Kleinhenz, 2006. *Influence of Supplemental Calcium Fertilization on Potato Tuber Size and Tuber Number.* ISHS Acta Horticulturae 619: XXVI International Horticultural Congress: Potatoes, Healthy Food for Humanity: International Developments in Breeding, Production, Protection and Utilization.

Ro, C.U., Vet, R.J. and Narayan, J. 2006. *Analyzed data fields from the National Atmospheric Chemistry Database (NAtChem) and Analysis Facility.* Atmospheric Science and Technology Directorate, Science and Technology Branch, Environment Canada, 4905 Dufferin St., Toronto, Ontario, Canada M3H 5T4.

Secondary and Micronutrients for Vegetables and Field Crops. August 1994. Michigan State University extension E-486.

Sprague, Howard D., ed. 1964. *Hunger Signs in Crops.* David McKay Company Inc.

For more detail

Barber, Stanley A. 1995. *Soil Nutrient Bioavailability: A Mechanistic Approach.* John Wiley and Sons, Inc.

Marschner, Horst. 1995. *Mineral Nutrition of Higher Plants.* 2nd ed. Academic Press.

4 SOIL pH, LIMING AND ACIDIFICATION

The effects of pH on plant growth are mostly indirect. Soil acidity affects nutrient availability, as shown in Figure 4-1. It can cause the concentration of some elements to rise to toxic levels. It also affects the activity of soil organisms that build soil structure, cycle organic matter or fix nitrogen in the nodules on the roots of legumes. Soil pH can have a drastic effect on the performance and breakdown of some pesticides.

Plant species differ in their requirements and tolerance of soil conditions that result from different pH regimes, just as they differ in their requirements and tolerance of differing soil moisture conditions. Correcting problems with soil pH is one of the first steps in good soil management.

Generally, plants take up nutrients only if they are dissolved in water. Soil pH influences the solubility of plant nutrients and other elements. Some nutrients are more soluble at high pH, others at low pH and still others at ranges in between.

As soil pH drops, aluminum dissolves more readily. Aluminum is not a plant nutrient but is a major component of the mineral (clay, silt and sand) fraction of soils. Dissolved aluminum reacts with dissolved phosphorus compounds rendering them insoluble and therefore unavailable. Levels of dissolved aluminum may reach toxic levels for intolerant species at pH values of 5.5 and below. High aluminum levels restrict the formation of nitrogen-fixing nodules on the roots of legumes. Manganese, which is a plant nutrient, may also reach toxic levels at pH values below 5.0 in some soils and for intolerant species.

When soil pH is high (above 7.5), we add nutrients to compensate for pH effects because it is uneconomical to lower soil pH for many crops. The same approach could be taken for low pH soils if toxicity were not an issue, but it is more cost-effective to correct soil pH by liming than to attempt to resolve multiple nutrient deficiencies by adding fertilizer. Neutral-to-high soil pH can have negative effects on some crops such as blueberries. Soil pH above 6.5 promotes scab disease in potatoes.

Aluminum, manganese and iron compounds abound in mineral soils but not in organic soils (mucks and peats). This limits the ability of these elements to interfere with the solubility of other nutrients in organic soils. Therefore, lower soil pH is more acceptable for organic soils than for mineral soils.

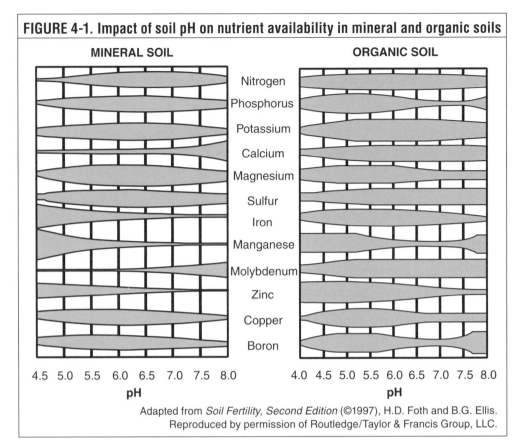

FIGURE 4-1. Impact of soil pH on nutrient availability in mineral and organic soils

MINERAL SOIL

ORGANIC SOIL

Nitrogen
Phosphorus
Potassium
Calcium
Magnesium
Sulfur
Iron
Manganese
Molybdenum
Zinc
Copper
Boron

4.5 5.0 5.5 6.0 6.5 7.0 7.5 8.0
pH

4.0 4.5 5.0 5.5 6.0 6.5 7.0 7.5 8.0
pH

Adapted from *Soil Fertility, Second Edition* (©1997), H.D. Foth and B.G. Ellis.
Reproduced by permission of Routledge/Taylor & Francis Group, LLC.

Factors in increasing soil acidity

Precipitation

Pure rainwater is slightly acidic because carbon dioxide is dissolved in the water, forming carbonic acid. Other acids, like nitric and sulphuric acid, are present in lower amounts, depending on the amount of air pollution. The addition of these acids over thousands of years, as they percolate down through the soil, creates a gradual reduction in soil pH at the surface of the soil. This is a normal part of soil development in humid climates.

Acid deposition (acid rain, acid snow and dry deposition) in most of southern Ontario does not contribute significantly to declining pH because of the ability of agricultural soils to resist change in pH and the low quantity of acid being deposited.

Unlike agricultural soils, many bodies of water, especially those located on the igneous rock of the Canadian Shield, have little or no ability to resist change in pH. Acid deposition is far more of a concern for aquatic systems and for the shallow soils of the Canadian Shield than for agricultural soils.

Organic matter decay

As organic materials break down, they release organic acids into the soil. This also contributes to the reduction of soil pH in the surface layers of the soil, where most of the organic matter is present.

Parent material

The primary soil factors that influence the potential rate of decline in pH are the starting pH, the amount of organic matter in the soil and the amount and type of clay. Mineral soils that are neutral to high in pH, high in organic matter content and have high clay contents, have greater buffering capacity than coarse textured soils, so pH declines much more slowly. Soils with high concentrations of free lime (carbonate minerals) neutralize acidity and resist decline of soil pH until the lime is depleted. Coarse textured soils low in organic matter and with pH in the 5–6 range have a poor ability to resist pH change.

Fertilizer application

The microbial conversion of the ammonium form of nitrogen to the nitrate form is one of the biological processes that release acid into the soil. The addition of large amounts of ammonium-containing fertilizers can accelerate the decline in pH, particularly in sandy soils low in organic matter.

Urea and anhydrous ammonia do not contain the ammonium form of nitrogen but are converted to ammonium nitrogen when in contact with the soil. The pH of sandy soils that receive the ammonium, ammonia or urea forms of nitrogen from fertilizers or manure should be monitored regularly.

How soil becomes basic (alkaline)

When the glaciers retreated from Ontario ten thousand years ago, the materials left behind were uniform in pH from the surface to the depth at which there was a change in the texture of the material. The materials were deposited directly by the glaciers, deposited by melt waters running from the retreating ice front or settled from the waters of post-glacial lakes. These became the materials from which our agricultural soils formed. Most of the materials were neutral-to-basic in pH.

The processes that make soils more acidic, work on the layers of soil closest to the surface. Over thousands of years the acidified surface layers thickened as the depth of biological processes increased and as the water moving downward through the soil removed bases. This has left soil profiles that have decreasing acidity (increasing alkalinity) with depth.

Many of Ontario's agricultural soils are alkaline (pH greater than 7) at depths of only 30 cm or more and have pH as high as 8.2 at about 1 m. As a result, most agricultural soils in Ontario allow plants to get ample supplies of basic nutrients such as calcium and magnesium within the rooting zone.

If soil pH increases over a series of soil tests, the likely causes are:
- The depth of soil collected when sampling has changed. It is much easier to collect soil samples to greater depth when the soil is moist and

friable than when it is dry or compacted.

- Tillage is mixing soil from deeper in the profile with the soil being sampled. Some farmers see this as a way of increasing pH without liming but it is rarely effective in making desirable changes in pH. The detrimental effects of diluting the organic matter content of the surface soil with sub-soil and on soil structure must be considered.
- Ditching, tile drainage or levelling has exposed sub-soil that is now being included in the soil sample.
- Erosion is removing the most acidic surface layers. Subsidence (oxidation, shrinkage and disappearance) of a layer of muck overlying mineral soil has the same effect.

In Ontario, precipitation exceeds the water lost through evaporation and transpiration. The net movement of water through the soil is downward and the net movement of basic cations is downward (albeit very slowly through all but coarse textured soils).

Alkali soils (sodium saturated) and deposits occur in dry regions such as the Prairies where evaporation and plant transpiration exceed precipitation. As a result, the net movement of water is upward carrying basic cations to the surface making the surface more alkaline.

Dealing with high pH soils

Assess soil pH levels. The optimum soil pH range for most crops is 6.0 to 7.5. Even above 7.5, the impact on field crop production is minor in most cases. Phosphorus availability is reduced somewhat, but this is reflected in the phosphorus soil test. As long as reasonable levels are maintained, it should not affect crop production. Band phosphorus fertilizer to reduce immobilization.

Don't try to reduce the pH of alkaline soils. If the soil pH is very high (7.8–8.2), the soil will contain a high concentration of free lime (calcium carbonate). The soil is extremely well buffered and will resist any attempts to bring the pH down. Adding sulphur to acidify the soil will not be effective but it will be costly.

Keep the pH from going any higher. Since most cases of elevated pH result from excessive tillage or soil erosion, a reduced tillage program will help keep the existing topsoil in place and prevent the subsoil from being brought to the surface.

Monitor crops for any signs of nutrient deficiencies induced by high pH. The most common deficiencies are manganese on soybeans or cereals or zinc on corn. If you see evidence of manganese deficiency, consider foliar application. For zinc deficiency, add zinc to the starter fertilizer.

Symptoms of pH problems

One principle of good soil management is to adjust soil pH to the optimal range for the crops you are growing. Then tackle soil fertility issues.

Soil testing is the only reliable means to determine whether the pH needs adjusting.

However, some areas within a field may show symptoms of low pH, even though the average pH for the field is acceptable. These areas, often sandy knolls, should be tested separately.

Symptoms that may indicate that there is a pH problem:

- poor nodulation of forage legumes even though the seed was inoculated (pale green colour results from the poor nodulation)
- only oats harvested, even though mixed grain was planted (barley is more sensitive to acid soil)
- poor persistence in perennial forages with adequate drainage and fertilization
- presence of mosses and weeds such as wild strawberry, devil's paintbrush, sheep sorrel
- poor performance of soil-applied triazine herbicides like atrazine and metribuzin
- longer than expected carryover of imazethepyr (Pursuit)

Do not make a diagnosis based only on symptoms. Always take a soil test to confirm pH problems.

Figure 4-2 shows the prevalence of acid soils in North American states and provinces.

Buffer pH

The buffering capacity of the soil is its ability to resist changes in pH. In an acid soil this ability to resist change is due to the reserve acidity. This reserve acidity is caused by hydrogen, aluminum and other cations held on the cation exchange complex. The greater the reserve

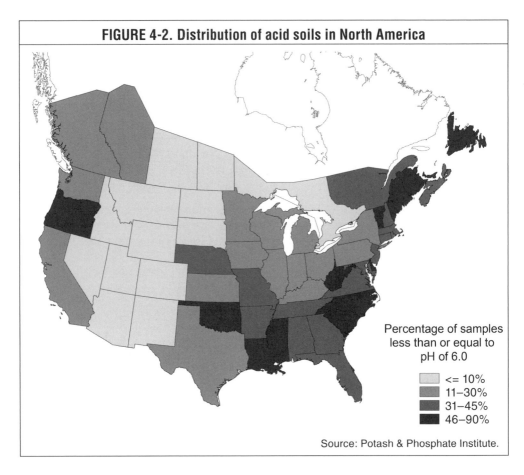

FIGURE 4-2. Distribution of acid soils in North America

Percentage of samples less than or equal to pH of 6.0

- <= 10%
- 11–30%
- 31–45%
- 46–90%

Source: Potash & Phosphate Institute.

acidity, the more lime is required to bring the pH into optimal range.

Soils differ in their buffering capacity depending mostly on the amount and type of clay in the soil, the soil organic matter content and the base saturation of the cation exchange sites. A simple measurement of soil pH does not depict its ability to resist changes in pH.

Buffer pH is a pH measurement after the soil sample is mixed with a buffered solution. The solution itself resists change in pH. See page 22 for more detail.

The pH resulting from the soil-buffer solution interaction is well correlated to the amount of limestone needed to adjust soil pH to a target level. Buffer pH is a simple, inexpensive and accurate means of determining lime requirements.

Recommendations from soil tests for crop nutrients are based on the relationship between soil test levels and crop response to the addition of nutrients. The buffer pH test differs in that it relates soil test levels to the soil response to the addition of lime.

The actual lime recommendation depends on the target pH for the crop as well as the buffer pH. Different crops require different pH ranges.

After determining the target pH, consult a chart for the lime requirement. See Table 4-1.

Some suggest that because aluminum becomes toxic under acid soil conditions the soils should be limed to neutralize the amount of exchangeable aluminum. This method is not any better, and may be worse, than adding lime according to the buffer pH.

	TABLE 4-1. Lime requirements to correct soil acidity based on soil pH and soil buffer pH			
Buffer pH	Target soil* pH = 7	Target soil pH = 6.5 (Lime if soil pH below 6.1)	Target soil pH = 6.0 (Lime if soil pH below 5.6)	Target soil pH = 5.5 (Lime if soil pH below 5.1)
Ground limestone required — t/ha (based on an Agricultural Index of 75)				
7.0	2	2	1	1
6.9	3	2	1	1
6.8	3	2	1	1
6.7	4	2	2	1
6.6	5	3	2	1
6.5	6	3	2	1
6.4	7	4	3	2
6.3	8	5	3	2
6.2	10	6	4	2
6.1	11	7	5	2
6.0	13	9	6	3
5.9	14	10	7	4
5.8	16	12	8	4
5.7	18	13	9	5
5.6	20	15	11	6
5.5	20	17	12	8
5.4	20	19	14	9
5.3	20	20	15	10
5.2	20	20	17	11
5.1	20	20	19	13
5.0	20	20	20	15
4.9	20	20	20	16
4.8	20	20	20	18
4.7	20	20	20	20
4.6	20	20	20	20
* Liming to pH 7.0 is recommended only for club-root control on cole crops.				

Limestone quality

Two parameters are normally used when assessing the quality of agricultural limestone. They are the neutralizing value and the fineness rating.

Neutralizing value

Acidity is neutralized when hydrogen ions (H^+) react with other compounds to form water (H_2O).

Certain compounds that fall into the general categories of carbonates, hydroxides and oxides are normally used to neutralize acidity.

Carbonates are most commonly used for agricultural purposes because they are readily available from the sedimentary limestone rocks found in many parts of the province and are relatively inexpensive.

When ground limestone is used, it is the carbonates in the lime that neutralize the acidity. The following reaction describes how calcium carbonate reacts with two hydrogen ions to produce water and carbon dioxide (CO_2). The up arrow indicates that the carbon dioxide is given off as a gas. This helps to keep the reaction from reversing itself.

$$CaCO_3 + 2H^+ \rightarrow H_2O + Ca^{2+} + CO_2\uparrow$$

This reaction is essentially the same as when vinegar, an acid that releases hydrogen ions, is added to baking soda (sodium bicarbonate).

Hydroxides (OH-) combine directly with hydrogen ions (H+) to form water (H_2O). Oxides of calcium, magnesium and potassium can combine with water to form hydroxides. Potential liming materials containing oxides and hydroxides are normally the result of heat treatment or combustion, e.g. wood ash. They tend to have high pH values and are more caustic to handle than limestone.

The neutralizing value is the ability of the material to neutralize acidity relative to the ability of pure calcium carbonate to do the same job. Because it is a relative value, it is expressed as a per cent of calcium carbonate's ($CaCO_3$) ability to neutralize acidity. Pure magnesium carbonate has a higher neutralizing value than calcium carbonate because magnesium atoms weigh less than calcium atoms. However, one magnesium carbonate molecule will neutralize as much acidity as one calcium carbonate molecule.

Pure compounds are never used for liming because they are too expensive. Normally, we use a source such as crushed limestone in which at least one of these compounds is found in relatively high proportions.

The pH of the material suspended in water is not a good indicator of the neutralizing ability of a material. For example, the pH of a potassium hydroxide may be greater than 13 (basic and caustic). The pH of a solution of calcium carbonate may only be 8.2, yet the calcium carbonate is a more effective liming agent.

Limestone is a sedimentary rock formed from corals in warm oceans. Limestone rock is not pure carbonate-minerals. Silts, clays, sand and other materials also accumulated in ocean bottoms. The degree of inclu-

TABLE 4-2. Neutralizing values of some liming materials		
	Formula	Neutralizing value relative to calcium carbonate
Calcitic lime (calcium carbonate)	$CaCO_3$	100
Magnesium carbonate	$MgCO_3$	119
Dolomitic lime (calcium magnesium carbonate)	$CaMg(CO_3)_2$	109
Calcium hydroxide	$Ca(OH)_2$	135
Calcium oxide	CaO	179
Magnesium hydroxide	$Mg(OH)_2$	172
Magnesium oxide	MgO	250
Potassium hydroxide	KOH	90
Gypsum (Calcium sulphate)	$CaSO_4 \cdot 2H_2O$	0
Wood Ashes	n/a	40–80

sion of these contaminants affects the purity of the limestone and therefore the neutralizing value.

Fineness

To be effective, any liming material must dissolve. Limestone does not dissolve quickly like salt or sugar and its rate of dissolution decreases as pH increases. The surface area of the limestone must be maximized to get satisfactory rates of dissolution. This is accomplished by having tiny particle sizes.

The fineness of liming materials is measured using sieves. The sieves are numbered according to the numbers of wires per inch and the size of the spaces between the wires. A #10 sieve has 10 wires per inch with openings that measure 1.65 mm per side. See Table 4-3.

Any material passing through a #60 sieve is considered to be fully effective. Material that passes through a #10 sieve but not a #60 sieve is considered only 40% effective. Materials that do not pass through a #10 sieve are considered ineffective. Figure 4-4. illustrates how the fineness rating for limestone is calculated.

Federal government standards dictate that liming materials be labeled with the percentages of the material that pass through a #10 and a #100 sieve. In Ontario, we use the #10 and #60 sieves to help determine the quality of agricultural limestone. It should feel like finely ground flour.

It is usually not economical to crush materials to the fineness needed to make effective agricultural limestone. Estimated usage in Ontario is a modest 100,000 to 300,000 tonnes a year. By comparison, retail sales of fertilizers in Ontario peaked in 1985 at 1,162,000 tonnes. The limestone is usually crushed for other purposes such as aggregate for construction or to

TABLE 4-3. Sieves used in determining limestone fineness

Sieve number	Wires (#/inch)	Opening size (mm/side)
10	10	1.65
60	60	0.25
100	100	0.15

TABLE 4-4. Determining a fineness rating for limestone

In this example, 75% of the sample passed through a #10 sieve and 40% passed through a #60 sieve.

Particle size	% of sample		Effectiveness factor		
Coarser than #10	25	×	0.0	=	0
Between #10 and #60	35	×	0.4	=	14
Finer than #60	40	×	1.0	=	40
			Fineness rating	=	54

produce limestone fluxes for smelting. Fine material is not wanted for those purposes and is sieved out. This byproduct may be sieved further to yield agricultural lime.

Dolomitic or calcitic lime

Liming materials made of crushed limestone rock are generally divided into two groups, calcitic and dolomitic, based on their content of calcium and magnesium.

Pure calcium carbonate (calcite) contains 40% calcium. Pure dolomite contains 21.7% calcium and 13.1% magnesium.

The division between calcitic and dolomitic limestone is not absolutely defined. Any limestone that is dominated by calcium and contains very little magnesium is considered calcitic. A 2006 survey reported 8 sources of dolomitic lime and 8 sources of calcitic lime in Ontario (K. Reid, 2006).

When liming is recommended, dolomitic lime should be used on soils with a magnesium soil test of 100 or less. When the magnesium soil test is greater than 100, either calcitic or dolomitic limestone can be used. Many Ontario soils contain lots of calcium or magnesium or both. High soil test values of either are not a concern and should not influence the choice of calcitic versus dolomitic limestone.

Anyone selling materials as an agricultural fertilizer source of calcium or magnesium must supply a guarantee of analysis. The calcium and magnesium content of the material are expressed as %Ca and %Mg.

Liquid lime

Lime suspensions, liquid lime and fluid lime are all names for a system of suspending lime in a fluid. The limestone used in suspensions is usually very fine and suspended in water or liquid fertilizer. Typically, suspensions contain 50% to 75% liming material, 0.5% to 5.0% clay and a small amount of a dispersing agent. The remainder is water or liquid fertilizer.

Suspended lime is usually associated with a fineness rating of 100 (passes through a #100 sieve). Lime that passes through a #60 sieve is considered 100% effective. Anything finer is not any more effective.

There is no evidence that liquid lime is more effective than regular lime.

Granulated or pelletized lime

Some companies promote the use of granulated lime. This material is a finely ground lime that is formed into granules similar in size to fertilizer granules. This helps overcome many of the handling and spreading difficulties with regular lime because regular fertilizer equipment can handle it.

There is no evidence that low rates of granulated lime are as effective as full rates of regular limestone.

The choice of liming materials must be based on the cost, availability and agricultural index of the product.

Alternative liming agents

Many industrial byproducts can be used as liming materials, such as wood ash, cement dust, beet lime, industrial precipitator sludges, slags and biosolids. Each must be evaluated for its ability to neutralize acidity, for metal content and

---

FIGURE 4-3. Agricultural index

$$\text{Agricultural index} = \frac{\text{Neutralizing value} \times \text{fineness rating}}{100}$$

---

sometimes for organic compounds. A certificate of approval must be obtained from the Ministry of the Environment before spreading on agricultural land. *Guidelines for the Utilization of Biosolids and Other Wastes on Agricultural Land*, available from offices of the Ministry of the Environment or Ministry of Agriculture, Food and Rural Affairs, describes the criteria by which the material will be evaluated.

Agricultural limestone has a pH of about 8.2. Some alternative liming agents, such as wood ash, may have much higher pHs. Extra caution must be taken when handling high pH materials. Seedling injury may occur if crops are seeded soon after a high pH material has been mixed into the soil.

Agricultural index

The agricultural index is an indicator of limestone quality that combines the neutralizing value and the fineness rating into a single value. See Figure 4-3.

The agricultural index can be used to compare the ability of agricultural limestones to neutralize soil acidity. The higher the agricultural index, the more effective the limestone is on an equal weight basis.

The average agricultural index of limestone sold in Ontario has been

FIGURE 4-4. Amount of lime to apply
Amount of lime to apply = recommend amount × $\dfrac{75}{\text{Agricultural index of lime used}}$

around 75. Limestone recommendations based on Ontario-accredited soil tests are based on the assumption that the limestone used has an agricultural index of 75.

The agricultural index of limestones sold in Ontario from 18 quarries in 2006 ranged from 36 to 102. The average was 74 (K. Reid, 2006).

Limestone recommendations should be adjusted according to the actual agricultural index of the limestone used. This calculation is illustrated in Figure 4-4.

Transportation to the farm usually accounts for most of the cost of using agricultural limestone because of its weight and volume. In general, using lime from the closest quarry will be the most economical. The cost per hectare should be calculated by multiplying the cost of each source applied to the field by the amount of lime required per hectare. This allows a fair comparison of alternative sources.

Lime application

Spreading

Conventional fertilizer spreaders are not designed to handle lime and the material will bridge in the spreader box. Commercial spreaders designed to handle lime are advised.

Check the distribution pattern by using the same method you would to check the distribution of manure from a manure spreader (lay 1 m × 1 m plastic sheets, collect and weigh the amount of lime spread on each sheet and compare lime spread across the width of distribution).

Because lime is finely ground powder, wind affects distribution patterns. Spreading in calm conditions is advised. Operators should be protected against dust hazards. Lime will drift over considerable distances even in moderate winds.

If lime must be stored on the farm prior to spreading, protect it from the elements and from drifting away. Lime will consolidate into unusable clumps if it gets wet.

Incorporation

As agricultural limestone does not dissolve quickly, it must be mixed uniformly with the soil to be effective. Tillage implements that mix the soil, such as the disc (offset disc-harrow), do the best job.

In no-till soils, correcting pH is a challenge. If the entire plough layer (15 cm) is acid, then tillage to incorporate limestone is the only practical option.

This does not mean that liming and no-till are completely incompatible. In no-till soils where nitrogen fertilizers have been surface applied, a shallow layer of acidic soil can develop. Sample the top 5 cm layer to check the surface pH. Frequent applications of low rates of limestone can neutralize the acidity in this zone.

Many farmers apply and incorporate a fraction of the total lime recommended over several years. This helps ensure the lime will be more uniformly distributed and mixed by tillage. This is an excellent preventive measure but will not correct severe acidity.

Time to work

Agricultural limestone does not dissolve quickly. The rate at which each limestone particle dissolves depends on how finely the limestone is ground. See Figure 4-5. The rate of dissolution decreases as the pH of the soil increases, which is the desired result of liming. After dissolution, the lime must diffuse through the soil and interact with the acidity held in the soil solution and on the cation exchange sites. Dry or frozen soil conditions will increase the length of time for this reaction to happen. As a result, it takes time for the full effects of liming to be realized. This may take up to three years.

It is especially important for crops sensitive to low pH, like alfalfa, to get the lime applied well in advance of seeding.

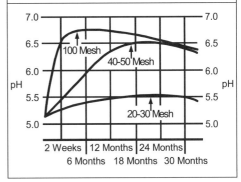

FIGURE 4-5. Reaction time for lime materials of different fineness

What about gypsum?

Gypsum is not a liming material, even though it is widely promoted as a source of calcium or sulphur and as a soil conditioner. Gypsum is used as a conditioner for sodic soils, which are present on the Prairies but not in Ontario.

The chemical make-up of gypsum is calcium sulphate, which breaks down into the calcium and sulphate ions when dissolved in the soil water. The calcium displaces hydrogen from the cation exchange sites, but this combines with the sulphate to form sulphuric acid, leaving no net effect on soil pH.

Gypsum is promoted as a calcium source because it is more soluble than lime in alkaline soils. While this is true, the solubility is still quite low (gypsum is the main ingredient in wallboard), so that you need large amounts to provide a significant amount of calcium. It is also a good source of sulphur where the need has been documented.

Soil acidification

Occasionally, growers want to lower the pH of their soil. This is a requirement for most commercial blueberry sites in Ontario and for home gardeners who want to grow rhododendrons and azaleas. These plants thrive in soils of pH 4 to 5 and develop micronutrient deficiencies when the soil pH rises above these levels.

Growers with alkaline soils, i.e. pH 7 or higher, may think lowering the pH will improve nutrient availability. Most crops thrive at soil pHs from 6 to 8 and the negative effect of low soil pH is much greater than the penalty for high soil pH. In addition, it is much cheaper to add extra nutrients than to lower soil pH.

Lowering soil pH

Soil pH is reduced by increasing the number of hydrogen ions in the soil, either directly by the addition of acids or by adding materials that will form acids when they react with the soil. Nitrogen fertilizers that contain ammonium will acidify the soil, as will elemental sulphur and iron or aluminum sulphate. Oxidized sulphur is available in the form of aluminum sulphate or iron (ferrous) sulphate, but these materials are required in much larger amounts (4 times and 8 times respectively) than elemental sulphur.

For crops like blueberries, which enjoy a high level of organic matter, the addition of acidic peat moss will have the double effect of increasing organic matter and lowering soil pH. Check that the pH of the peat is low, as several brands of peat moss raise the pH for use in potting mixes. For large areas peat moss will be too expensive and it is usually applied only in the rooting area of the plants.

Taking a soil test before and three months after the sulphur is applied will provide baseline information on soil pH. Annual soil testing to monitor pH is important.

Soils that can be acidified

The success of soil acidification will depend on the soil's buffering capacity. In general, it is easier to modify a sandy soil with low organic matter and low exchange capacity than a clay soil with high exchange capacity. On highly buffered soils, the reduction in soil pH may be short lived. The other factor

TABLE 4-5. Sulphur for soil acidification		
Soil type	for each 1.0 pH unit kg/ha (lb/ac)	for each 0.1 pH unit kg/ha (lb/ac)
sand	350 (313)	35 (31)
sandy loam	750 (670)	75 (67)
loam	1,100 (980)	110 (98)
Example: the initial pH of a sandy loam soil is 6.2, and the desired pH for blueberries is 4.8. The soil pH must be lowered 6.2 – 4.8 = 1.4 units. Therefore, 1.4 × 750 = 1,050 kg/ha of sulphur must be applied.		

in soil acidification is the amount of free lime in the soil. Soils above pH of 7 often contain undissolved calcium and magnesium carbonates, which react immediately with the acid produced by the sulphur, neutralizing it and preventing the desired drop in pH.

The natural soil pH also has an effect on the ease of lowering the pH. Remember that the pH scale is logarithmic: to move from 7 to 5 is 10 times more difficult than to move from 6 to 5. Soils with a natural pH of two units above the desired pH are almost impossible to alter. For example, if 750 kg/ha of sulphur are required to reduce the soil pH from 6 to 5, it could easily take 8000 kg of sulphur or more to reduce the pH from 7 to 5, plus enough S to neutralize any free lime that is in the soil at the higher pH. For home gardens, replacing soil with acidic soil or building a raised bed of acidic peat may be more practical.

There are often patches in fields that show greater resistance to lowering pH. Symptoms of nutrient deficiency (e.g. nitrogen in blueberries) are a good indication of areas that need separate treatment. Test and treat these areas individually.

Using sulphur

Sulphur (S) is the most economical way to lower soil pH, though still expensive. This is a biological process where certain soil bacteria convert elemental sulphur to sulphate sulphur. During this process, acid is formed. The drawbacks to using elemental sulphur are:

- A soil must have a viable population of the correct bacteria.
- It is a slow process requiring time where the soil temperature and moisture conditions are proper for microbial activity. It takes three months to a year for the reaction to be complete.
- Many soils need yearly applications of sulphur to maintain a lower pH.

Guidelines for the amount of sulphur required to lower soil pH are shown in Table 4-5. When treating the soil with sulphur to lower the soil pH, apply sulphur before the planting is established and incorporate it throughout the soil. Powdered sulphur acts more quickly than granular sulphur but it is also more expensive and unpleasant to spread. Sulphur can be applied in any season.

Alternatives to elemental sulphur and conversions between the materials are listed in Table 4-6.

TABLE 4-6. Relative effectiveness of various materials for reducing soil pH			
Material	Chemical Formula	Percent Sulphur	Kg of material to neutralize 100 kg of Calcium Carbonate*
Elemental Sulphur	S	100	32
Granular Sulphur	S	90	36
Sulphuric Acid	H_2SO_4	32	98
Iron Sulphate	$FeSO_4 \cdot 7H_2O$	11.5	278
Aluminum Sulphate	$Al_2(SO_4)_3$	14.4	114
Ammonium Sulphate	$(NH_4)_2SO_4$	23.7	66

* These are theoretical values, based on all the material reacting with the soil to produce acidity. Actual effectiveness will be less than this, often by as much as 50%, because of immobilization of the materials on soil surface, in soil microbes or by plant uptake.

References

Fixen, P.E. 1989. *Agronomic evaluations of MAP and DAP.* Proceedings of the 1989 North Central Extension-Industry Soil Fertility Conference, St. Louis, MO. Potash & Phosphate Institute, Norcross, GA.

Foth, Henry D. and Boyd G. Ellis, 1997. *Soil Fertility, Second Edition.* CRC Press, Inc. Boca Raton, FL 33431.

Miller, M.H., C.P. Mamaril, and C.J. Blair. 1970. *Ammonium effects on phosphorus absorption through pH changes and phosphorus precipitation at the soil-root interface.* Agron. J. 62:524-527.

OMAFRA/MOE, 1996. *Guidelines for the Utilization of Biosolids and Other Wastes on Agricultural Land.*

Reid, Keith, 2006. *Sources of Agricultural Limestone for 2006.* Ontario Ministry of Agriculture, Food and Rural Affairs (*www.ontario.ca/crops*).

5 ORGANIC NUTRIENT SOURCES: MANURE, BIOSOLIDS, LEGUMES

Organic nutrient sources are materials that contain carbon and were once part of a living organism. The most commonly used organic nutrient sources on Ontario farms are livestock manure and residues from crops like forage legumes. There are also materials from municipal or industrial sources known collectively as biosolids that are suitable for land application. Urea fertilizer, while it contains carbon in its chemical structure, is manufactured and so it is not normally considered to be an organic nutrient source.

For management purposes, organic nutrient sources can be divided into two groups: land applied materials and crop residues. The land applied materials, like manure, biosolids and compost, can be applied at different rates, timings and locations, to meet the nutrient requirements of a particular crop in a field. In contrast, crop residues are limited to the field where they were grown. While any type of crop residue will influence the cycling of nutrients through the soil, forage legumes provide the greatest quantity of nutrients to the following crop. Cover crops may also be used to capture excess nutrients and relay them to the next crop.

> ### *Organic nutrients – not just for organic agriculture*
> While organic agriculture uses organic nutrient sources, these materials fit just as well in a conventional cropping system. The key in both systems is managing the organic materials to provide nutrients, in available forms, to the crop while avoiding over-application. The difference is that in conventional systems the grower has the option of making up any shortfall in the organic materials with commercial fertilizer. Organic farmers will also occasionally use supplemental nutrients but from a more restrictive list of permitted substances.

Nutrients from land applied materials

Similarities among materials

There is a wide range of organic materials that can be used as nutrient sources but they have some characteristics in common. They all contain a mix of mineral nutrient sources and organic materials, in various proportions depending on the bedding or dilution materials and how the material was stored or treated.

The mineral forms of nutrients in an organic material are chemically identical to the nutrients in commercial fertilizer and are in the form that crops can take up immediately. These forms, however, can be lost to the environment more easily than the same nutrient bound within an organic compound. In manure, for example, the nitrogen is split between organic compounds and ammonium. The ammonium nitrogen is the same chemical compound as aqua ammonia or as anhydrous ammonia that has dissolved in soil water. Ammonium is immediately available for plant uptake but like aqua ammonia, if this material is left on the soil surface, it will vaporize into the air and be lost as ammonia. This results in a significant reduction in available nitrogen from manure not incorporated into the soil. The proportion of ammonium nitrogen in various organic materials is shown in Table 5-1.

The organic compounds are less subject to loss. They are not available to plants until they are mineralized (broken down to the mineral forms) by bacteria and other soil organisms or by chemical reduction. The speed at which this mineralization happens depends on how easy or difficult the organic compounds are to break down, the soil conditions (temperature, moisture, aeration, pH, etc.) and the physical contact between the materials and the soil.

Whether the material is of human or animal origin matters less than how it has been managed. Each material will go through similar chemical and biological transformations in the soil.

TABLE 5-1. Proportion of total nitrogen present as ammonium*

(typical values expressed as % of total N, as applied to land)

Nutrient type	Ammonium-N
Liquid hog	66%
Liquid dairy	42%
Liquid beef	43%
Liquid poultry	67%
Solid hog	26%
Solid dairy	21%
Solid beef (high bedding)	12%
Solid horse	15%
Solid poultry (broilers)	6%
Solid poultry (layers)	46%
Composted cattle manure	0.6%
Municipal sewage biosolids:	
Aerobic	1.6%
Anaerobic	35%
Dewatered	12%
Lime Stabilized	trace
Paper mill biosolids	trace
Spent mushroom compost	5%

* as the liquid concentration of the material increases, the ammonium content also increases.

Differences between materials

The fundamental difference between different types of manure and between manure and biosolids, is the amount and type of dilution material added and the way the mixture of materials is processed before it is applied to the field. On most livestock farms, the urine and faeces are diluted with either bedding, to form a solid manure, or water to form a liquid. All of the resulting material is usually applied to land. Municipal sewage biosolids on the other hand, are highly diluted when they enter the treatment plant. The goal of sewage treatment is to remove and clean most of the water for release into the environment, while the part that is land-applied is a by-product of this process.

Manure will vary between farms in form and nutrient content. Livestock species vary in the type of ration they are normally fed, with ruminants generally receiving diets that are high in forages, while monogastric (hog or poultry) diets are more concentrated. This means that ruminant manure will contain more fiber and have a lower nutrient concentration than most hog or poultry manure. Rations for young livestock are normally higher in protein and minerals than the feed for mature animals, so the nutrient content of the manure will be higher from these animals as well. Changes in the ration, such as the inclusion of phytase in the diet or amino acid balancing to reduce the protein requirements will have significant effects on the nutrient content of the manure excreted by the animal. Average nutrient contents for various manure types are shown in Table 5-2.

The manure handling and collection system in the barn will mix the manure with various dilution materials. In solid manure systems this is the straw or wood shavings used for bedding, while in liquid systems it is water spilled from drinkers or washwater. There is tremendous variability in the amount of dilution

Options to reduce the nutrient content of manure

1. Balance the ration properly. Nutrients in excess of livestock requirements will simply be excreted in the manure. Phase feeding and split-sex feeding will match nutrient needs at different stages in production.

2. Minimize feed wastage. Inspecting, adjusting and cleaning feeders regularly and using feed equipment designs that minimize spillage will reduce feed nutrients in manure.

3. Add Phytase enzyme to rations for hogs or poultry. This enables them to digest much of the phosphorus in grains that would be otherwise unavailable and reduces the amount of supplemental phosphorus needed.

4. Balance the amino acids in the feed, so the livestock have enough to meet their needs without feeding excess protein. This will reduce the nitrogen content of the manure.

in various systems. Typical available nutrient contents for various manure types are shown in Tables 5-3 and 5-4.

Some manures undergo further treatment to reduce odours and weed seed populations or to produce energy. Composting is an aerobic process where most of the nitrogen is combined into complex organic compounds and the remaining mineral nitrogen is primarily in the nitrate form. Anaerobic digestion is a process that converts part of the organic compounds in the manure into methane gas for heating or electrical generation and leaves much of the nitrogen in the ammonium form.

Sewage biosolids enter the treatment plant as an extremely dilute liquid material, since water is used as the carrier to transport these materials to the plant. Prior to requirements for Certificates of Approval for land application of biosolids, the sewage could contain significant quantities of contaminants if the system collected wastewater from industrial as well as domestic sources. Sewer use bylaws in most communities have now restricted these contaminants to very low concentrations, so the biosolids produced by the plant meet the criteria for a Certificate of Approval. During the treatment process, the solids are concentrated and the phosphates are precipitated out of the water in insoluble forms, while most of the potassium remains in solution and is not retained. The biosolids at the end of the process contain both organic and ammonium nitrogen, plus a significant amount of phosphorus. The availability of this phosphorus to plants may vary depending on the specific treatment process used. These biosolids may undergo further treatment before land application. This further treatment can significantly alter the quantity and availability of the nutrients.

Other materials from industrial or municipal sources may be suitable for land application. These can vary widely depending on the source of the material and the treatment to which it has been subject. Paper mill biosolids are primarily carbon compounds, with relatively low amounts of nutrients. Yard waste composts will vary widely in nitrogen, phosphorus and potassium contents, depending on the source of the material. These materials need to be assessed on a case-by-case basis if they are to be used as a nutrient source. Typical nutrient values for some non-agricultural source materials are shown in Table 5-5.

The physical and chemical characteristics of the various manure types and the various biosolids, overlap. This means that the management to optimize the use of the nutrients from these materials will be the same and will depend more on the characteristic of the individual material rather than the source. However, biosolids are subject to additional rules intended to ensure that their application is done in a way that benefits crop production.

Nutrient contents of various organic materials

Manure Type	(# of samples)	Dry Matter %	Total N[1] %	NH4-N %	P[2] %	K %	Ca %	Mg %	S %	Zn ppm	Cu ppm	Mn ppm
						Fresh Weight Basis						
SWINE — liquid	(924)	3.8	0.40	0.265	0.13	0.17	0.12	0.06	0.06	85	30	22
SWINE — solid	(54)	29.8	0.90	0.258	0.47	0.56	–	–	0.14	172	103	–
POULTRY — liquid	(137)	10.6	0.83	0.558	0.3	0.3	1.6	0.08	0.08	70	11	64
POULTRY — solid	(623)	52.6	2.37	0.550	1.11	1.17	4.6	0.28	0.16	238	33	204
DAIRY — liquid	(860)	8.5	0.36	0.153	0.09	0.24	0.49	0.14	0.04	48	17	40
DAIRY — solid	(150)	24.2	0.61	0.128	0.17	0.50	1.54	0.36	0.08	95	29	107
BEEF — liquid	(81)	7.95	0.52	0.179	0.13	0.43	0.7	0.3	0.04	57	14	61
BEEF — solid	(176)	28.6	0.73	0.101	0.23	0.57	1.5	0.41	0.09	129	36	112
SHEEP — solid	(54)	31.3	0.76	0.186	0.27	0.70	1.5	0.38	n/a[3]	170	20	140
HORSE — solid	(32)	33.41	0.42	0.068	0.13	0.36	1.7	0.56	n/a[3]	73	23	113

TABLE 5-2. Average nutrient analyses of livestock manures

Data from manure analysis provided from Ontario Labs collected between 1992 and 2004. Micro nutrient data is obtained from a smaller subset of data. Micronutrient concentration is highly dependent on animal diet, so will vary widely between farms.

[1] Total N = Ammonium-N + Organic N
[2] %P = total phosphorus
[3] n/a = data not available

TABLE 5-3. Average amounts of available nutrients from liquid manure
(AS APPLIED)

| | Average dry matter | Available Nitrogen | | | | Available P_2O_5 | Available K_2O |
		Late Summer*	Late Fall*	Spring, not incorporated	Spring, injected		
	%	lb/1000 gal					
Liquid hog							
6–10%	7.5	15	30	24	43	22	27
2–6%	3.5	9.4	20	16	30	12	20
0–2%	1.3	5.3	11	9.6	18	4.6	13
Average	3.8	9.2	19	16	29	12	18
Liquid dairy							
10–18%	13.6	14	20	15	24	13	35
6–10%	8.1	10	15	12	20	7	26
2–6%	4.5	7.3	10	8.7	15	6.4	21
0–2%	1.0	2.9	4.1	3.8	6.8	4.6	13
Average	8.5	10	15	12	19	8.3	26
Liquid beef							
Average	7.1	9	13	10	17	7	22
Liquid poultry							
10–18%	13.8	25	49	41	72	35	37
6–10%	8.2	21	41	35	63	25	31
2–6%	4.4	13	26	23	42	11	24
Average	10.6	22	42	36	64	28	32
Liquid runoff							
Average	0.6	1.2	2.5	2.0	3.6	1.5	9.6

* Manure incorporated within 24 hours of application.

Available phosphate is calculated as 40% of total phosphate in the manure. Available K_2O is calculated as 90% of the total K_2O.

To convert pounds per 1,000 gallons to kilograms per cubic metre, multiply by 10.

Data from manure analysis performed at University of Guelph, Stratford Agri-Analysis, A&L Canada Labs and Agrifood Labs between 1991 and 2003.

TABLE 5-4. Average amounts of available nutrients from solid manure
(AS APPLIED)

| | Average dry matter | Available Nitrogen | | | | Available P_2O_5 | Available K_2O |
		Late Summer	Late Fall	Spring, not incorporated	Spring, immediate incorporation		
	%	kg/t (lb/ton) fresh weight					
Hog	28.2	2.3 (6.1)	2.3 (6.1)	2.6 (5.6)	3.6 (7.9)	5.5 (12)	7.7 (17)
Dairy	24.2	1.5 (3.3)	1.7 (3.7)	1.2 (2.7)	1.8 (4.0)	1.3 (2.9)	5.0 (11)
Beef	28.6	1.8 (3.9)	2.0 (4.4)	1.3 (2.8)	1.6 (3.6)	1.3 (2.9)	6.4 (14)
Broiler	60	7.8 (17)	7.3 (16)	7.8 (17)	10.0 (22)	8.2 (18)	11.8 (26)

Available phosphate is calculated as 40% of total phosphate in the manure. Available K_2O is calculated as 90% of the total K_2O.

Data from manure analysis performed at University of Guelph, Stratford Agri-Analysis, A&L Canada Labs and Agrifood Labs between 1991 and 2003.

TABLE 5-5. Typical nutrient contents of biosolids
(DRY WEIGHT)

Material	Average dry matter	Total nitrogen	NH4-N	Usable N in year applied	Available P_2O_5	Available K_2O
	%	% of dry matter				
Municipal Sewage Biosolids						
Aerobic	1.7	5.0	.01–.75	.08	2.5	>0.01
Anaerobic	3.0	6.4	.33–3.4	2.7	3.3	>0.01
Dewatered	26	3.6	.35–.65	1.0	2.5	>0.01
Pelletized			Trace	0.8	4.5	>0.01
Paper Mill Biosolids						
Primary	50	0.3	Trace	0.1	Trace	Trace
Primary + Secondary	32.8	2.5		1.4	.08	0.02
Distillers Grains						
Dried		5.0		1.5	0.6	0.9

The quality and nutrient content of non-ag source materials is unique and must be determined on a case-by-case basis. Generators are required to sample and analyze these materials on a regular basis. This information should be used to determine accurate application rates for crop fertility requirements.

	TABLE 5-6. Nutrient contents of composts					
	(DRY WEIGHT)					
Material	Average dry matter	Total nitrogen	NH4-N	Usable N in year applied	Available P_2O_5	Available K_2O
	%	% of dry matter				
Composted Cattle Manure	38.3	2.25	0.14	0.67	0.68	3.1
Spent Mushroom Compost	35	2.1	0.05	0.63	0.75	1.25

Factors affecting nutrient availability to the crop

Nitrogen

Nitrogen uptake by crops is in the mineral form, as either nitrate (NO_3^-) or ammonium (NH_4^+). This means the ammonium portion of the manure is immediately available to the crop, while the organic nitrogen needs to be mineralized before it can be used. For optimum use of the nutrients in manure, they should be available where and when the crop can utilize them but it is not always easy—or even possible—to meet this goal with current manure management options.

For more detail about nitrogen transformations, see the section on the nitrogen cycle in Chapter 3 on page 53.

Ammonia volatilization

Ammonium nitrogen can easily convert to ammonia gas when the manure is exposed to the air, which results in the loss of a large part of the available N from the manure. Conditions that favour rapid loss of ammonium-N from the surface of the soil are high concentration of ammonium in the manure, warm temperatures, dry soils and windy conditions. Crop canopy or residue has an inconsistent effect on ammonia volatilization. While it can reduce the amount of loss from manure placed below the cover, loss can actually increase from manure spread on top of the canopy because of increased surface area. Incorporation of the manure effectively stops ammonia volatilization, since any ammonia that is released is quickly re-absorbed in the soil water and adsorbed on the surfaces of clay particles.

Mineralization

The organic nitrogen in manure needs to be converted to ammonium before it is available for plant uptake. This happens when microbes feed on the organic compounds and release ammonium as a waste product, so the rate of mineralization increases when conditions are favourable for microbial activity. The nature of the organic materials in the manure will also affect the rate of mineralization. About 20% of the organic N from ruminant manure is considered to be available in the first cropping season after application, while up to 30% of the organic N from poultry manure is available. Swine manure is intermediate.

Mineralization will be slow when soil conditions are cool. This can lead to temporary nitrogen deficiency during cool spring weather in crops that are planted on manured fields. A starter application of nitrogen can help to overcome this.

Immobilization

Microbes can immobilize soil nitrogen while they break down the carbon compounds in materials high in carbon that have been added to the soil, such as very strawy manure or primary papermill biosolids. See Carbon-to-Nitrogen Ratio, below and Table 5-7. This can reduce the nitrogen availability to crops if these materials are applied before planting. There is potential for using these materials to tie up soil nitrogen in the fall and reduce leaching losses over winter, but the effectiveness has not been proven.

TABLE 5-7. Typical C:N ratios of some common materials

Material	C:N ratio
Soil microorganisms	7–9
Soil organic matter	10–12
Alfalfa	13
Fall rye	
Vegetative	14
Flowering	20
Mature	80
Cereal straw	80
Corn stalks	60
Sawdust	200–400
Paper mill biosolids	
Primary	80–100
Secondary	7–10
Distillers grains	9
Solid cattle manure	20–30
Solid poultry manure	10
Composted manure	10–40
Yard waste compost	25–40
Spent mushroom compost	25–30

Carbon-to-nitrogen (C:N) ratio

The C:N ratio is the balance between the amount of carbon in an organic material and the amount of nitrogen. The carbon is a constituent of organic compounds, like cellulose, lignin and protein, which are food sources for soil microorganisms. As the microorganisms multiply to take advantage of increased food supply, they also need nitrogen. If there isn't enough N in the organic material, they will absorb nitrogen out of the soil to meet their needs. This immobilized N will be released after the extra carbon is used up and the microbial population starts to die off. As a rule of thumb, mineralization occurs if the C:N ratio of the organic material is less than 20 while immobilization occurs if the C:N ratio is greater than 30. Additionally, the balance between mineralization and immobilization will depend on temperature and moisture conditions, as well as the nature of the organic material.

Phosphorus

Most of the phosphorus in manure is associated with the solid portion and is found in either in the ortho-phosphate form (PO_4^{3-}) or in readily degraded organic compounds. This means that, chemically, the phosphorus in manure does not differ greatly from the phosphorus in fertilizer. Despite this, phosphorus from manure is assumed to be less available than fertilizer to crops in the year of application. In Ontario, the availability of manure P, in the year of application, is assumed to be 40% that of fertilizer P.

Recent greenhouse studies have shown that equal amounts of phosphorus from either liquid hog manure or fertilizer, when mixed evenly with the soil, result in equal plant uptake. The difference in apparent availability of the phosphorus could stem from the inability to place the manure in a band close to the seed for maximum availability and to uneven application rates across the field.

Nutrient management plans in Ontario credit 80% of the total P in the manure towards building soil fertility. Other jurisdictions may use a figure of up to 100%. Regular soil testing is the best way to track the actual build-up of soil P in individual fields.

Many municipal biosolids are treated with alum, iron sulphate or lime during the secondary treatment process to remove phosphate from the discharge water. A similar treatment is used in some poultry barns. This results in a high proportion of the P tied up in insoluble aluminum, iron or calcium phosphates, which can greatly reduce the nutrient availability from these materials in both the short and long term.

Potassium

Essentially all of the potassium in manure is in soluble forms and available to crops. With solid manure, losses can occur from storage if the runoff is not contained. High rates of manure application on dairy farms can result in luxury consumption of K by alfalfa and mineral imbalances for dry cows in the dairy ration. Sewage biosolids contain very little potassium, since it is not retained with the solids during the treatment process.

The phosphorus and potassium content of manure varies significantly from farm to farm. The best estimates come from lab analysis.

Secondary and micronutrients

In addition to NPK and organic matter, manure contains significant quantities of calcium, magnesium, sulphur and micronutrients. Deficiencies of these elements are uncommon on livestock farms that regularly apply livestock manure.

Biosolids also contain micronutrients. The levels will often depend on the mix of residential, institutional and industrial contributors to the system. With sewer use bylaws, industrial contributions to sewage systems are often lower in contaminants than those from other sources.

Some of the micronutrients are regulated under the *Environmental*

Protection Act (e.g. zinc, copper). The levels of these elements are limited in biosolids and if the level of any of the elements is too high, the material cannot be used for land application. Most manure is low in these elements, unless they have been added to feed to reduce antibiotic use. The rate or frequency of manure application may need to be limited for these specific manures.

Predicting available nutrients from land applied materials

Optimizing the use of nutrients in organic materials depends on knowing how much nutrient is in the material being applied and what proportion of that will be available to the crop. Since most nutrient response calibrations have been done with mineral fertilizers, the availability of nutrients from organic sources is often expressed relative to fertilizer.

There are tables available with average nutrient values for various manure and biosolid types and these are good planning tools. Given the variability among nutrient sources, however, analysis of the material will give better information if the sample collected is representative of the material to be land applied.

Interpreting manure analyses

Results from a manure analysis must be read carefully, since there can be wide variation in how the results are expressed. The analytical results may be expressed as a percentage of the dry matter in the manure or as a percentage of the fresh (wet) weight. Further, the results may have been converted into a fertilizer replacement value, based on information provided when the sample was submitted.

The formulas for calculating the available phosphorus and potassium are found in Table 5-8. Table 5-9 gives the conversions from percentages to the commonly used units of weight.

TABLE 5-8. Calculating available phosphorus and potassium from manure
Most labs in Ontario report the amount of available P_2O_5 and K_2O from manure, but occasionally you see a sample reported as %P and %K. If this occurs, you will have to convert the figures to match the units of the fertilizer recommendation.
Total P to available P_2O_5
% P × 2.29 = % total P_2O_5
% total P_2O_5 × 0.40 = % available P_2O_5 in application year
% total P_2O_5 × 0.80 = % available P_2O_5 for soil build-up
Total K to available K_2O
% K × 1.20 = % total K_2O
% total K_2O × 0.90 = % available K_2O

TABLE 5-9. Conversion from per cent to units of weight
% available nutrient to unit of weight
% available nutrient × 10 = kg/t
% available nutrient × 20 = lb/ton
% available nutrient × 10 = kg/1,000 L = kg/m³
% available nutrient × 100 = lb/1,000 gal (Imperial)

Total vs. ammonium vs. organic N

In most organic materials, the nitrogen is divided between the ammonium and organic forms, so the total N is the sum of these two quantities. The measurements made in the lab are actually of total N and ammonium N, and the organic N is determined by subtraction.

Composted materials may contain a significant amount of nitrate N. Check with the lab that the compost analysis package includes all aspects relevant to nitrogen availability: nitrate, ammonium and total N, as well as C:N ratio.

Estimates of available N from manure can be made as a proportion of the total N, which assumes both the manure and the application management are "average." This is a good tool for planning, on a broad basis, the distribution of manure among different fields. More precise estimates of available N from manure can be made following application when the precise timing, weather conditions at application and the time before incorporation is known. Using the actual split between ammonium and organic N from the manure analysis can also make more precise estimates.

Impact of application timing/method

Application timing and method has the greatest impact on nitrogen availability and much less on phosphorus or potassium. Because of the varying proportions of mineral and organic N in organic materials, the impact of application timing

TABLE 5-10. Ammonium-nitrogen loss from manure under different weather and soil conditions

Days After Application	Average	Cool (<10°C)		Warm (>20°C)	
		Wet	Dry	Wet	Dry
Injected	0	0	0	0	0
Incorporated within 1 day	25	10	15	25	50
Incorporated within 2 days	30	13	19	31	57
Incorporated within 3 days	35	15	22	38	65
Incorporated within 4 days	40	17	26	44	73
Incorporated within 5 days	45	20	30	50	80
Not Incorporated					
Spring/Summer/Early Fall					
– bare soil	66	40	50	75	90
– crop residue	50	30	35	60	70
– standing crop	33	20	25	40	50
Late Fall (air temp < 10°C)	25	25	25	N/A	N/A

Source: adapted from Best Management Practices booklet, "Manure Management", 2006.

and method is not the same for all materials.

Ammonia volatilization results in an immediate loss of available N. The amount lost varies with the time between application and incorporation and the conditions at the time of application. See Table 5-10. The ammonium N retained in the soil can still be lost following conversion to nitrate, through leaching or denitrification. Organic materials high in mineral nitrogen will provide the greatest amount of N to the crop when it is applied as close to the time of N uptake by the crop as possible.

Organic N is not available to the crop until it has mineralized to ammonium. This process proceeds slowly when soils are cold. Materials that are predominantly organic N (e.g. solid beef or dairy) will show much less difference in N availability between spring and fall application, since the loss of the mineral N is balanced by greater availability of the organic portion. There is an advantage, in terms of optimizing N availability, if these materials are applied in early spring and incorporated. This retains the ammonium N but also provides time for mineralization to occur. A similar benefit could be gained from a late fall application of this material, as it is applied to soils that are already cold enough to inhibit nitrification. The difficulty with this approach is the variability of fall and winter weather conditions.

Impact of treatment systems – composting, anaerobic digestion, etc.

Treatment systems change the form of the nitrogen in the material and can also significantly reduce the nitrogen content of the material. Sampling and analysis is critical to knowing what value to place in a treated material and how best to manage it.

Composting is an aerobic process that seeks to convert most of the nitrogen in the material to an organic form. This is accomplished by adding materials with a high C:N ratio to manure or biosolids and then providing conditions that encourage microbial growth. In a properly managed composting system, microbes take up most of the nitrogen as they consume the high-carbon material. In improperly managed compost, up to half of the total N can be lost through volatilization. Not all of the nitrogen is bound in organic forms in finished compost. Because of the aerobic conditions, the mineral N that remains is primarily in the nitrate form. Composts can be surface applied with negligible loss of N through volatilization but the availability of the organic N depends on conditions that favour mineralization. Typical available nutrient contents of some composts are shown in Table 5-6 on page 104.

Anaerobic digestion is used to reduce odours and pathogens in organic materials, as well as to produce methane gas that can be used for heating or electricity generation.

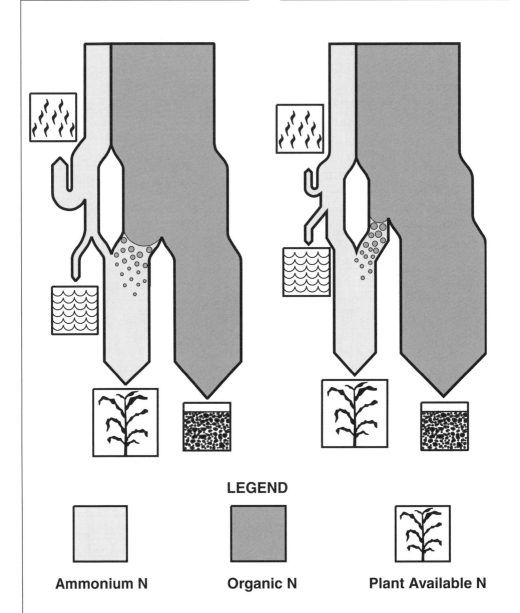

FIGURE 5-1. Solid manure, fall surface applied

FIGURE 5-2. Solid manure, spring applied, incorporated within one day

LEGEND

Ammonium N

Organic N

Plant Available N

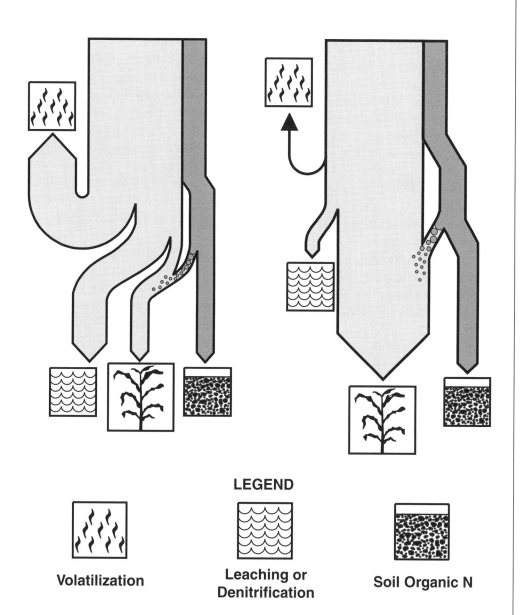

FIGURE 5-3. Liquid manure, fall surface applied

FIGURE 5-4. Liquid manure, spring injected

LEGEND

Volatilization

Leaching or Denitrification

Soil Organic N

N from manure is in both mineral and organic forms, in varying proportions. Some of the N is lost to the air or water, some remains in the organic form and the balance is available to be taken up by crops.

The end product has lost much of the readily degraded organic material and has left a greater proportion of the N in the ammonium form than in the original material. This increases the immediate availability of the N from the digested material but it should be incorporated quickly. N volatilization losses from surface application of this material will generally be greater than from undigested materials.

Predicting available N from manure

For general planning, nitrogen availability from organic materials can be estimated from table values. For fine-tuning fertilizer application rates however, a more precise estimate is desirable. This involves estimating the retention of the ammonium N in the manure, the mineralization from the organic N pool and the losses from the soil between manure application and crop uptake. Figures 5-1 to 5-4 show examples of manure application systems with different relative amounts of ammonium and organic nitrogen in the manure, and different application timing and methods. The amount of nitrogen that is available for plant uptake is determined by the initial manure nitrogen, and also by the transformations and losses that the manure nitrogen undergoes. Predictions of manure nitrogen availability try to account for these factors, but tables cannot capture all of the variability in management, or the influence of weather. The uncertainty of predictions will be much greater with late

summer or fall manure application, than with applications near planting time.

Available nitrogen from previous manure applications

Most of the available nitrogen in manure is used by the crop or is lost during the first growing season following application. The remaining organic nitrogen becomes available in small, diminishing quantities in the succeeding years. This availability is most often assumed to be 10% of the organic N applied one year ago, 5% from two years ago and 2% from three years ago. This is not normally enough to make a practical difference in nitrogen recommendations from a single application of manure. However, where solid manure is applied regularly to the same field, there can be significant residual nitrogen.

Calibrating application equipment

Calibrating manure application equipment is essential. Several methods can be used to measure spreading rates.

For solid materials:

- Weigh a load and measure the area it covers.

or

- Spread a metre-square plastic bag on the ground and spread solid manure on it as you would on the field. Weigh the bag and manure and find the equivalent in Table 5-12.

Estimating the rate of solid manure application by the volume of the spreader is not accurate, because of the variation in how high the spreader is heaped and because of the variation in density of solid manure types. See Table 5-11.

TABLE 5-11. Densities of manure

	kg/m³	lb/cu ft	lbs/bu
Liquid	1,000	62.4	80
Semi-solid	960	60	76
Thick solid	800	50	64
Light solid	560	35	45

For liquid materials:
- The application rate can be determined from the volume of the tanker divided by the area covered by one tanker load. The area covered by a tanker load of manure can be calculated from the width of spread, the speed of travel and the time it takes to empty the tanker.

or

- Place a straight-walled pail on the ground you intend to cover. Spread the manure then measure the depth of manure in the pail and find the application rate in Table 5-12.

Take overlap into account.

Nutrient management planning

Nutrient management planning is simply matching the needs of the crop and the nutrients already in the soil with the nutrients available from manure or other organic sources and then balancing any deficits with mineral fertilizer. Many jurisdictions, including Ontario, have legal requirements for nutrient management plans on intensive livestock farms and some only think of nutrient management planning in terms of regulation. Although it is a regulatory requirement on some farms, in reality every farm can benefit from planning to optimize their nutrient use.

TABLE 5-12. Calibrating manure spreaders

Solid Manure Calibration

Weight/sheet		Application rate	
kg	lb	t/ha	tons/ac
0.5	1	3.6	1.6
1	2	7.2	3.2
1.5	3	10.8	4.8
2	4	14.3	6.4
2.5	5	17.9	8.0
3	7	25.1	11.2
5	10	35.8	16.0
7.5	15	53.8	24.0

using 1 m × 1 m (40 in. × 40 in.) sheet

Liquid Manure Calibration using a straight-walled pail

Depth of manure		Application rate	
mm	L/ha	in.	gal/ac
2.5	25,000	1/10	2,265
3.1	31,000	1/8	2,825
6.3	63,000	1/4	5,650
9.4	94,000	3/8	8,500
12.5	125,000	1/2	11,325
15.6	156,000	5/8	14,150
18.8	188,000	3/4	17,000
25	250,000	1	22,650

Challenges with different livestock intensities

Livestock farms can be roughly divided into three classes based on the intensity of their production.

Whole farm nutrient balances: Where does Ontario fit?

Some critics imply that intensification of agriculture will inevitably lead to excesses of nutrients and over-application of manure. For justification, they point to areas like North Carolina and Delaware because regions within these states have expanded livestock and poultry production beyond the capacity of the land base to absorb nutrients. The result has been significant degradation of the surface and ground water quality in these regions, as well as complaints about odour and poor air quality.

The situation in Ontario is much different. In 2002, the State of Delaware had almost 1 nutrient unit per hectare, averaged over all the crop land in the state, while North Carolina had 1.25 nutrient units per hectare. In contrast, in the 2001 Census of Agriculture, the province of Ontario had 0.65 nutrient units per hectare of cropland. (The figure for all of Canada was 0.43 nutrient units per hectare.) A nutrient unit is the number of livestock that produce the lesser of 43 kilograms of nitrogen or 55 kilograms of phosphate (fertilizer replacement value) and is used to compare different livestock on an equal nutrient basis.

It is certain that there are some small areas of nutrient excess but the problem is one of distribution rather than over-supply.

Each class has very different challenges in nutrient management.

The members of first group are highly intensive, with a significant portion of the livestock diet coming from purchased feed rather than grown on-farm. This results in a surplus of nutrients coming on to the farm over what is sold as meat, eggs and milk. These farms are faced with the challenge of exporting manure to other farms or having a build-up of nutrients in their soils from over-application of manure.

The second group represents farms where the nutrient inputs to the farm in feed and fertilizer are close to balanced with the exports in meat, eggs and milk. Most of the feed is grown on-farm and the manure is returned back to that land base. The challenge on this farm is distributing the manure properly among the available fields. Mineral fertilizers will still need to be used on most of these farms to balance the nutrients supplied by manure.

The third group has very low livestock intensities and does not generate nearly enough manure to meet the requirements for crop production. If these farms do not apply nutrients in the form of mineral fertilizers or import organic nutrient sources such as livestock manure or biosolids, productivity will gradually decline as nutrients are exported off the farm.

Optimizing manure as a nutrient source

The value of manure as a fertilizer has been limited by uncertainty about the quantity of nutrients in the manure, the availability of these nutrients and the amount actually applied to the field. Following a systems approach to manure utilization can remove much of this uncertainty.

Manure application should aim to supply up to about three-quarters of the nitrogen requirements of the crop. During application, samples should be collected for analysis and records should be kept of actual application rates, time to incorporation and weather conditions at application. This will allow a more precise estimate of the nutrients available from the manure and any deficits can be filled with an application of mineral fertilizer.

Crops that benefit

Grain corn is a common recipient of manure because it has a high demand for nitrogen and is often grown as a feed crop on livestock farms. Using manure to supply all the nitrogen required by a corn crop however, provides more phosphorus and potassium than the crop removes from the soil. Over the years, the concentrations of these two nutrients in the soil can become excessively high.

This build-up can be alleviated. Grain corn can be rotated with other crops that use large quantities of phosphorus and potassium, such as alfalfa. The manure application rates can also be reduced to two-thirds or three-quarters of the nitrogen requirements and the balance supplied as nitrogen fertilizer. This brings the additions of phosphorus and potassium more into line with the amount removed by the crop.

For summer application to standing crops such as corn or forages, rates should be kept below 40 m³/ha and less for highly concentrated manures. Application to forages should be done as soon as possible after harvest to avoid nitrogen burn (from ammonia) to new leaf growth. Older forage stands with higher grass content benefit most from the manure nitrogen. Vegetable and small fruit crops can benefit from manure applications in the rotation, provided food safety requirements are met.

Cautions on applying

Manure applications to cereal crops, spring grains or soybeans should be done with caution, since too high a rate will increase the incidence of lodging.

Avoid application into standing crops of concentrated manure with high ammonium-nitrogen levels, like manure from covered storages or swine barns with wet-dry feeders, which may result in leaf burn.

No-till and manure

Manure is still one of the factors that makes livestock farmers think twice about no-till. Farmers who have to deal with manure but also engage in a no-till cropping system have to compromise — some tillage or some loss of nutrients from manure.

Crop rotation is important in a no-till system. The most popular options are to:

- **apply manure to wheat fields after harvest and follow with shallow tillage.** This allows faster breakdown of the wheat residue and alleviates risk of allelopathic interference for the planned corn crop while providing minimal soil disturbance and reduced risk of compaction. This system also makes good use of manure nutrients, especially if combined with a fall cover crop. On sandy soils prone to leaching, application rates should reflect nitrogen quantity and type being applied. In most cases, solid manure containing a higher percentage of organic nitrogen will have less risk of loss through leaching.

- **use manure on forages**. Although not the most economic use of manure nitrogen, legume forages do use the phosphorus and potassium. Grassy forages will make more efficient use nitrogen and also benefit from the phosphorus and potassium.
- **side-dress liquid manure into a standing corn crop by injection**. The manure reaches the crop when the nutrients are most needed and the risk of compaction is often lower. The biggest drawback is the time needed. There is also a risk of reducing plant population due to tramping or damaged plants from injectors.

Environmental concerns

The use of manure or other organic nutrient sources for crop nutrient needs is better for the environment.

As with any nutrient source, using too much or not applying it carefully can cause harm from contaminated streams, run-off and leaching.

Avoid spreading manure in winter or early spring because of the potential for runoff to surface water. Frozen soils cannot absorb the nutrients that are applied and there are no growing crops to utilize them. In those years when winter spreading may be necessary, select fields to minimize risk of runoff by choosing ones far from surface water.

Do not spread manure immediately adjacent to surface water. A vegetated buffer will help to trap any material that runs off the field and keep it out of streams and lakes.

Rain can cause organic nitrogen to wash into streams if manure has been applied to unprotected cropland. Phosphorus attached to soil particles can be carried to streams by soil erosion. Minimizing runoff from fields that receive manure will reduce the risk of harmful bacteria reaching streams and waterways.

Flow into tile drains can become contaminated if manure enters a catch basin. With liquid manure, maintain a 9 m buffer around a catch basin or surface inlet — 4.5 m with solid manure — or block the tile run during and after spreading. All tile inlets should be regarded as direct connections to surface water and managed accordingly.

Flow can also become contaminated if manure travels through soil cracks and macropores to the tiles. This problem is most likely to occur in clay or clay loam soils where there is shrinking and swelling of the soil. A light tillage pass before spreading will disrupt the channels and significantly minimize the risk of movement. Blocking the tile run during and after spreading may also work.

Safe utilization of manure above crop requirements

Large livestock operations on a small land base have special challenges. To avoid over-application of nutrients, exporting manure to non-livestock farms or composting operations may be needed. If this is not possible, limit manure applications to the nitrogen requirements of the crop, since over-application of nitrogen will most likely lead to some form of environmental impact. Although the risk from excess nitrogen leaching is minimal on heavy textured soils, losses through denitrification can be substantial and

this leads to greenhouse gas emissions. Nitrogen-based application rates can also result in over-supply of phosphorus and potassium. Excess phosphorus is a concern if it can reach surface water, leading to algae blooms. High rates should not be applied in areas where there is the potential for surface runoff or erosion. Incorporating the manure may also help to reduce the concentration of phosphorus in runoff water.

Regulatory requirements

Every province and state has some type of regulatory control on the application of manure and biosolids. This ranges from the environmental protection laws that apply to everyone, to specific regulations dictating when and where a particular material can be applied. In Ontario, the first category is represented by the *Environmental Protection Act* and the

Ontario Water Resources Act, which lay out penalties for anyone who pollutes surface or groundwater or causes an adverse effect. The federal *Fisheries Act* also mandates that no deleterious substance can be allowed to enter surface water. In the second category, the *Nutrient Management Act (2002)* gives force to regulations on the storage, handling and application of materials containing nutrients to land.

You should be aware of the most recent versions of any specific laws and regulations that apply in your jurisdiction.

Manure

Manure applications on livestock farms in Ontario are regulated under the *Nutrient Management Act (2002)*, which gives force to Ontario Regulation 267/03 (as amended). Phased-in farms are required to complete a nutrient management plan and to follow that plan for any nutrient applications. Growers and advisors should refer to the regulation for details. The most current version of the regulation can be found at *www.e-laws.gov.on.ca*.

Biosolids

In Ontario, biosolids are currently regulated under both the *Nutrient Management Act* and the *Environmental Protection Act*. The materials must meet quality criteria for pathogens and metals before they are approved for land application. Biosolids must be applied according to the criteria set out in a Certificate of Approval, including restrictions on setbacks from surface water and limits on the time between application and the harvest of various crops. Application of biosolids is not permitted on home lawns and gardens, golf courses or recreational land.

Detailed requirements for biosolids application can be found in the most recent version of the *Guidelines for the Utilization of Biosolids and Other Wastes on Agricultural Land* and in Ontario Regulation 267/03.

Nutrients from crop residues

As they break down, crop residues can provide significant quantities of nitrogen to succeeding crops. The value of legumes is well established in this regard but there is also potential for nitrogen mineralization from the residues of non-legume crops. Conditions where this can be significant are where large quantities of residue are left following harvest (as in some horticultural crops) and the residue is relatively immature. This is a source of nitrogen that has been under-utilized.

Legumes are unique among crops because they form symbiotic relationships with bacteria (Rhizobia) that convert nitrogen from the air into ammonium, which is then available to plants. The legumes grown primarily for seed production, such as soybeans, use all of this nitrogen for crop growth and yield and leave little or none in the soil for the next crop.

Perennial forage legumes on the other hand, are a source of additional nitrogen because they tend to fix more nitrogen than is needed for the current crop. The nitrogen from legumes is held almost completely in the organic form and is not available until the residues are broken down. This residual nitrogen must be considered when planning a fertilizer program for the succeeding crop. Cool spring weather may delay the breakdown of residues and hence nitrogen release.

When considering the effects of legumes on the growth of succeeding crops, it is important to separate the effect of improved physical properties, such as soil structure and tilth, from the effect of residual nitrogen.

Legumes in a cropping system

The predominant forage legumes included in Ontario crop rotations are alfalfa, trefoil and red clover. Alfalfa and trefoil are usually harvested as hay and maintained for at least two years. Red clover is usually included as a cover crop following small grains, with growth terminated at the end of the first year or early during the next growing season, just before corn planting.

The greatest benefits occur during the first year after plowdown. However, there may be residual benefits during subsequent years. Late May soil nitrate-nitrogen concentrations and indexed yields shown in Table 5-13 show that potential nitrogen availability and yield increases following forage legumes are greater during the first year after forage legumes.

Total nitrogen accumulation

Ploughdown red clover, established as a cover crop following cereals, can also accumulate a substantial amount of nitrogen, about 40 kg/ha for every tonne per hectare of top growth. A relatively thick 30 cm tall stand of ploughdown red clover produces about 4 t/ha of top growth containing about 160 kg N/ha.

TABLE 5-13. Effects of crop rotation on post-planting soil nitrate-N concentration and corn yields				
	First Year Corn		Second Year Corn	
Rotation	Soil NO$_3$-N kg/ha	Yield %	Soil NO$_3$-N kg/ha	Yield %
Continuous corn	9.1	100	9.5	100
Soy–soy–corn–corn	12.6	104	10.6	97
Soy–wheat–corn–corn	10.9	104	12.0	98
Soy–wheat + clover–corn–corn	16.7	107	12.7	99
Alfalfa–alfalfa–corn–corn	17.8	108	14.7	102

Effects of crop rotation on soil nitrate-N concentration 2 weeks after planting and corn yields. Indexed relative to continuous corn for the first and second year of production. From a long-term rotation experiment.

Source: T. Vyn, Crop Science Department, University of Guelph.

However, more typical ploughdown red clover yields, when established as a cover crop following cereals, range from 1 to 3 t/ha.

Available nitrogen from legumes

Not all the nitrogen produced by a legume crop is available. The rate of mineralization may limit the availability of the nitrogen during the time the subsequent crop needs it and some of the nitrogen may be incorporated into soil organic matter or lost through volatilization or leaching. Despite this, the amount of nitrogen available from forage legumes can be considerable, often totally fulfilling the nitrogen requirement of a succeeding corn crop. See Table 5-14 on page 122.

Accurately predicting the nitrogen available from forage legumes is difficult and depends on a number of factors, including the amount of legume growth, spring soil moisture conditions and the tillage system and timing of legume kill.

Obviously, you should not apply all the recommended nitrogen credits if legume growth is poor or if the stand is variable across the field. However, when excellent legume (alfalfa, trefoil or red clover) growth has occurred, the recommended credits are quite conservative. Several Ontario studies indicate that fertilizer nitrogen is not required when corn is planted following excellent forage legume stands.

The potential nitrogen availability from forage legumes to corn can be reduced if early (May and June) weather conditions are extremely dry or wet. Excessive rainfall can result in denitrification or leaching losses. If soil conditions are extremely dry, especially during May or June, mineralization rates of legume-nitrogen can be decreased, thereby decreasing the amount available to corn.

How much is a full stand?

A full stand of clover, alfalfa or trefoil is anything greater than 12 plants per square foot (120 plants per m²). Therefore, a 50% stand is 6 plants per square foot, and a 33% stand is 4 plants. The nitrogen credit is the same whether the space between plants is empty or filled with grass and weeds.

Optimizing nitrogen recovery

To be useful, the nitrogen must be released when the crop needs it. If the nitrogen is mineralized too soon, it can move deeper in the soil profile where it may be beyond the reach of roots. If it is released too late, the crop suffers from a shortage. This is illustrated in Figure 5-5.

Tillage systems that mix the legume top growth into the soil (mouldboard plough, chisel plough, disc) release the nitrogen from the crop residues faster than in a no-till system. Analysis of nitrogen response data in corn shows about 10% less nitrogen availability from a red clover cover crop in no-till than tilled systems.

Also, studies in no-till systems using red clover indicate that even though spring-killed red clover accumulated more nitrogen, fall-killed red clover produced greater corn yields in the absence of fer-

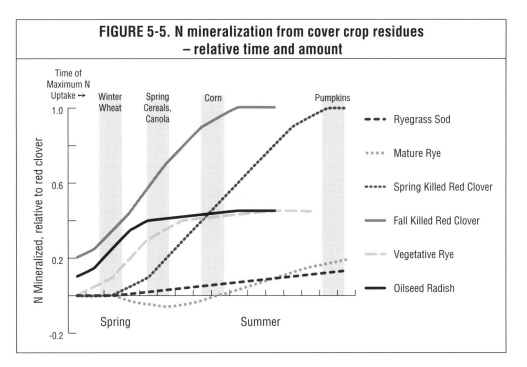

FIGURE 5-5. N mineralization from cover crop residues – relative time and amount

Time of Maximum N Uptake →

Winter Wheat

Spring Cereals, Canola

Corn

Pumpkins

N Mineralized, relative to red clover

1.0

0.6

0.2

-0.2

Spring   Summer

- - - Ryegrass Sod

..... Mature Rye

---- Spring Killed Red Clover

▬▬ Fall Killed Red Clover

- - Vegetative Rye

▬▬ Oilseed Radish

tilizer nitrogen and required less fertilizer nitrogen to optimize yields. This suggests that fall-killed red clover nitrogen is more available when the corn plant needs it than spring-killed red clover in no-till systems. Therefore, no-till farmers should consider killing the legume in the fall.

A simple credit system can only give a general idea of nitrogen availability. The variability in the growth of the crop (and hence, the amount of nitrogen in the residue) and the variability in the soil and weather conditions that control mineralization, mean that the precise N availability will vary year to year. However, it's possible for soil nitrate tests to predict the need for supplemental nitrogen.

A survey of 25 corn fields planted following red clover in southern Ontario in 1994 and 1996 dem-

onstrated that a pre-side-dress soil nitrate test was as good as or better a predictor of fertilizer nitrogen requirements for corn than the OMAFRA fertilizer nitrogen recommendations.

Nitrogen availability from non-legume residues

Many horticultural crops are harvested before the plants reach physiological maturity and a relatively small part of the plant is removed from the field. This leaves a large quantity of green, succulent material in the field, which can rapidly break down to release mineral N into the soil. In cases where multiple crops are grown in the same field, this nitrogen can reduce the fertilizer requirement of the succeeding crops.

TABLE 5-14. Adjustment of nitrogen requirement where legumes ploughed down		
Type of crop	kg/ha	lb/ac
Established forages		
less than 1/3 legume	0	0
1/3 –1/2 legume	55	50
1/2 or more legume	110	100
Perennial legumes seeded and ploughed in same year	78 (for field corn) 45 (all other crops)	70 (for field corn) 40 (all other crops)
Soybean and field bean residue	30 (for field corn) 0 (all other crops)	27 (for field corn) 0 (all other crops)

Cover crops for nitrogen management

Relatively good stands of actively growing cover crops, including legumes such as red clover, will take up (i.e. sequester) significant amounts of soil mineral nitrogen. Cover crops following winter wheat in Ontario have reduced the level of nitrate left in the soil in October and November by 50%, compared to where no cover crop was planted. This results in less nitrate-N available to be lost over winter.

Under optimal growing conditions, non-legume cover crops (ryegrass, cereal grains) can take up substantial amounts of soil mineral nitrogen. Oilseed radish has been reported to contain up to 100 kg/ha of nitrogen in above-ground growth under optimal growing conditions.

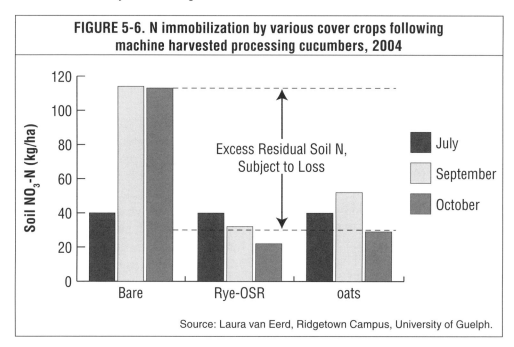

FIGURE 5-6. N immobilization by various cover crops following machine harvested processing cucumbers, 2004

Source: Laura van Eerd, Ridgetown Campus, University of Guelph.

Although non-legume cover crops can sequester a significant amount of nitrogen, subsequent corn yields may not be increased to the same extent as following legume cover crops. To date, it has been difficult to show a consistent reduction in N fertilizer requirement for crops grown following a non-legume cover crop.

Cover crops vary widely in the timing of nitrogen mineralization. See Figure 5-5. Oilseed radish and spring cereals tend to start to release nitrogen early in the spring when it may be subject to losses.

Some cover crops, like ryegrass, are extremely resistant to breakdown. Although they absorb significant quantities of nitrogen, little is released to the next crop during the growing season.

There are circumstances where cover crops can inhibit the growth of the following crop. A heavy layer of crop residue can keep the soil cool and wet in the spring, slowing crop germination and development as well as slowing nutrient mineralization. It may physically impede the operation of planting equipment, reducing the stand. It may also harbour pests like slugs or nematodes, which can harm the crop. However, cover crops protect the soil from wind and water erosion, and some species help to reduce the numbers of pests like nematodes.

Manure Amount	Cover Crop	2003 Cover Crop Nitrogen	2004 Corn Yield (No N Fertilizer)	2004 Corn Yield (Fertilized)	Optimum Fertilizer N Rate
m³/ha		kg/ha			
0	No Cover	—	6590	9100	96
	Oats	38	7840	9410	82
	OSR*	42	7470	8350	67
	Peas	37	6900	9980	102
75	No Cover	—	9410	10790	79
	Oats	64	10730	10730	0
	OSR*	80	10420	10420	0
	Peas	53	10980	10980	0

TABLE 5-15. Cover crop effects on corn yield and nitrogen requirements, Embro

* OSR = Oilseed Radish

Source: Ontario Greenhouse Gas Mitigation Project.

References

Ontario Regulation 267/03 (Amended to O. Reg. 511/05). Ontario Ministry of Agriculture, Food and Rural Affairs, 2005.

Guidelines for Utilization of Biosolids and Other Wastes. Ontario Ministry of Agriculture, Food and Rural Affairs and Ontario Ministry of the Environment, 1996.

Statistics Canada. 2001 Census of Agriculture.

National Agricultural Statistics Service, USDA. 2002 Census.

6 FERTILIZER RECOMMENDATIONS

There is no single correct fertilizer recommendation. Crop and site-specific fertilizer recommendations are developed using information from:

- soil testing
- tissue analysis
- specific requirements for crop quality
- desired economic, production and yield goals
- production practices
- potential environmental risks

Factors limiting yield response to fertilizer

Many interacting factors affect a crop's yield response to fertilizer applications. Some of these factors are within a producer's control, while others are not. General production practices — how a producer manages water, soil, insects and crop diseases — can improve or reduce yield response to applied fertilizers. These factors are summarized in Table 6-1.

TABLE 6-1. Factors limiting crop response to applied fertilizers		
Factor	How it affects response	Example
Soil water management		
Dry soil	reduces nutrient flow to roots and within plant	boron deficiency in alfalfa
	limits root growth and activity	lack of response to surface applied fertilizer
	increases salt concentration	risk of fertilizer burn
Wet soil	reduces root growth and ability to absorb nutrients	yellow corn in flooded soil
	changes chemical state of nutrients in low oxygen soils	denitrification of N; enhanced Mn availability in tire tracks
Cold, wet soils	reduces growth and activity of roots	phosphorus deficiency in corn seedlings
Crop rotation		
Soil structure	proportion of soil volume that roots will explore	corn in compacted soil has higher optimum P & K levels
Residual nutrients in the deeper soil profile	deeper rooted crops within a rotation will use nutrients from lower in the soil profile	sugar beets and carrots pull nitrogen from deep in the soil profile
Previous crop	accumulation and availability of soil nutrients	corn following alfalfa rarely needs N fertilizer

TABLE 6-1. Factors limiting crop response to applied fertilizers

Factor	How it affects response	Example
Agronomic Factors		
Choice of tillage system	more tillage leads to less mycorrhizae	greater response to starter P in conventionally tilled than no-till soils
	more tillage increases N mineralization	increased N credit where red clover cover crops are tilled
	deep tillage can dilute soil nutrient concentrations	low fertility on eroded knolls where tillage brings subsoil to the surface
	no-till leads to stratification of immobile nutrients	increased corn response to banded K in no-till
Pest Control		
Weeds	high soil fertility favours growth of weeds as well as crop	banding fertilizer places nutrients where they are less accessible to the weeds
Diseases	root diseases affect the root surface area and uptake of nutrients	white beans with root rots require more N
Nematodes	interferes with root uptake efficiency	soybean cyst nematode increases optimum soil K level
Insects	root pruning reduces root surface area and nutrient uptake	corn rootworm feeding induces N and K deficiencies
Agronomic Factors		
Cultivar selection	genetic differences in rooting habit	potato varieties with smaller root systems tend to respond to higher levels of fertility
	end use/quality	N recommendations for wheat and potatoes are specific to cultivar
Lodging	where crops are susceptible, excess N reduces yield by increasing lodging	optimum N rates are lower for cereals susceptible to lodging
Plant population and spacing	populations with higher yields remove more nutrients	in maximum yield research, high corn populations have sometimes been shown to respond more to fertility

Developing fertilizer recommendations

The need for additional fertilizer is determined through a diagnostic approach. It is essential for managing soil fertility and making recommendations. The tools of the diagnostic approach are:

- soil testing
- plant analysis and tissue testing
- visual nutrient deficiency symptoms

The challenge in making any fertilizer recommendations based on these diagnostic approaches is to determine an effective and economical rate of fertilizer. There are two common methods to develop fertilizer recommendations from soil test results: the "sufficiency" approach and the "build-up and maintenance" approach. Both concepts have their own strengths and weaknesses. One method may be more applicable than the other for a particular nutrient or a particular cropping system. Neither system will be effective, however, without soil test calibration.

Soil test calibration

Since its inception, soil testing has been used for most of the major crops produced in Western Europe and North America. Soil testing can index the availability of a wide range of plant nutrients and monitor changes in the levels of soil fertility over time.

No reasonable fertilizer recommendation can be made for annual crops without using the soil test as the starting point. For perennial horticultural crops, tissue testing is the foundation of fertilizer recommendations.

The soil test provides only an index of availability of a nutrient. This index must be calibrated against actual measurements of crop response in the field.

Different interpretations to soil test calibration are possible. One approach places more emphasis on crop response to applied nutrient. Another considers the yield in relation to the soil test level of a nutrient.

It is not possible to rely solely on the soil test for recommendations. The test does not reflect the external variables such as cool growing temperatures or high rainfall after the soil sample was taken. Nor does the soil test predict whether the crop will be managed to its full yield potential. External factors that affect the yield response to applied fertilizer must be considered in addition to the soil test.

Yield response to fertilizer applied

Field experiments are used to determine how much nutrient is required for each soil test level. This is determined by applying at least four different rates, including a zero rate, of a nutrient to different plots of a fairly uniform soil. A graph is developed by plotting the yields against the fertilizer rates applied. The resulting graph is used to define a response curve. A common response curve is shown in

Figure 6-1. A mathematical equation is fitted to the yield data.

There are several mathematical equations that can describe the response curve. The choice of equation is arbitrary. No single equation can represent all the processes controlling the response of crops to applied nutrients. The choice of equation can make substantial differences in the amount of fertilizer recommended. Despite that, the response curve can be used to apply economics to fertilizer decisions. Examining the response data visually is useful. It ensures that the response curve chosen represents the financial impact of fertilizer rate decisions.

By knowing the response curve, it is possible to use fertilizer price information. As shown in Figure 6-1, this information can calculate the economically optimum fertilizer rate to apply. As the rate of fertilizer applied increases, the slope of the response (the curved line) is steep at first, and then decreases. At point "A" in Figure 6-1 the increase in crop yield returns no more value than the increase in fertilizer cost. After this point, increasing the fertilizer rate does not increase economic return to fertilizer. This is the highest fertilizer rate that can be justified in one year.

Point "A" is called the maximum economic rate or the economically optimum rate. At nutrient rates higher than this point, yield may increase slightly, but not enough to justify the added cost.

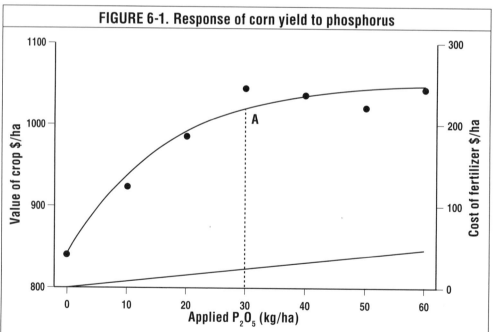

FIGURE 6-1. Response of corn yield to phosphorus

Response of corn yield to applied phosphorus at one of 17 locations in an Ontario study conducted by Philom Bios and Dow Elanco. The sloping straight line shows the fertilizer cost. The vertical dotted line indicates the optimum rate where the difference between crop value and fertilizer cost is maximum.

Choosing a yield response equation

Fertilizer response trials, no matter how extensive, produce data for yield responses at discrete points, either fertilizer additions or soil test levels. These data are fitted to a curve and the equation for this curve is used to predict fertilizer requirements more precisely. The type of equation used to describe this curve can influence the results.

No one curve is clearly better than any other for describing how crop yields increase with fertilizer additions. The common element of most equations is that the calculated response to fertilizer decreases as the amount of fertilizer added increases, so that at some point, the value of the added yield is less than the cost of fertilizer needed to achieve that yield. This point is the maximum economic yield.

The quadratic equation and the Mitscherlich equation are the most common ones used to fit fertilizer response data. A quadratic equation (Yield = $a + bx - cx^2$, where x is fertilizer rate and a, b and c are constants used to fit the curve) gives a curve that shows large responses to fertilizer at low rates. The response gradually decreases, so that eventually there is no more response to added fertilizer. Finally, the curve turns down, so that it predicts a decrease in yield with added fertilizer. The cost of the fertilizer added can be included on the same graph as the value of the crop yield. The maximum economic yield is the point of greatest difference between the value of the yield and the cost of the fertilizer.

The Mitscherlich equation has a similar form in the lower parts of the curve but this equation never reaches a maximum yield. The Mitscherlich equation is RY (relative yield) = $1 - (10^{(-x+b)^*c})$ where x is either fertilizer added or soil test value and b and c are constants relating to the efficiency of fertilizer use.

Both equations give similar maximum economic yield figures at moderate fertilizer and crop values. The differences arise if the value of the crop is high or the cost of the fertilizer is low. In this case, the Mitscherlich equation predicts a significantly higher maximum economic yield than the quadratic.

Yield response equations are useful tools for predicting maximum economic fertilizer rates but is important to remember, like any tool, they have limits.

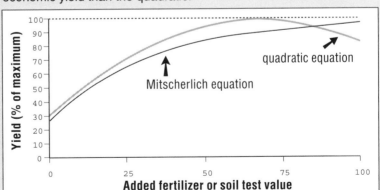

Although the Mitscherlich and quadratic equations have similar shapes in the lower parts of the curve, the Mitscherlich equation never reaches the maximum yield, while the quadratic equation reaches the maximum and then begins to drop off. It is extremely important not to extrapolate either curve beyond the data used to generate the curve. The risk of incorrect interpretation is too great.

Response to soil test level

Soil test calibration relates crop responses to soil test levels. This is most important for soil-immobile nutrients like phosphorus and potassium.

To determine this relationship, scientists conduct experiments in which the soil test is brought to various levels. At each level, two yields need to be measured: the yield without the applied nutrient and the yield with a non-limiting rate (more than the plant could possibly use) of applied nutrient. Relative yields, the unfertilized yield as a fraction of the non-limited yield, are plotted against soil test level. This determines the critical level above which the crop rarely responds economically to the applied nutrient.

Probability of response versus soil test level

When experiments are conducted over many years, a single response curve, while accurate for the average, may not represent actual results in a given year. Recognizing the variability in yield response leads to different approaches to interpreting the soil test results. In this approach, the frequency of positive yield responses is plotted against the soil test level. The soil test rating then becomes an index of the probability of response to the nutrient.

Table 6-2 describes the probability of response to added nutrients at different soil test levels. In general, crops grown in soils with low soil tests will respond to added nutrients most of the time and the optimum rate of fertilizer to apply will be high. On soils with high levels of fertility, profitable responses to fertilizer occur only rarely and optimum rates of application are lower.

Profitable responses to starter or seed-placed phosphorus in some crops continue at higher soil test levels than responses from broadcast applications.

Do high soil tests harm the environment?

Losses of nutrients from soil can harm water quality. The risk depends on both the source and transport of the nutrients. Higher soil test levels increase the source but not the transport. This is why a soil test level is one component of the Phosphorus Index. On land where risks of erosion and runoff are high, controlling soil test levels is relatively more important. On the other hand, on soils with low runoff risk, large applications of manure that provide benefits to soil quality may build up soil test P with relatively little risk of harm to water quality.

TABLE 6-2. Probability of response to added nutrients at different soil test levels

Level of soil fertility	Response rating	Probability of profitable response	Optimum fertilizer rates
low	high	most cases	high
medium	medium	about half the cases	medium
high	low	occasional	low
very high	very low	sporadic	very low
excessive	non-responsive	negligible*	nil

*The addition of nutrients to soils that already have above optimum levels of nutrients may reduce crop yields or quality by interfering with the uptake of other nutrients.

Developing fertilizer recommendations: "fertilize the crop" or "fertilize the soil"

There are two approaches to making fertilizer recommendations. One is to "fertilize the crop," often called the sufficiency approach. The second is to "fertilize the soil," frequently called the build-up and maintenance approach. Table 6-3 summarizes these two approaches to making fertilizer recommendations.

The sufficiency approach aims to supply the needs of the current crop. This approach is the basis for OMAFRA recommendations, as well as for those in some adjoining states, including New York. It considers the amount of nutrient available from the soil based on a soil test. Additional fertilizer recommendations are made that aim to provide an optimum payback in increased value of the current crop. It is the approach of choice for nutrients that are subject to losses from the soil like nitrogen. It can also be used for other nutrients, including phosphorus and potassium.

Building the soil test level to a specific target is not the goal of this method. Higher amounts of fertilizer are recommended at low soil test levels, lower amounts at high soil test levels. It tends to maintain soil test levels near the critical level.

The build-up and maintenance approach emphasizes soil fertility levels rather than direct crop responses. Fertilizers are applied to build or increase the soil test to a level at which crop growth is not limited by the nutrient.

In the build-up phase, nutrients are added to increase the soil test level. The maintenance phase involves adding nutrients to maintain a targeted level of fertility. For soils above the targeted range, nutrient recommendations decline to zero. See Figure 6-3, on page 136.

The benefits of an investment in building up soil fertility do not all occur in one year. While the costs and returns to added fertilizer in a single year may only justify fertilizing to 90% of maximum yield, adding the returns to residual fertility over a longer term will justify fertilizing for a greater percentage of maximum yield (Reetz and Fixen, 1992).

It's important to consider all the costs of this approach, including amortizing the investment over several years. The cost of investing includes both interest rates and opportunity costs. If other opportunities for investment yield better returns, it would be better not to invest in the additional fertilizer for building soil test levels.

Many commercial, state and university labs, including Pennsylvania, Ohio, Michigan and Indiana, use the build-up and maintenance approach. Major differences between laboratory recommendations can occur when using this approach. Assumptions used for soil test increase per unit of fertilizer and the time allowed for the soil test build-up will affect recommendations.

Developing fertilizer recommendations: the Ontario Corn Nitrogen Calculator

The nitrogen recommendations for corn were updated in 2006. Data was collected from 41 years of nitrogen trials and response curves were re-calculated to fit a quadratic-plateau model. Optimum rates of N for each site-year were determined and the factors with the greatest impact on optimum N rates were used to develop a model to predict N requirements for individual fields.

The factors included in the model were the yield potential for the field (average yield for the past five years), soil texture, previous crop, crop heat unit rating, application timing, and the relative price of corn and nitrogen fertilizer.

More information on the Ontario Corn Nitrogen Calculator can be found on the OMAFRA website at *www.ontario.ca/crops* by clicking on 'Corn'.

TABLE 6-3. Sufficiency versus build-up approaches to developing fertilizer recommendations

Sufficiency approach	Build-up and maintenance approach
Assumptions	
• Cost of the applied nutrient is paid for by the yield increase in the current crop. • No economic value is given to the residual effect of the fertilizer. • The yields obtained at low soil test with high added fertilizer are about the same as the yields at high soil test with less added fertilizer.	• Nutrient to be applied is not irreversibly fixed by the soil. • Nutrient is not subject to losses from the soil by leaching or volatile escape. • Producer can profit from future returns to investments in soil fertility.
Strengths	
• In a single year analysis, gives the greatest net return to fertilizer. • Can be used for both mobile and immobile nutrients.	• Accounts for residual benefits of fertilizer application. • Gives the greatest assurance that crop yields will not be limited by nutrients.
Challenges	
• Can be difficult to predict precisely the most economic rate for a particular set of circumstances because response can vary with soil type, tillage practice, variability in soil, crop variety and the weather. • Entails a greater risk of under-fertilizing, see Table 6-7, page 141.	• Applies only to immobile nutrients and therefore is not appropriate for nitrogen. • Requires amortization of fertilizer costs over several years to obtain full economic return.

TABLE 6-4. Which system?

Uncertainty exists in dealing with any biological system. We cannot predict exactly how crop yields will react in a specific set of factors.

Over time, the differences in net income between the two main approaches to fertilizer recommendations are not large, as long as they are based on valid data. However, there are factors that favour each system.

Factors favouring sufficiency approach:	Factors favouring build-up and maintenance approach:
• Short land tenure, annual rental agreements. • Not wanting to spend any more than necessary. • Low crop value, high fertilizer prices. • Alternative uses for capital with higher rate of return. • Nutrients converting to unavailable forms. • Nutrients easily lost from the soil. • Limitations to yield other than fertility. • Expectation that crop value and fertilizer prices will remain stable.	• Long-term land tenure. • Not wanting fertility to be limiting factor. • High value, high yielding crops. • No other use for capital or large investment in equipment. • Low-cost source of nutrients like manure or biosolids. • Nutrients held in soils in available forms. • Expectation that crop value and fertilizer prices will rise. • Rotational crops requiring high level of soil fertility.

Example of soil test calibration using sufficiency and build-up approaches

Examples of corn yield response curves at three levels of soil test phosphorus, each at a different site, are shown in Figure 6-2. The soil test extractant was sodium bicarbonate. The most economic rates were calculated on a corn price of $150 per tonne and a fertilizer price of $0.80 per kilogram of fertilizer phosphorus (P_2O_5).

Using the sufficiency approach strictly, from this one-year set of data, would result in the maximum economic rates of phosphorus fertilizer additions shown in Table 6-5. This table is only an example. A much larger number of experiments are needed to assemble a complete recommendation table. Soils of different type and texture may show different response curves at the same soil test level. For this reason, the three sites chosen for the example show some difference from the current recommendations.

Current recommendations are based on the sufficiency approach but allowances have been made for soil variability and for starter responses, particularly for phosphorus. Also remember that the current recommendations are derived from a far greater number of experiments than in the example and thus are more appropriate to use as general guidelines.

Figure 6-5 shows relative yield of unfertilized corn as a per cent of fertilized corn yield, using the phosphorus response data for corn

from the same source as used for the sufficiency approach example. The horizontal line is set at 95%, the relative yield chosen as economically attainable. The vertical line is positioned so that the fewest points are in quadrants B and D. This line represents the critical level.

In this case, a critical level of 16 ppm is suggested. Above this level, you would recommend maintenance doses only. Below this level, the amount of fertilizer recommended is that required to raise the soil test level plus maintenance. Rates recommended will vary according to length of time allowed for build-up.

A recommendation based on the build-up and maintenance approach is shown in Table 6-5. It assumes three things:

- It takes 37 kg of P_2O_5 per hectare to increase the soil test by 1 ppm (Richards et al, 1995).
- A target of building the soil test to the critical level over four years.
- The maintenance value is equal to the expected crop removal of 55 kg/ha.

Figure 6-4 explains the calculation for the phosphorus recommendation. In this example, the existing soil test level is 9 ppm. The recommended rate is calculated as the target soil test, 16 ppm, less the existing soil test level, 9 ppm, multiplied by the amount needed to raise the soil test one unit, 37, divided by the number of years, 4, plus maintenance, 55. These amounts are higher than those for the sufficiency

---

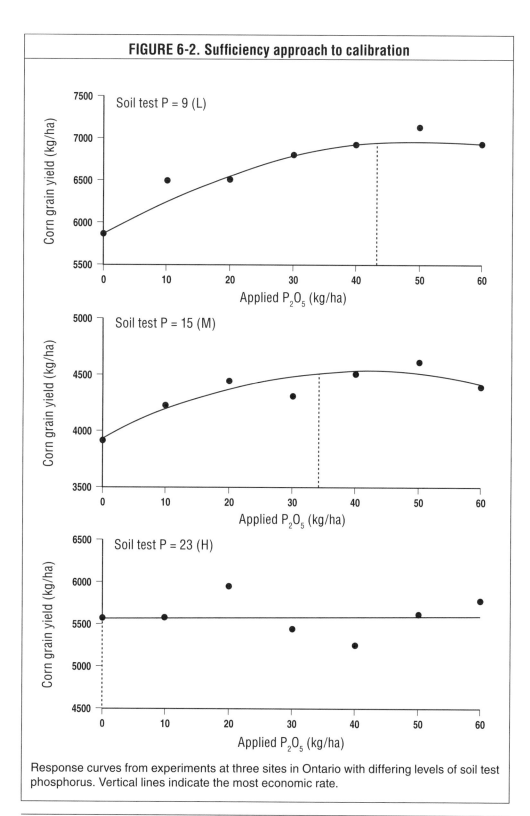

FIGURE 6-2. Sufficiency approach to calibration

Response curves from experiments at three sites in Ontario with differing levels of soil test phosphorus. Vertical lines indicate the most economic rate.

TABLE 6-5. Comparison of P recommendations from different approaches			
Soil test P (ppm)	P_2O_5 recommended (build-up & maintenance) (kg/ha)	Maximum economic rate of P_2O_5 (one year, one site) (kg/ha)	Current Ontario P_2O_5 recommendation (kg/ha)*
9	120	43	70
15	64	34	20
23	55	0	20
* OMAFRA Publication 811, *Agronomy Guide for Field Crops.*			

approach even though the same data are used.

An economic justification for these rates is quite complex. It involves the assumptions already mentioned above plus the following:

- An interest rate lower than 20%.
- An amortization period of at least 6 years.
- Attainable yield of 9 tonnes/ha (150 bu/ac).
- Relative yield curve as in Figure 6-6.

In practice, maintenance applications are recommended over a range of soil test levels. Beyond the maintenance limits, the rates begin to decline. See Figure 6-3.

Maintenance is based on removal by crop and has no direct bearing on crop response. Therefore, the maintenance portion should be based on average crop yield for the field rather than a yield goal.

FIGURE 6-3. Build-up and maintenance approach to calibration

Critical Level Maintenance Limit

Fertilizer Rate

Buildup Range | Maintenance Range | Drawdown Range

Soil Test Level

FIGURE 6-4. Build-up and maintenance requirement calculation

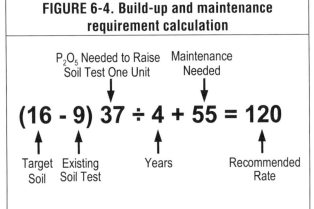

P_2O_5 Needed to Raise Soil Test One Unit   Maintenance Needed

$$(16 - 9)\ 37 \div 4 + 55 = 120$$

Target Soil Existing Soil Test   Years   Recommended Rate

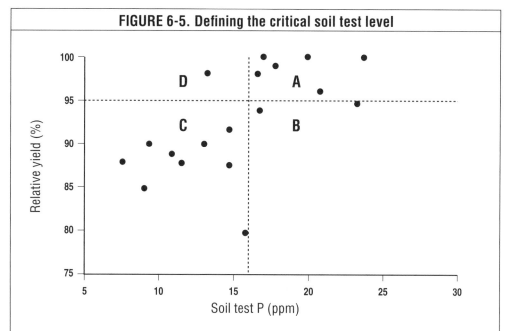

FIGURE 6-5. Defining the critical soil test level

Relative yield of corn versus soil test phosphorus from 18 site-years in an Ontario study conducted by Philom Bios and Dow Elanco (1993–1994).

Other things to consider

Yield goal

Expected yield influences fertilizer rate decisions. Obviously, the final yield is what pays for the input costs, so that higher yielding and higher value crops tend to receive more fertilizer.

In the long term, higher yields remove more nutrients from soil and require more to be added. In the short term, yield goal or yield level may have little or no effect on maximum economic rate of fertilizer (except for nitrogen). Soils with high yield potential have deep topsoil and excellent structure. This allows roots to explore larger volumes of soil for nutrients and moisture.

For example, research at the Ridgetown College of Agricultural Technology recorded a corn yield of 18.4 tonnes/ha in 1985 on research plots near Chatham. (Stevenson, 1983). Many things contributed to the high yield, including soil factors, irrigation and high inputs of fertilizer and manure nutrients. The most important factors were considered to be hybrid selection and population. The soil test levels for the plot before adding fertilizer were:

pH	P	K	Mg	Ca
	ppm	ppm	ppm	ppm
6.8	48 VH	161 VH	405 H	2774

It would be foolhardy to try to match these levels and expect the

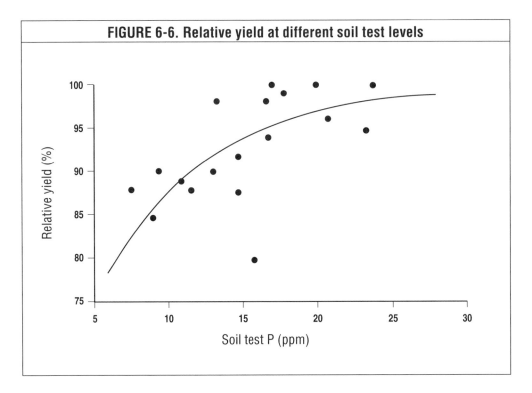

FIGURE 6-6. Relative yield at different soil test levels

Relative yield (%)

Soil test P (ppm)

same yield results from fertility response alone.

Basic cation saturation ratios and percentages

The ratios or percentages of the basic cation nutrients, calcium (Ca), magnesium (Mg) and potassium (K), are sometimes used as indicators of their availability. The aim is to recognize interactions among the cations.

These basic cations are known to have antagonistic effects on each other. This means a very high soil test level of one cation may reduce the availability to plants of one of the others. For practical purposes, these interactions are only important when one of the nutrients is approaching deficiency.

The basic cation saturation concept originated in New Jersey in the 1940s. In a series of greenhouse experiments over eight years, infertile, acid soils were limed and fertilized to grow alfalfa and the cation saturation of the soils was measured. The investigators suggested the cation exchange complex should be occupied by 65% calcium, 10% magnesium, 5% potassium and 20% hydrogen. It is important to note that the crop grew well with these levels of nutrients in the soil but this does not imply that these exact proportions are required for crop growth.

In many trials since the original study, crop growth has not been adversely affected over a wide range of Ca:Mg:K ratios or percentages, as long as one of the nutrients was not clearly deficient. A study on alfalfa and trefoil in New York State, found that Ca:Mg ratios ranging from 267:1 to 1:1 had no significant influence on yields (Reid, 1996).

There are two main drawbacks to the use of basic cation saturation ratios or percentages in making fertilizer recommendations:

- No economic analysis is included in the recommendations, particularly on soils high in calcium and magnesium. The cost of these fertilizer programs can be extremely high.
- Many alkaline Ontario soils have high levels of carbonate minerals. These minerals can be dissolved by the soil test extractant, releasing calcium and magnesium into the extract. This will inflate the calculated CEC and the calcium and magnesium percentages, leading to unrealistically high potassium recommendations.

The basic cation saturation ratio concept does have merit in recognizing extremes in the ratios between cations, especially in soils with very low CEC and fertility. In particular, potassium can interfere with magnesium uptake. Extra care must be taken to ensure adequate magnesium supplies where soils test high in potassium and low in magnesium. This interaction is particularly important in the management of ruminant nutritional problems such as grass tetany.

Adjusting potassium recommendations for cation exchange capacity (CEC)

Some states adjust potassium recommendations for CEC. In Michigan, Ohio and Indiana, the potassium recommendations increase with increasing CEC. This recommendation is based on trials in southern Ohio. Clay soils in this area can fix significant amounts of potassium. This leads to a greater requirement for potassium on the heavier textured soils, both for optimum crop yield and to build the potassium soil test. The younger soils of northern Ohio contain more native potassium in the clays and do not fix potassium as readily. In these soils, the clay content or CEC has only a very minor effect on the amount of potassium required.

In New York, for a given level of soil test potassium, potassium recommendations are higher on sandier, low CEC soils. Research there has shown soils higher in clay release more potassium through weathering, so that less potassium fertilizer is required for optimum crop yields.

Ontario research has not found any significant effect of CEC on the amount of potassium required.

Spatial variability

Most fertilizer calibrations have been done on small plots where soil fertility is relatively uniform. Most fields, however, show large variations in soil test levels. Ontario fields that have been intensively sampled show a coefficient of variation of 18-54% for nitrate, 20%–140% for phosphorus, 12%–70% for potassium and 50%–60% for micronutrients.

This variation in soil test means part of the field has above average fertility and a lower than average response to applied fertilizer. Another part of the field has below average fertility and shows a larger than average response to fertilizer.

The yield gain from extra fertilizer on the low-testing areas generally is larger than the cost of the extra fertilizer on the high-testing areas. As the field becomes more variable, the part that is highly responsive becomes larger in relation to the low- or no-response part of the field. The net result is that, in variable fields, the most profitable single rate of fertilizer to apply to the whole field is higher than the requirement for a uniform field.

An example of the effect of soil test variability on optimum fertilizer rate is shown in Table 6-6. Note how spatial variability increases the optimum constant rate of potassium, particularly in high testing soils.

If the spatial variability within a field can be mapped accurately, the same yields could be attained with less increase in fertilizer use than shown in the table. This could be done by using variable rate application of fertilizer on the most responsive areas.

However, sampling fields on the scale of one sample per hectare can miss some of this variability. The variable rate technology for such applications is available but the development of accurate application maps is just beginning.

In fields with highly variable soil test values, you can improve profitability of fertilizer use with variable rate application, providing that significant areas of the field are in the responsive soil test range.

Cost of under- versus over-fertilizing

In yield response curves (Figure 6-2), the slope decreases as applied fertilizer increases. Therefore, the change in yield for a given percentage of under-fertilization is greater than the change in yield for the same amount of over-fertilization. See Table 6-7.

If you are unsure whether a recommendation is accurate, erring on the side of over-fertilization entails smaller profit losses than those arising from under-fertilizing. The actual difference depends on the

TABLE 6-6. Influence of soil test K variability on optimum K fertilizer rate in Ontario			
	Soil test variability		
Average soil test K ppm	Uniform	Moderate	High
		Optimum K_2O rate (kg/ha)	
45	100	101	106
90	50	58	77
135	0	30	58
Coefficient of variation for low variability site = 0%, medium = 53% and high = 131%.			
		Source: Kachanoski and Fairchild, 1994.	

TABLE 6-7. Effect of under-fertilizing versus over-fertilizing on net return

Fertilizer rate (lb N/ac)	Yield (bu/ac)	Crop value	Nutrient cost	Net return	Difference
		$/ac			
64 (1/3 less)	129	359.80	25.64	334.16	5.88
96 (recommended)	135	378.28	38.24	340.04	
127 (1/3 more)	138	386.68	50.96	335.72	4.32

Price assumptions: Corn @ $2.80/bu, N @ $0.40/lb.
Source: mean of 109 OMAFRA N fertilizer rate trials, 2001–2005.

shape of the response curve. This is most likely to be apparent for nutrients like nitrogen, where yield increases are relatively linear until a plateau is reached.

For nutrients that can have a negative environmental impact, over-fertilization is a concern. It's important to make every attempt to be accurate in determining recommendations and to use every means possible to get information on the particular recommendation.

Agronomic and environmental impacts of fertilizer application

Under the humid conditions of eastern North America, the amount of mineral nitrogen left in the soil is a reliable indicator of the risk of loss through either leaching or denitrification. Post harvest residual nitrate levels increase greatly when application rates exceed the amount required for optimum yield. This is clearly shown in Figure. 6-7, where the crop yield increases to a plateau while the level of residual soil N increases.

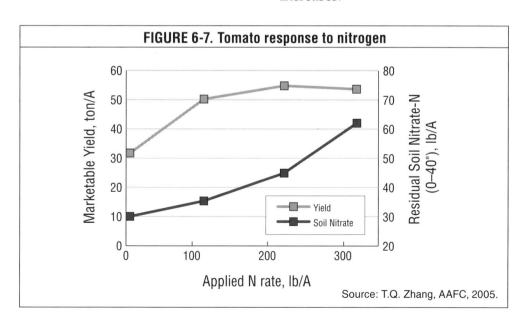

FIGURE 6-7. Tomato response to nitrogen

Source: T.Q. Zhang, AAFC, 2005.

Crop nutrient uptake and removal per unit of yield

Nutrient uptake refers to the maximum quantity of nutrient taken up into the above-ground portion of the crop. Nutrient removal is the amount of nutrient removed in the harvested portion of the crop. The two are nearly equal in crops harvested as whole plants like silage corn, alfalfa and cabbage.

The amounts shown in Tables 6-9 and 6-10 are based on Ontario field data where possible and general North American crops where local data was insufficient. To do precise nutrient budgeting, it is necessary to have the particular crop analyzed for nutrient content.

The forage crop figures are specific to Ontario and are ranges observed in samples submitted for analysis to Agri-Food Laboratories, Guelph, over five years in the early 1990s.

Nutrient recommendations based on plant tissue analysis

Tissue, leaf or plant analysis can be used to:
- determine the nutrient needs of established perennial crops such as cane berries, tree fruit and grapes
- confirm the diagnosis of visual symptoms of unusual plant growth so remedies can be used immediately

When used in perennial crops, it is often preferred over soil analysis because of the difficulty of taking soil samples in the root zone of perennial crops. Tissue analysis also helps show what nutrients are being taken up by the crop as opposed to what is available in the soil. Occasional soil analysis from orchards and vineyards is often useful when done along with tissue analysis, particularly for monitoring pH levels.

Extensive calibration trials in the field have resulted in fertilizer recommendations based on tissue analysis for Ontario fruit crops. Thus, tissue analysis is the major factor determining fertilizer application for the following growing season.

Used along with a soil test, tissue analysis can identify possible nutrient limitations or deficiencies. A tissue analysis may indicate a nutrient could be deficient or limiting but it is not easy to make a fertilizer recommendation rate from a tissue analysis. Tissue analysis may not provide information in time for correction for annual crops in the current growing season.

Deficient, critical and sufficient concentrations

Plant analysis identifies a nutrient as being deficient when its concentration falls below a critical level for a given plant part in a given crop for a given stage of plant development. The concept of the critical level

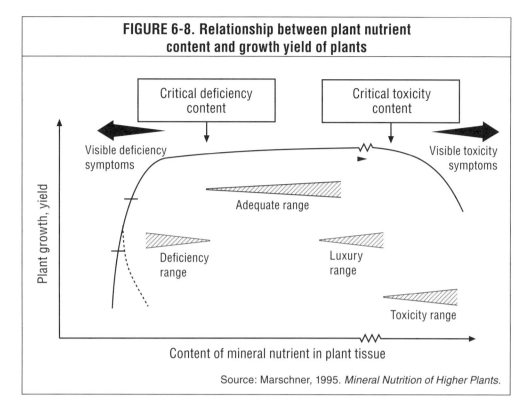

FIGURE 6-8. Relationship between plant nutrient content and growth yield of plants

Critical deficiency content

Critical toxicity content

Visible deficiency symptoms

Visible toxicity symptoms

Plant growth, yield

Adequate range

Deficiency range

Luxury range

Toxicity range

Content of mineral nutrient in plant tissue

Source: Marschner, 1995. *Mineral Nutrition of Higher Plants.*

separating deficient and adequate ranges is illustrated in Figure 6-8.

In order to interpret the tissue analysis, the timing or stage of plant growth and the plant part being sampled is very important. For more details on sampling plant tissue, refer to Chapter 1, pages 7–9.

OMAFRA crop recommendation and production guides list critical nutrient ranges for most crops grown in Ontario. Many publications on field and horticultural crops list critical values. Most labs that do tissue analysis have their own set of critical values, developed from their own experience. It is important to follow closely the laboratory's instructions regarding the

plant part sampled, stage of plant development and sample handling.

When investigating crop growth peculiarities, if the time of sampling does not correspond to the stage of plant development for which there are established critical values, separately sample a portion of the normal crop as well as the affected area. See Figure 1-7, page 13.

Table 6-8 shows the probable causes for excessive or deficient levels of nutrients in plant tissue samples. Interpretations of these results are more complex than simply looking at the numbers on the analytical report.

TABLE 6-8. Possible causes for variation in plant tissue nutrient levels

Nutrient	Excessive	Deficient
All Nutrients	reduced plant growth due to weather conditions (frost injury, drought), disease or deficiency of another nutrient	inadequate supply of any nutrient from the soil will tend to produce low plant tissue levels
Nitrogen	over application of nitrogen, from commercial sources and or manure, high soil organic matter, high rates of mineralization	low organic matter, soil compaction, dry soil conditions, water logged conditions causing denitrification
Phosphorus	high soil test, low or deficient zinc, high rates of P nutrient application	low pH, or high soil pH, soil compaction, drought, cold soils, root disease
Potassium	high rates of application, high soil test level	excessive nitrogen, soil compaction, cold soils
Magnesium	old plant part, over application of magnesium fertilizer	low pH, high potassium availability, high nitrogen levels
Calcium	old plant part, diseased leaf, contamination of sample with soil. High calcium levels are rare.	leached sandy soil, high rates of potassium in low CEC soils, high nitrogen availability, low pH, inadequate rates of limestone
Zinc	naturally high soil zinc, heavy application of swine manures, high organic matter, contamination from galvanized sampling equipment	high soil pH, high soil phosphorus, eroded soil areas, low soil organic matter
Manganese	high nitrogen and phosphorus applications, low pH, soil compaction, low oxygen root environment, contamination from sprays, dust	high soil pH, highly aerated soil, high organic matter
Copper	high soil copper, spray materials (fungicides), soil splash up on leaves	high soil organic matter, leached soil, high levels of zinc and manganese
Iron	wet soil conditions, soil on leaves, zinc deficiency	excessive phosphorus, zinc, copper and manganese
Boron	improper application rates, lowered soil pH	sandy leached soils, low organic matter
Sulphur	high application rates of sulphate-sulphur, foliar spray residues on leaves	excessive rates of nitrogen application or high mineralization rates from soil organic matter, leaching losses
Molybdenum	high soil pH, foliar application residues	low soil pH, high phosphorus, sulphur applications, (ion antagonism at root site)

Diagnosis and recommendation integrated system (DRIS)

The DRIS was initially designed to apply to both soil and plant analysis. In North America, it has been used more frequently for plant analysis.

The system relates complete sets of nutrient concentrations and ratios for a particular crop to those of crops grown under optimum conditions at the highest attainable yield levels. The values and ratios obtained from these crops are referred to as DRIS norms.

The DRIS approach applied to plant analysis places a relative ranking of the essential elements from the most to the least deficient. In some cases, this analysis has been found to be more sensitive than the critical, or sufficiency, level in identifying the need for higher levels of one or more nutrients. Because DRIS uses ratios of nutrients, dry matter dilution due to the maturing of the crop is minimized and the time of sampling has less influence on the test results.

Initially it was thought DRIS norms were applicable across wide areas. However, studies on major agronomic crops show that locally or regionally developed norms are more accurate in diagnosing deficiencies. While the DRIS has not yet become a completely reliable system for fertilizer recommendations, it provides the possibility of bringing together all the elements of plant nutrition and evaluating them simultaneously with yield level as part of the process. Providing that adequate calibration data becomes available, the DRIS approach may be used more often in the future.

Fertilizer recommendations: not a production prescription

No one table of recommendations can cover all situations. A recommendation is not a production prescription. The amounts recommended by any source may be adjusted using local experience and knowledge of the particular soils and financial conditions of the producer. It is more valid to make such an adjustment than to use the general recommendations.

The fertilizer retailer is often in a good position to know the peculiarities of the soils, owing to the geographic limitations of distribution from a fertilizer blending plant. For this reason, each retail outlet should have at least one experienced agronomist or Certified Crop Adviser qualified to make sound recommendations.

TABLE 6-9. Field crop nutrient uptake and removal in Ontario							
Crop	Yield	N*	P₂O₅	K₂O	Ca	Mg	S
	bu/ac	lb/ac					
Grains, oilseeds							
Grain corn	150	uptake	173–239	74–109	133–243	26–49	18–30	13–16
		removal	97–149	55–66	39–44	1	13	10–11
Soybean	50	uptake	230–290	40–50	120–220	25–30	20–25	17
		removal	187–200	40–44	69–70	9–11	7–9	5
Winter wheat	75	uptake	140–155	51–56	94–152	13	17–23	15–19
		removal	86–94	41–47	26–28	2	12	6
Barley	75	uptake	93–112	36–41	75–112	17	8–13	13–15
		removal	65–83	28–30	19–26	2	4	6
Oats	75	uptake	70–86	30–33	89–109	9	10–15	14
		removal	47–60	19	14–15	2	3	5
Winter rye	50	uptake	83–84	28–42	50–120	13	7	14–15
		removal	54–61	17–23	17–18	3	4	5–10
Dry beans	30	removal	75	25	25	2	2	5
Canola	45	uptake	135–144	59–75	107–120	**	**	27–28
		removal	90–100	50–60	25–30	9–12	12–15	15
Forages	**ton/ac DM†**						
Corn silage	8	173–239	74–109	133–243	26–49	18–30	13–16
Legume haylage	5	266–367	53–79	224–354	113–177	19–36	19–20
Mixed haylage	5	228–338	52–78	224–355	95–164	16–34	15–29
Grass haylage	4	129–219	39–62	163–287	42–90	10–21	**
Legume hay, 1st cut	5	223–331	52–80	206–350	101–154	21–34	19–27
Mixed hay, 1st cut	5	172–273	50–72	170–297	82–135	18–30	13–21
Grass hay, 1st cut	4	103–181	35–56	111–224	42–85	11–21	11–16
Hay, 2nd cut	3	152–215	34–47	119–191	68–102	14–23	11–17

* Soybeans, dry beans and forage legumes get most of their nitrogen from the air.
† Tons per acre of dry matter.
** Data not available.

Ranges of nutrient uptake and removal for yield levels typical of good growing conditions for field crops. Figures are based on Ontario field data where possible and are estimates. Actual uptake and removal will vary with yield, and nutrient concentrations will also vary with year, level of soil fertility and crop variety. Precise nutrient management planning would require analysis of each crop each year. Actual changes to soil fertility may differ from the amount removed by the crop.

In some instances, weathering of soil materials and organic matter may compensate for part of the nutrient removal by crops. In other instances, nutrients may be chemically fixed by the soil or lost to leaching, and the loss of nutrients will exceed crop removal.

TABLE 6-10. Horticultural crop nutrient uptake and removal in Ontario

	Yield ton/ac		N*	P_2O_5	K_2O lb/ac	Ca	Mg	S
Beans, green	3	uptake	102	10–24	60–122	**	13	**
		removal	17	3	34	**	**	**
Broccoli	4	uptake	133	8	165	**	**	**
		removal	36	5	36	**	**	**
Cabbage	30	uptake	180–210	50–66	195–220	66	27	50–60
		removal	120	24	215	66	27	50
Carrot	25	uptake	145	25	345	**	**	**
		removal	80	20	200	**	**	**
Corn, sweet	6	uptake	155–187	20–63	105–181	**	27	15
		removal	50	4	30	**	**	**
Onion	20	uptake	120–145	25–53	105–155	30	9	20–36
		removal	75	15	80–85	23	4–9	20–36
Peas, green	2	uptake	170–260	22–56	80–168	**	29	16
		removal	40	2	30	**	**	**
Potato	15	uptake	160–170	50-55	220–330	**	30	15
		removal	63	12	108–125	2.5	5	5–6
Sugar beets	22	uptake	186–211	29–67	386–403	**	59	32–33
		removal	88–92	11–40	143–183	**	**	13
Tobacco	1	uptake	84–110	17–30	170–171	**	16	13
		removal	56–75	4–6	104–120	75	18	14
Tomato	40	uptake	232	87	463	**	36	54
		removal	144–160	24	280–288	14–24	22–24	28
Apple	20	uptake	165	75	300	**	40	**
Grapes	6	uptake	51	18	80	**	9	**
Peaches	15	uptake	50	20	60	11	**	**

Ranges of nutrient uptake and removal for yield levels typical of good growing conditions for horticultural crops.
* Legumes such as beans and peas get much of their nitrogen from the air.
** Data not available.

References

Black, Charles A. 1993. *Soil Fertility Evaluation and Control.* Lewis Publishers, Boca Raton.

Foth, H.D., and B.G. Ellis. 1996. *Soil Fertility.* 2nd ed. CRC Press, Inc.

Kachanoski, R.G., and G.L. Fairchild. 1994. Field scale fertilizer recommendations and spatial variability of soil test values. *Better Crops* 78(4):20-23.

Marschner, H. 1995. *Mineral Nutrition of Higher Plants.* San Diego, California: Academic Press, Inc.

Reid, W.S. 1996. Influence of lime and calcium:magnesium ratio on alfalfa and birdsfoot trefoil yields. *Communications in Soil Science and Plant Analysis 27:* 1885-1900.

Reetz, H.F. Jr., and P.E. Fixen. 1992. Economics of long-term and short-term soil fertility management. *Better Crops* 76(2):8-11.

Richards, J.E., Bates, T.E., and Sheppard, S.C. 1995. Changes in the form and distribution of soil phosphorus due to long-term corn production. *Can. J. Soil Sci.* 75:311-318.

Stevenson, C.K. 1983. Maximum yield research progress at Ridgetown College in Ontario. *Better Crops* 68 (1):4–5.

Stevenson, C.K., and MacAlpine, M.C. . 1996. Penicillium bilaii phosphorus research with corn. Report No. 51, Ridgetown College of Agricultural Technology.

7 FERTILIZER MATERIALS, BLENDING AND APPLICATION

Fertilizer materials

No matter what fertilizer you apply, the materials you choose and the way you blend and apply them will have great impact on your fertilizer program. Most of the fertilizer applied in Ontario is in the granular form but liquids and gases are also used. Each form is listed below and in Table 7-1 with its specific grade (% N-P_2O_5-K_2O by weight), chemical analysis and handling and use characteristics.

About 70% of the mineral nutrients applied to Ontario fields are in the form of granular fertilizers. They generally have a higher analysis than liquid fertilizers and are relatively less expensive. Their storage, handling and transport requirements differ from those of liquid or gaseous fertilizers. Granular materials can be blended to meet a wide range of crop requirements.

In general, liquid fertilizers are more expensive per unit of nutrient than granular fertilizers because of the extra weight and volume that must be transported and, in some cases, extra processing. This is balanced by the convenience of being able to pump it and the ease and accuracy of metering and placement. See Table 7-1, page 152.

In 2006, 10-34-0 cost 54% more than the same amount of nutrient purchased as diammonium phosphate. The difference is even greater for complete N-P-K fertilizers, where liquids may cost double the equivalent in granular fertilizer.

Nitrogen (N) sources

Urea (46-0-0)

- white; $CO(NH_2)_2$
- produced synthetically from ammonia and carbon dioxide
- most commonly used fertilizer N source worldwide
- may contain small amounts (0.5%–1.5%) of biuret, about 0.3% conditioning agent (formaldehyde or methylene di-urea) and less than 0.5% moisture
- grades for foliar application should contain less biuret

Urea converts to the ammonium form of N in the soil. The urease enzyme—present in soils, bacteria and crop residues—speeds the process. Surface-applied urea is subject to losses of ammonia. Losses increase with higher soil pH, more crop residues and with higher temperatures.

Ammonium nitrate (34-0-0)

- NH_4NO_3
- produced by combining ammonia with nitric acid
- may contain about 1% conditioning agent and 0.5% moisture

- more expensive per unit of N than urea
- no longer produced in Canada
- regulations apply to its transport (Transport of Dangerous Goods Class 5.1)
- needs to be kept away from oils and other flammable materials as it can form an explosive mixture
- more hygroscopic than urea and may deteriorate in storage during hot weather as crystal phase changes result in a break down of the prills

When applied to the soil, ammonium nitrate dissolves in the soil water and separates into ammonium and nitrate, both of which can be absorbed by plants. It is slightly more quickly available to plants at low temperatures than urea but under normal growing conditions there is no practical difference.

Calcium ammonium nitrate (27-0-0)

- uniform mixture of 80% ammonium nitrate and either calcitic or dolomitic limestone
- limestone reduces explosion hazard

When applied at equal weights of N, calcium ammonium nitrate is similar to ammonium nitrate. The lime included in the granules balances part of the acidity released by the N so that it does not acidify the soil as quickly as ammonium nitrate does.

Urea-ammonium nitrate solution (UAN) (28-0-0 to 32-0-0)

- produced by dissolving urea and ammonium nitrate (50:50) in water
- 28-0-0 can salt out (precipitate out of solution) if temperature drops below -18°C (0°F)
- more concentrated solution (32-0-0) is available but not often used in Ontario because the salting out temperature is 0°C (32°F)
- similar to urea, is subject to loss as ammonia if UAN applied to soil surface
- herbicides and other pesticides commonly added to UAN for broadcast application on the soil
- avoid application onto crop foliage because severe burning will result
- lends itself to side-dress applications

Urea-ammonium nitrate solution is the most commonly used liquid fertilizer in Ontario.

Anhydrous ammonia (82-0-0)

- NH_3
- manufactured by reacting natural gas with atmospheric N under high pressures and temperatures
- colourless, pungent gas at atmospheric pressure
- handled as a pressurized liquid; at -2°C (28°F) pressure same as surrounding air, at 16°C (60°F) it is 655 kPa (93 psi)
- building block for all manufactured N fertilizers

- similar to urea and ammonium nitrate in acidifying effect (1.8 lb $CaCO_3$ to neutralize acidity generated per lb of N supplied)

Anhydrous ammonia is applied directly by injecting it into the soil where it vapourizes and dissolves in the soil moisture. To avoid vapour losses to the air the anhydrous band must be placed deep enough in the soil that the injection slot closes over.

There is some concern that anhydrous ammonia is harmful to soil life. Within the injection band high soil pH and hygroscopic conditions are severe enough to kill earthworms and other soil fauna and microflora but this zone is relatively small and dissipates quickly. The population of soil organisms quickly recovers and is actually increased by the addition of N to the soil ecosystem.

Those little puffs

Have you wondered about those little puffs of vapour behind the anhydrous applicator?

Many farmers worry they are losing large quantities of N fertilizer. In fact, most of what they are seeing is a fog created by the cold ammonia gas condensing water vapour. It has been estimated that each millilitre of ammonia can produce over a litre of mist. The average emission loss is only 4% and is less in good conditions.

Ammonium sulphate (21-0-0)

- $(NH_4)_2SO_4$
- white-to-brown crystalline industrial byproduct obtained by neutralizing ammonia from coke ovens with recycled sulphuric acid or from nylon manufacturing
- may contain about 0.5% moisture and minute amounts of nutrients such as K, calcium, copper, iron, manganese and zinc
- generally more expensive per unit of N than urea

Ammonium sulphate breaks down to ammonium and sulphate when dissolved in the soil water. It is useful for surface broadcast applications as there is less risk of ammonia volatilization. Depending on the source, its form is granular or coarse powder.

Calcium nitrate (15-0-0)

- $Ca(NO_3)_2$
- expensive source of N
- used only where both calcium and N are required and soil acidification is undesirable
- contains N in nitrate form and water soluble calcium
- highly hygroscopic, may liquefy completely when exposed to air with a relative humidity above 47%. Store any broken bag in a tightly closed waterproof bag

The highly soluble nitrate-N and calcium are immediately available to the plant.

TABLE 7-1. Common fertilizer ingredients

	Grade[1] (%)	Other nutrients[2]	Salt index[3]	CaCO$_3$ equivalent[4] lb/lb N	Bulk density[5] lb/ft^3	kg/L	Relative cost/unit nutrient[6]
GRANULAR							
Urea	46-0-0		74	1.8	50	0.80	1.00
Ammonium nitrate	34-0-0		104	1.8	56	0.90	1.42
Calcium ammonium nitrate	27-0-0	4–6% Ca 0–2% Mg	93	0.9	68	1.10	1.46
Ammonium sulphate	21-0-0	24% S	88	3.6	68	1.10	1.41–2.04
Calcium nitrate	15-0-0	19% Ca	65	-1.3 (B)	75	1.20	3.72
Potassium nitrate	12-0-44		70	-1.9 (B)	75	1.20	2.54
Sodium nitrate	16-0-0		100	-1.8 (B)	78	1.25	n/a
Single superphosphate	0-20-0	20% Ca 12% S	8	neutral	68	1.10	1.77
Triple superphosphate	0-46-0	21% Ca	10	neutral	68	1.10	1.00
Monoammonium phosphate	11-52-0		27	5.4	62	1.00	0.82
Diammonium phosphate	18-46-0		29	3.6	62	1.00	0.81
Muriate of potash (red)	0-0-60	45% Cl	115	neutral	70	1.10	1.00
Muriate of potash (white)	0-0-62	46% Cl	116	neutral	75	1.20	1.00
Potassium sulphate	0-0-50	18% S	43	neutral	75	1.20	2.34
Sulphate of potash-magnesia	0-0-22	20% S 11% Mg	43	neutral	94	1.50	3.71
LIQUID							
Anhydrous ammonia	82-0-0		47	1.8	37	0.6	0.83
Urea-ammonium nitrate (UAN)	28-0-0 32-0-0		63 71	1.8	80 82	1.28 1.32	1.10
Ammonium polyphosphate	10-34-0 11-37-0		20	3.6	87	1.40	1.27

[1] Grade: guaranteed minimum percentage by weight of total N, available phosphoric acid (P_2O_5) and soluble potash (K_2O) in each fertilizer material.
[2] Other nutrients: nutrients other than N, P or K.
[3] Salt index: comparison of relative solubilities of fertilizer compounds with sodium nitrate (100) per weight of material. When applied too close to the seed or on the foliage the higher salt index materials are more likely to cause injury.
[4] CaCO$_3$ equivalent: pounds of lime required to neutralize the acid formed by one pound of the N supplied by the fertilizer material. "B" following the lime index indicates a basic (acid-neutralizing or alkaline) ingredient. Note: acid-forming effects can be up to twice as great as indicated, depending on plant uptake processes.
[5] Bulk density: expressed as pounds per cubic foot or kg/L, important since fertilizers are metered by volume rather than weight in spreaders or planting equipment.
[6] Relative cost/unit: based on 2006 prices of urea for N, triple superphosphate for P and muriate of potash for K.

Potassium nitrate (12-0-44)

- KNO_3
- extracted from dry brine lakes (e.g. Dead Sea) or manufactured by reacting potassium chloride and nitric acid
- expensive source of N and K
- used mainly for horticultural crops, tobacco and hydroponics

Phosphorus (P) sources

Single superphosphate (0-20-0)

- about one half mono-calcium phosphate and one half gypsum [$Ca(H_2PO_4)_2 \bullet H_2O + CaSO_4 \bullet 2H_2O$]
- made by reacting phosphate rock with sulphuric acid
- usually contains 20% available phosphate, 12% sulphur and 20% calcium

The oldest commercial fertilizer, single superphosphate has been on the market since 1840 and is no longer handled by major fertilizer suppliers in Ontario. It has been largely replaced by triple superphosphate.

Triple superphosphate (0-46-0)

- mostly mono-calcium phosphate [$Ca(H_2PO_4)_2 \bullet H_2O$]
- made by reacting phosphate rock with phosphoric acid
- contains about 83% mono-calcium phosphate, 2% moisture, balance mostly unreacted phosphate rock and other insoluble phosphates

Mono-calcium phosphate is an acidic salt that can break down urea fairly easily. Triple superphosphate should not be blended with urea.

Monoammonium phosphate (MAP; 11-52-0)

- $NH_4H_2PO_4$
- produced by reacting anhydrous ammonia with phosphoric acid
- off-white-to-grey colour
- usually contains 85% pure chemical compound, 3%–5% diammonium phosphate, 1% moisture, balance magnesium and other phosphates and sulphates
- economical source of N (10%–12.5%) and P_2O_5 (48%–52%)

Monoammonium phosphate is the P source of choice in Ontario because of its high nutrient concentration and relative crop safety in starter fertilizers. It's well-suited for use in starter bands.

Diammonium phosphate (DAP; 18-46-0)

- $(NH_4)_2HPO_4$
- produced by reacting anhydrous ammonia and phosphoric acid
- relatively low cost per unit
- light-to-dark grey colour
- usually contains about 80% pure chemical compound, 10% monoammonium phosphate, 1%–2% moisture, balance magnesium and other phosphates or sulphates. May also contain a small amount of ammonium nitrate or urea added during manufacturing to bring the N content up to the guaranteed 18%

- nitrogen 100% water soluble, available phosphate usually 90% water soluble

Diammonium phosphate has been the main source of P for several decades because of its cost and high nutrient content. However, it is not always the most suitable choice because of the risk of ammonia injury when used in starter fertilizers, particularly in alkaline soils.

Ammonium polyphosphate

- $(NH_4)_3HP_2O_7$
- liquid solution, 10-34-0 analysis (can also be 11-37-0)
- about 75% of the P is polyphosphate, 25% orthophosphate
- made by reacting ammonia with pyrophosphoric acid, which is made by dehydrating orthophosphoric acid
- solution pH of 6, near neutral
- blends well with UAN

A 10-34-0 solution also blends well with micronutrients. For example, it can maintain 2% Zn in solution compared to 0.05% with H_3PO_4.

Rock phosphate

- sedimentary rock made up primarily of calcium fluorophosphate with impurities of iron, aluminum and magnesium
- raw material for production of P fertilizers
- sometimes promoted as a "natural" source of P
- none of the P is water soluble
- citrate solubility of the P ranges from 5 to 17%

- finely ground, it can supply sufficient plant-available P in low pH (acidic) soils when applied at 2 to 3 times the rates of superphosphates
- availability to plants is low-to-nil in neutral or alkaline soils

Potassium (K) sources

Muriate of potash (0-0-60 or 0-0-62)

- KCl, potassium chloride
- most common and least expensive source of K
- contains chlorine (47%), an essential plant nutrient needed for cell division, photosynthesis and disease suppression
- a small amount (less than 100 grams per tonne) of an amine/oil anti-caking agent is often included in the shipped product
- the availability of the K to plants is equal from red and white forms

Red muriate of potash (0-0-60)

- mined primarily in Saskatchewan, and some in New Brunswick
- contains about 97% potassium chloride (KCl)
- iron impurities are responsible for the colour; they do not affect solubility

White muriate of potash (0-0-62)

- obtained by crystallizing potassium chloride out of the solution mining liquor
- almost pure potassium chloride

Potassium sulphate (0-0-50)

- K_2SO_4
- extracted from the brines of Great Salt Lake in Utah
- also contains 17% sulphur in the water soluble form

Potassium sulphate, or sulphate of potash, has a lower salt index and is more expensive than muriate of potash. It is used mainly on crops sensitive to chloride, such as tobacco, potatoes, tree fruits and some vegetables.

Sulphate of potash-magnesia (0-0-22)

- potassium-magnesium sulphate $K_2SO_4 \cdot 2MgSO_4$
- mined from deposits in New Mexico
- commonly referred to as K-Mag and Sul-Po-Mag

Potassium-magnesium sulphate, or sulphate of potash-magnesia, has a higher cost per unit of K than the muriate form. It also contains 11% magnesium and 22% sulphur in water-soluble form and therefore readily available to plants. It is useful as a source of soluble magnesium in fields where lime is not required.

Clear solutions

- wide range available of N-P and N-P-K fertilizers with neutral pH (see Table 7-2)
- based on ammonium polyphosphate (10-34-0)
- made by adding urea, aqua ammonia, phosphoric acid, potassium chloride or potassium hydroxide to the ammonium polyphosphate
- micronutrients can be added but must be in the chelated form
- all ingredients must be high quality, since impurities can lead to salting out or gelling of the fertilizer solution
- generally of high agronomic quality, although salt injury to seeds and roots becomes a concern with higher amounts of N and K
- most commonly used as starter fertilizer applied in the seed furrow
- reduces time and labour at planting because of low use rates and the ability to pump the material from nurse tanks into the planter
- equipment cost for planters can be reduced because separate fertilizer opener not required

Acid solutions

- combinations of phosphoric acid, sulfuric acid and urea
- micronutrients do not have to be added in chelated form

Acid solutions are not commonly used in Ontario because they are corrosive and expensive compared

		Weight/				
Analyses	Weight/ US gal (lb)	Imp. gal (lb)	Weight/ litre (lb)	Imp. gal/ tonne	US gal/ tonne	Litre/ tonne
8-25-3	11.11	13.35	2.94	165.1	198.4	749.9
6-18-6	10.69	12.85	2.83	171.6	206.2	779.0
3-11-11	10.45	12.55	2.76	175.7	211.0	798.8
9-9-9	10.49	12.60	2.77	175.0	210.2	795.9
7-7-7	10.41	12.50	2.75	176.4	211.8	801.7
6-24-6	11.07	13.30	2.93	165.8	199.2	752.4
9-18-9	11.07	13.30	2.92	165.8	199.2	755.0
5-10-15	10.70	12.85	2.83	171.6	206.0	799.0
2-10-15	10.62	12.75	2.81	172.9	207.6	784.6
10-34-0	11.60	14.00	3.09	157.0	188.5	715.8

TABLE 7-2. Blended liquid fertilizers

1 Imperial gallon = 1.201 US gallons   1 US gallon = 0.8326 Imperial gallons
1 US gallon = 3.785 litres   1 Imperial gallon = 4.546 litres

to granular fertilizers. These solutions are promoted on the basis that nutrients are more available at the low pH created in the fertilizer band, particularly in alkaline soils.

Most soils are well enough buffered, however, that the acid addition has no effect on soil pH. These materials are equal to but not better than, other fertilizer materials in nutrient availability.

Suspensions

- produced by mixing finely ground dry ingredients with water and a suspending agent such as clay
- can produce a complete fertilizer with a higher analysis than dissolved fertilizer
- mix needs agitation to keep it suspended and special handling and application equipment

Suspensions form an almost insignificant part of the Ontario fertilizer market, although they are common in western Canada.

Secondary nutrient sources

Secondary nutrients are needed occasionally in Ontario soils. If required, they may be applied as part of a fertilizer blend or added as part of a lime application to correct soil acidity. Common sources for secondary and micronutrients are shown in Table 7-3.

Calcium

Limestone (either calcitic or dolomitic) is the most common source of calcium. It also increases the pH of acidic soils. To be effective, it must be finely ground. Limestone is available in powder form or in pellets made from finely ground limestone. The solubility of limestone drops quickly as soil pH increases.

In soils with neutral or alkaline pH, gypsum (calcium sulfate) is the preferred form of calcium because it is more soluble than lime. Gypsum has no effect on soil pH.

Calcium chloride or calcium nitrate are occasionally used as foliar sources of calcium.

Magnesium

Magnesium deficiency is most common in acidic soils. If dolomitic limestone is added to correct the acidity, it will also supply enough magnesium to correct the deficiency. The solubility of dolomitic limestone decreases as the soil pH increases, thus it is not appropriate for alkaline soils.

In neutral or alkaline soils, Epsom salts (magnesium sulphate) or sulphate of potash magnesia can be used for supplemental magnesium.

Sulphur

Sulphate sulphur is present in a number of common fertilizer materials and can be included in a fertilizer blend in these ingredients. Most common are ammonium sulphate, potassium sulphate and sulphate of potash magnesia. Gypsum (calcium sulphate) can also be used as a sulphur source. Product availability, transportation costs and crop requirements for other nutrients will dictate which source of sulphur is most economic.

Granular elemental sulphur (90% S) can be another source. It will also acidify the soil. The sulphur must be oxidized to sulphate before it is available to the crop, which can take several months. Some of the intermediate products in the oxidation process can be toxic to crops; therefore high rates should be broadcast rather than banded.

TABLE 7-3. Common secondary and micronutrient sources					
Nutrient	Source	% Nutrient	Other nutrients	Application Soil	Application Foliar
Calcium (Ca)	calcitic limestone	22%–40%		*	
	dolomitic limestone	16%–22%	6%–13% Mg	*	
	gypsum ($CaSO_4 \cdot 2H_2O$)	23%	19% S	*	
	calcium chloride ($CaCl_2$)	36%	64% Cl	*	*
	calcium nitrate ($Ca(NO_3)_2$)	19%	15.5% N	*	*
	pelletized lime	16%–40%	0%–13% Mg	*	
	cement kiln dust	26%–32%	2%–9% K_2O	*	
Magnesium (Mg)	dolomitic limestone	6%–13%	16%–22% Ca	*	
	Epsom salts ($MgSO_4$)	9%	13% S	*	*
	sulphate of potash magnesia	11%	22% K_2O; 20% S	*	
Sulphur (S)	ammonium sulphate	24%	21% N	*	
	potassium sulphate	18%	50% K_2O	*	
	sulphate of potash magnesia	22%	22% K_2O; 11% Mg	*	
	calcium sulphate	19%	23% Ca	*	
	granular sulphur	90%			
Boron (B)	various granular materials	12%–15%		*	
	Solubor	20%			*
Copper (Cu)	copper sulphate	25%		*	
	copper chelates	5%–13%			
Manganese (Mn)	manganese sulphate	28%–32%			*
	manganese chelates	5%–12%			*
Molybdenum (Mo)	sodium molybdate	39%			*
Zinc (Zn)	zinc sulphate	36%		*	*
	zinc oxysulphate	8%–36%		*	
	zinc chelates	9%–14%			*

Micronutrient sources

Since micronutrients are required and applied in relatively small quantities, even distribution during application is important. The main classes of micronutrient products are granules intended for mixing with granular fertilizers and liquids or soluble powders for foliar application. The most appropriate form for application will depend on the specific nutrient, as well as the crop species and soil conditions.

Granular micronutrient products are blended with other fertilizer ingredients for broadcast application or use as a starter fertilizer. Compatibility with the other ingredients is important, both chemically and in granule size. Since many micronutrients are toxic to plants if over-applied, segregation of the fertilizer blends must be avoided.

Oxy-sulphates

- combinations of the oxide and sulphate forms of the micronutrient
- sulphates much more soluble and available than the oxides
- oxides much more stable in a blended product
- oxides only slowly available to the crop

These products have been declining in popularity because of the inconsistency in plant availability and crop response.

Sulphates

- quite soluble
- tend to be hygroscopic and can cause problems with caking or clumping when mixed with other fertilizer ingredients

Despite these concerns, their consistent plant availability has made them popular in fertilizer blends.

Liquid and soluble micronutrients

These materials may be mixed with water and sprayed on crop foliage or mixed with liquid fertilizers for use as starters.

Chelates

- complex organic molecules that bind metallic ions held in soluble forms where they would normally react with other minerals to form insoluble compounds
- allows many of these nutrients to be mixed with liquid fertilizers without forming insoluble precipitates
- may increase the availability of the nutrients in soil

- most commonly used chelating agents are EDTA and DTPA
- other organic materials (humic acids, lignosulphonates, glucoheptonates) will form complexes with metallic ions but do not hold them as tightly as a true chelate

Chelates are considerably more expensive than other soluble forms of micronutrients. They should be used with care, since they can complex minerals already in the soil and make the deficiency worse.

Soluble powders

- least expensive form of micronutrients for foliar application and the most consistently reliable
- most require a sprayer with good agitation to keep material in solution
- sticker-spreader needed to get the nutrient through the cuticle and into the leaf.

Materials to enhance fertilizer efficiency

Nitrogen

Most products designed to enhance the efficiency of N uptake delay the release of its soluble forms, ammonium and nitrate. Use of these products is increasing. Hall (2005) reports that sales of such fertilizers amounted to about 120 thousand tonnes of N in 2003, accounting for about 1% of the total North American N fertilizer market.

The products fall into one or more of the following categories:

- **Slow or controlled-release fertilizers**. These are materials that contain N in a form that delays its availability for plant uptake and thus makes it available over a longer period of time, in comparison to the regular ammonium, nitrate or urea fertilizers. The delay in release can be attained by a variety of mechanisms, including polymer or sulphur coatings, occlusions, or incorporation into compounds that are either insoluble or require mineralization to release the N. Examples include ESN® Polymer Coated Urea 44-0-0, DURATION CR®, Multicote®, NUTRI-PAK®, Osmocote® or POLYON® Coated Urea. Some of these are available in a range of grades varying in release profiles. Note that each material is designed for a specific application and specific crop.
- **Urease inhibitors**. A substance that inhibits the hydrolytic action on urea by the urease enzyme. An example is Agrotain®, which contains N-(n-butyl) thiophosphoric triamide (NBPT).
- **Nitrification inhibitors**. A substance that inhibits the biological oxidation of ammonium to nitrate. Examples include N-Serve® (nitrapyrin) and DCD (dicyandiamide). Ammonium thiosulfate also inhibits nitrification to some extent.
- **Stabilized Fertilizers**. A nitrogen stabilizer is a substance added to a fertilizer which extends the time the fertilizer remains in the urea or ammoniacal form. An example is SuperU®, a urea fertilizer containing both NBPT (a urease inhibitor) and DCD (a nitrification inhibitor).

Based on research in Western Canada, Dr. Cynthia Grant (2005) listed seven benefits of enhanced efficiency N fertilizers. She pointed out that these products can help to:

- minimize inorganic soil N thus reducing potential loss
- substitute for capital investment in specialised machinery for placement
- allow reduction of labour
- increase flexibility in timing of application
- avoid the potential for "missing" window of application
- manage the ratio of ammonium to nitrate according to crop preference
- require less specialized knowledge for their use

Controlling the release of soluble nitrogen can have disadvantages if the use of these materials is not carefully planned. Most fertilizer materials are supplied in a soluble form to maximize plant availability. It is only in specific situations—where the amount applied exceeds what plants can take up within a reasonable time frame—that the above materials will enhance efficiency.

Phosphorus

Products designed to enhance efficiency of P uptake prevent the fixation of P by the soil. These may include organic or humic materials and polymer coatings that reduce the rate of diffusion from the granule to the fixation sites in the soil. As an example, a grade of 11-52-0 monoammonium phosphate coated with maleic itaconic copolymer (AVAIL®) is being marketed in North America.

In certain soil conditions, slowing the release of phosphate could potentially reduce fixation reactions that make applied P unavailable. For instance, Garcia et al. (1997) found that urea phosphate or lignin-coated triple superphosphate increased soil P availability in a highly calcareous P-fixing soil, while uncoated superphosphate or diammonium phosphate did not. However, the timing of release is a critical factor for most starter fertilizers. Most field crops require available P release to the seedling within a few weeks from planting.

Some products that inoculate the soil with micro-organisms that make phosphorus more available have been tested in Ontario. Generally, they have not been found to provide an economic benefit. For example, two years of research with *Penicillium bilaii* found the inoculant to be ineffective in increasing seedling growth and yields of corn. (Stevenson, 1994).

Materials for organic production systems

Many of the materials listed above are not approved for use in organic production systems. According to the Canadian General Standards Board, substances used to improve the fertility of soils in organic production systems must be of plant, animal, microbial or mineral origin and may undergo the following processes: physical, enzymatic or microbial. Since most N, P and K fertilizers undergo some degree of chemical processing, they are considered "synthetic." Exceptions include some grades of rock phosphate, muriate of potash, potassium sulfate and sulfate of potash magnesia. For a detailed list of permitted substances, contact the Canadian General Standards Board.

Fertilizer blending

Blended fertilizers have been available for much of this century but the early forms left much to be desired. For many years, fertilizers were shipped to the farm as fine powders in paper bags. These powders tended to bridge in the drill boxes or cake if they got damp.

In the 1950s, mixed granulated fertilizers were introduced in Ontario. These materials incorporated the same raw materials into a multi-nutrient granule. The equipment to produce these mixed granules, however, was cumbersome and expensive and mixed granulated fertilizers were soon supplanted by bulk blends.

Bulk blending is the act of mixing granular fertilizer ingredients to produce the desired ratio. In Ontario, these operations are generally carried out at retail blenders serving a relatively small area.

These operators make custom blends on short notice for immediate spreading on the farmer's field. Custom blends, or Customer Formula Fertilizers, are obtained by mixing granular fertilizer materials according to a formula calculated to suit the fertilization recommendation for a given field and crop.

Custom blends are efficient because they:

- provide the exact amount of nutrients required to grow the crop
- are less likely to absorb moisture and cake in storage
- minimize the cost of fertilization with high analysis, filler-free materials

Even though the cost per tonne may be higher, the cost per hectare is reduced. The ability to blend a wide range of analyses from a small group of ingredients also saves storage costs.

Limitations to blends

Bulk blends, and custom blends in particular, are subject to a few limitations. For instance, the high analysis obtained with today's concentrated materials makes it difficult to meter low plant food application rates.

For some applications, there are advantages to fertilizers that combine several nutrients in the same granule. Examples include starter fertilizers incorporating small amounts of micronutrients and home lawn fertilizers. These homogenized fertilizers spread all nutrients uniformly and are convenient to use. Their main limitation, however, is that their nutrient ratios are fixed and thus it is difficult to match specific soil requirements.

Physical and chemical compatibility of blending materials

Fertilizer materials are generally compatible with each other as long as they remain dry.

There are some exceptions:

- **Do not blend ammonium nitrate with urea.** When these two are brought together, the mix is so hygroscopic that it turns into a soaking mess in minutes. Take precautions to avoid cross contamination while in storage and during handling. Before mixing two blended fertilizers, check the ingredients to ensure you are not bringing ammonium nitrate and urea together.
- **Do not blend single or triple superphosphate with urea.** Superphosphates (0-20-0 or 0-46-0) may react with urea, especially if they are not dry and hard. When this reaction takes place the urea is broken

DO NOT BLEND
- AMMONIUM NITRATE with UREA
- SUPERPHOSPHATE with UREA

down and the mix becomes sticky.

- **Spread blends containing a superphosphate and diammonium phosphate as soon as possible**. Single or triple superphosphates may react with diammonium phosphate in the presence of moisture. The mix becomes sticky and eventually cakes.
- **Spread mixes containing micronutrients as soon as possible**. Some micronutrient ingredients (particularly sulphates) may absorb moisture from the air.

Consistent particle size critical

Consistent particle size is critical in mixing and applying bulk blends. If particle sizes of ingredients differ, the ingredients will segregate when they are dropped into a bin, with the largest particles at the outside of the pile and the finer materials in the centre. This can result in a large variation in the make-up of the fertilizer from one part of the pile to another.

Particle size also influences the spreading pattern of the fertilizer. Tests conducted by the Tennessee Valley Authority showed a range of spreading widths from 10.5 m for material with a 1.7mm diameter, to 19.5 m for materials with a 3mm diameter. If the materials in the blend are different sizes, the application of the different ingredients is not uniform.

The fertilizer blender should use materials with similar sizes. The Canadian Fertilizer Institute published the SGN System of Materials Identification in 1986.

SGN, or size guide number, is the average dimension of the fertilizer particles, measured in millimetres times 100. For example, SGN 280 means that one half the fertilizer sample is retained on a testing sieve of 2.80 mm opening. SGN and the uniformity index, a measure of size uniformity, are the two characteristics used to simplify the selection of size-compatible materials.

Figure 7-1 clearly shows the impact of mixing two materials of different sizes. A fertilizer blend made with the materials in the box on the right (SGN 240 + 170) will show significant segregation in the bin or fertilizer box, resulting in uneven application of the nutrients across the field.

Formula calculations

A custom blend is one formulated to meet the fertilization recommendation exactly. The formula is nothing more than a recipe calculated to use available materials to supply the desired plant foods.

The same calculations work with any combination of ingredients but most fertilizer blenders have a limited range of ingredients. This normally includes a N source (46-0-0, 27-0-0, etc.), a P source (18-46-0, 11-52-0, 0-46-0, etc.) and a K source (0-0-60, 0-0-62, etc.).

The exact analyses of the ingredients may vary, depending on the source, making it important to know what ingredients are avail-

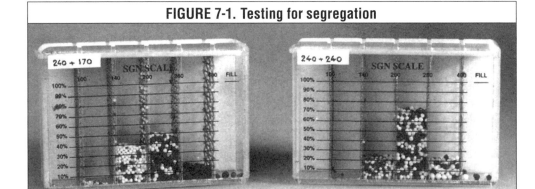

FIGURE 7-1. Testing for segregation

There is no segregation in the box tagged 240 + 240. But the box tagged 240 + 170 show segregation between the white material SGN 170 and the grey material SGN 240.

able. Some blenders also stock specialty ingredients for crops like tobacco.

A pocket calculator is the main tool you need to calculate fertilizer blends. The most important calculation is determining the amount of fertilizer required to provide each nutrient. Do this by using the proportion of each nutrient in the ingredient (the proportion is the percentage divided by 100— the decimal parts in 1 rather than the parts in 100. For example, 46% becomes 0.46). Calculate the amount of ingredient required by dividing the amount of nutrient required by the proportion of nutrient in the ingredient. An example is shown in Figure 7-2. A blank worksheet is in Appendix A.

Calculating fertilizer blends that contain N and P is similar to calculating N-K or P-K blends, except you will want to take advantage of the savings possible with MAP or DAP. This adds a couple of steps to the process, because you will have to calculate the amount of ingredient to meet one requirement and then deduct the contribution of that ingredient from the other requirement. See Figure 7-3 and Appendix B.

Which requirement you calculate first depends on the ratio of N:P required and the choice of ammonium phosphate (MAP or DAP). In general, fill the P requirement first in high N fertilizers (N:P ratio of 1:2 and higher). Fill the N requirement first in fertilizers with N:P ratio of 1:4 and lower. Computer software to facilitate blend calculations is also available. For example, the Fertilizer Chooser at *http://soilfertility.unl.edu/* finds least-cost blends from a list of materials with user-entered price information.

Legalities

The Canadian Food Inspection Agency monitors and controls fertilizers and supplements sold in or imported into Canada. The purpose of the *Fertilizers Act* and Regulations is to ensure that fertilizer and supplement products are safe, efficacious and accurately represented in the market place.

Most fertilizer and supplement products are regulated, however, not all of these products require registration. Micronutrient products, fertilizer-pesticide products and supplements not found in Schedule II of the *Fertilizers Act* and Regulations (such as plant growth regulators, soil conditioners, wetting agents and microbial inoculants etc) require registration before they can be legally imported into and/or sold in Canada.

All products must be safe for plants, animals, humans and the environment. They must be effective and they must be properly labeled. The minimum required information that must appear on a fertilizer or supplement product label is the name, grade (if any), brand (if any), name and address of the manufacturer or registrant, lot number (if any), registration number (where applicable), guaranteed analysis, directions for use (where applicable), product weight and appropriate cautionary statements. Some specialty fertilizer products and supplements will require additional information to appear on the label. In addition, the guarantees displayed on the product label must be met, as all products are subject to monitoring and inspection.

Many fertilizer manufacturers and blend producers are part of the Canadian Fertilizer Quality Assurance Program. Under this voluntary program, participants take their own samples and send them to accredited labs that submit the analyses to the Canadian Food Inspection Agency. The results are tabulated and each manufacturer or blend plant that submits the minimum number of required samples is given a performance rating. The ratings are published annually in the Canadian Fertilizer Quality Assurance Report, which is distributed widely. A customer can ask for a supplier's CFQAP rating.

For more information, contact the Fertilizer Section, Canadian Food Inspection Agency, 2 Constellation Crescent, Ottawa, Ontario K1A 0Y9.

> All fertilizers must be properly labelled, whether they are registered or not. Information that appears on the label must include the name, grade, guaranteed minimum analysis, manufacturer, packager and product weight. Specific types of products need more information. The guarantees on a label must be met and all products are subject to monitoring and inspection.

FIGURE 7-2. Fertilizer blend worksheet:
Example for N-K or P-K blend

1. List materials on hand and grades.

Ingredient	Grade
urea	46-0-0
triple superphosphate	0-46-0
muriate of potash	0-0-60

2. Obtain nutrient requirement (or desired ratio or grade): 130-0-90 kg/ha

3. Calculate ingredient required for each nutrient. Repeat for each nutrient.

$$\frac{\text{nutrient requirement}}{\text{proportion of nutrient}} \quad \frac{130}{0.46} = \text{ingredient amount} \quad 283$$

$$\frac{\text{nutrient requirement}}{\text{proportion of nutrient}} \quad \frac{90}{0.60} = \text{ingredient amount} \quad 150$$

$$\frac{\text{nutrient requirement}}{\text{proportion of nutrient}} \quad \underline{\hspace{1.5cm}} = \text{ingredient amount}$$

4. Add weights of materials and calculate nutrients provided.

Material	Weight	N	P_2O_5	K_2O
urea	283	130	0	0
KCl	150	0	0	90
Total	433	130	0	90

The total weight of the blend at this point is the application rate. The units will be the same as the initial nutrient requirements.

5. Calculate the total amount of fertilizer required.

application rate × size of field = total weight of fertilizer

433 kg/ha × 20 ha = 8,640 kg

6. Adjust material weights to give formula in kilograms per tonne.

Divide the weights of the individual materials by the total weight and multiplying by 1,000.

Material	Weight	N	P_2O_5	K_2O
urea	654	301	0	0
KCl	346	0	0	208
Total	1000 kg	301	0	208
Grade (divide total NPK by 10)		30.1	0	20.8

Blank charts for you to copy and use are in Appendix A.

FIGURE 7-3. Fertilizer blend worksheet:
Example of NPK blend

1. List materials on hand and grades.

Ingredient	Grade
urea	46-0-0
monoammonium phosphate (MAP)	11-52-0
triple superphosphate	0-46-0
muriate of potash (KCl)	0-0-60

2. Obtain nutrient requirement (or desired ratio or grade):   90-90-110 lb/ac

3. Calculate ingredient (MAP) required for either N (for high P ratios) or P (for high N ratios).

$$\frac{\text{nutrient requirement}}{\text{proportion of nutrient}} \quad \frac{90}{0.52} = \text{amount of MAP (lb/ac)} \quad 173$$

4. Calculate contribution of ingredient to other nutrient.

ingredient required × proportion of nutrient = contribution $173 \times 0.11 = 19$

5. Deduct contribution from requirement to determine the residual nutrient requirement. (Note: if contribution is greater than requirement, you calculated the wrong nutrient first. Return to step 3.)

Requirement – contribution = residual requirement $90 - 19 = 71$

6. Determine amount of ingredient to provide residual requirement (N source or P source).

$$\frac{\text{residual requirement}}{\text{proportion of nutrient}} \quad \frac{71}{0.46} = \text{ingredient amount} \quad 154$$

7. Determine amount of muriate of potash to meet K requirement.

$$\frac{\text{K nutrient requirement}}{\text{proportion of nutrient}} \quad \frac{110}{0.60} = \text{ingredient amount} \quad 183$$

8. Calculate any ingredients needed for any other micronutrients in the same way.

9. Add weights of materials and calculate nutrients provided.

Material	Weight	N	P_2O_5	K_2O
MAP	173	19	90	0
urea	154	71	0	0
potash	183	0	0	110
Total	510	90	90	110

The total weight of the blend at this point is the application rate. The units will be the same as the initial nutrient requirements.

10. Calculate the total amount of fertilizer required.

application rate × size of field   = total weight of fertilizer

510 lb/ac × 40 ac   = 20,400 lb (9,251 kg)

11. Adjust material weights to give formula in kilograms per tonne.

Divide the weights of the individual materials by the total weight and multiply by 1,000

Material	Weight	N	P_2O_5	K_2O
MAP	339	37	176	0
urea	302	139	0	0
potash	359	0	0	215
Total	1000 kg	176	176	215
Grade (divide total NPK by 10)		17.6	17.6	21.5

Now you can calculate the price of the fertilizer.

A blank chart for you to copy and use is in Appendix B.

Fertilizer application

The aim of any fertilizer program is to get the nutrient into the crop plants where it will be used to improve yield and quality of the crop. Fertilizer not placed where the roots can reach it when the crop needs it won't do the job.

Fertilizer placement is a compromise between applying the fertilizer in optimum concentrations precisely where and when the plant needs it and the practical considerations of the time and equipment available for applying the fertilizer. If you are considering a more costly fertilizer application system, there should be advantages in increased crop yield or reduced fertilizer cost that compensate.

The best placement for a particular nutrient (or combination) depends on how mobile the nutrient is in the soil, the concentration required by crop plants, how toxic the nutrient is at high concentrations, the soil texture and moisture status and the crop being fertilized.

Crop safety

Plant tissue is sensitive to injury from high salt concentrations (osmotic pressure) or free ammonia, both of which can be produced by too much fertilizer in too small a volume of soil.

The symptoms of fertilizer burn are reduced root growth and blackened or discoloured areas on the roots, as if they were burned. Injury will be most severe with seedlings because young tissues are more sensitive; larger proportions of the plant tissue are affected by any injury and there is less reserve for re-growth following injury. Also, there is less opportunity for the plant to grow around the area of high concentration.

The key factor in fertilizer injury is concentration rather than the total amount applied. Banded fertilizers are much more likely to cause injury than broadcast fertilizers.

If fertilizer is applied with a corn planter in a 2.5 cm band in rows 0.75 m apart, the concentration within the band is 30 times what it would have been if the fertilizer had been broadcast over the whole area. Also, the distribution along the row is not always even so the fertilizer rates can be much higher at some points.

The concentration can be diluted as the fertilizer diffuses out of the band but the amount of dilution depends on the texture and moisture content of the soil. Moist soils cause greater dilution. We commonly see fertilizer burn in dry springs and on coarse textured, well-drained soils. Since coarse textured soils with low organic matter also have less surface area to react with and adsorb fertilizer, the concentration in the soil solution will remain higher than in clay soils.

The risk of injury also increases with the proximity of the seed or transplant to the fertilizer band. With the fertilizer too close, there is little opportunity for dilution by the soil water. There is also little or no chance for the roots to grow beyond the zone of concentration. Nitrogen and potassium in particular can be harmful to seedlings and to seed germination. Cold soils, which slow root growth, can magnify these effects.

When a fertilizer is banded with the seed, the safe rate of nutrients is much less than that of fertilizer banded 5 cm to the side and 5 cm below the seed. Even at recommended rates, seed-applied fertilizer will slow germination and emergence slightly, as the salt effect slows the absorption of water. Applying fertilizer with seed is not appropriate for all crops.

Salt injury occurs when the concentration of ions in the soil solution is greater than the concentration within the plant. When this happens, water is pulled across the cell membranes and out of the root. The root tissues are injured by desiccation, as if they had been singed by heated air.

Any soluble compound in high enough concentration will cause salt injury. The greater the solubility of a fertilizer, the greater the potential to cause salt injury. The acids and hydroxides are somewhat less likely to cause injury, but these ingredients as used in fertilizer manufacture are combined into other soluble compounds before application.

Ammonia injury occurs when there is free ammonia in the soil solution. Normally, this compound would be dissolved as the ammonium ion but with high concentrations and particularly with alkaline conditions, some of the ammonium will be released as ammonia. This could occur with applications of anhydrous ammonia or high rates of liquid manure or if urea or diammonium phosphate (DAP, 18-46-0) is banded near the row. The symptoms of ammonia injury are similar to salt injury and they often happen together.

Not every crop is equally sensitive to fertilizer injury. In general, grasses (monocots) are much less susceptible than broadleaf crops (dicots). Within the grasses, cereals are more tolerant of high-banded fertilizer rates than corn. Among the broadleaf crops, soybeans and edible beans are more susceptible than forage legumes or canola, but they are all much more sensitive than corn.

In general, seeded vegetables are quite sensitive to fertilizer injury.

Maximum safe rates of fertilizer are shown in Table 7-4.

Application methods

Broadcast

Broadcast fertilizer application is by far the fastest and least expensive method. The fertilizer is spread evenly over the soil surface, then incorporated into the soil for most field crops. This gives the greatest possible dilution, minimizing the risk of fertilizer burn. It may, however, interfere with the uptake of nutrients such as P, where the concentration of the nutrient is critical for uptake by a small root system. Broadcast application also maximizes the contact between the fertilizer and the soil, making

TABLE 7-4. Maximum safe rates of nutrients

Excess fertilizer can harm seedlings owing to effects of ammonia and salt. These effects are related to fertilizer nitrogen (N) and potassium (K) content. Toxicity varies widely depending on soil texture, moisture conditions, crop, fertilizer source and placement. This table provides guidelines that will most likely limit injury to less than 10% of the cases where they are used. Injurious effects include reduced or delayed germination or retarded growth. Weather, stress and other conditions that affect growth may increase the chances of injury.

Spring oats and barley (fertilizer with seed)	N (kg/ha)	N+K_2O (kg/ha)
Sands, sandy loam Urea (46-0-0):	10	30
Diammonium phosphate (18-46-0):	20	35
Other fertilizers:	35	55
Loams, silt, clay loams Urea (46-0-0):	10	30
Diammonium phosphate (18-46-0):	30	55
Other fertilizers:	45	70
Winter wheat, triticale or barley (fertilizer with seed)		
All soils Urea (46-0-0):	0 (fall)	0 (fall)
Diammonium phosphate (18-46-0):	0 (fall)	0 (fall)
Other fertilizers:	15	30
Corn (fertilizer banded with the seed)		
All soils Urea (46-0-0):	0	0
Diammonium phosphate (18-46-0):	0	0
Other fertilizers — 100 cm rows:		7
— 75 cm rows:		10
— 50 cm rows:		14

Sweet corn can be more sensitive to fertilizer placed with the seed. Do not apply fertilizer with the seed of super sweet hybrid sweet corn.

Corn (fertilizer banded 5 cm to the side and 5 cm below the seed)		
All soils Urea (46-0-0):	39	60
Other fertilizers:	55	90

If higher rates are banded, band should be at least 15 cm from seed. At row widths other than 100 cm, the rate may be adjusted to provide the same maximum concentration in the row (for example, in 50 cm row the safe rate = 100/50 × 55 = 110 N).

Corn (fertilizer broadcast)		
Sands, sandy loam Urea (46-0-0):	200	250

Canola (fertilizer with the seed)

Up to 20 kg/ha phosphate fertilizer may be drilled with the seed as superphosphate or monoammonium phosphate. N (except as monoammonium phosphate) and K should not be applied with the seed.

Flax (no fertilizer with the seed)

Rates recommended are normally safe when broadcast.

Peas, beans and soybeans (no fertilizer with the seed)		
All soils, fertilizer banded 5 cm to the side and 5 cm below the seed:	30	90

Fertilizers containing more than half as much N as P_2O_5 (e.g.16-16-16) often contain urea. Fertilizers containing urea are not suitable for banding at seeding in many cases.

immobilization reactions quicker than with banded fertilizer.

Fertilizer burn can still occur on very sandy soils with low organic matter. High rates of urea and potash spread on these soils can cause seedling injury under dry conditions, especially if combined with banded or seed applied fertilizer.

Whether a granular fertilizer is spread by a pull-type or self-propelled spreader, there are two types of delivery systems: spinners and pneumatic (air-stream). Either will do a good job if properly operated and maintained.

Spinner spreaders

Spinner spreaders use one or two rapidly spinning disks with paddles to throw the fertilizer granules out from the spreader. A consistent granule size is important as smaller particles do not travel as far and spread out in an uneven pattern. Windy conditions can also distort the spread pattern, as does a build-up of fertilizer on the distributor or the paddles. Frequent cleaning is necessary but the areas needing cleaning are easily accessible.

Spinner type spreaders are relatively simple mechanically and relatively inexpensive. The power requirements are modest so that any tractor capable of pulling the spreader has lots of power for the spinners. These are the most popular types of spreaders for rental units because of their low cost, generally trouble-free operation and ease of repair in the field.

Pneumatic spreaders

Pneumatic spreaders use a high velocity air stream to carry the granules through a boom to distributors spaced about 1.7 m apart. These spreaders have a higher power requirement because the fan that creates the air stream runs at high speeds. These spreaders are also more complicated because of the moving parts in the fan and the metering system that distributes the fertilizer evenly to each of the boom sections.

However, the metering can be more precise than the spinner type spreaders and the mixing action of the air stream allows the addition of small quantities of granular herbicides or micronutrients in the field.

Because the distributors are relatively close together, these spreaders are not affected by wind as much as the spinner type. The self-propelled units often have a wider spread pattern than spinner spreaders, allowing greater through-put from the same power unit. Plugging is not a frequent problem because of the high velocity of the air stream but the spreader does need to be monitored in humid conditions or when using damp materials.

The pneumatic spreader is relatively expensive and complicated and thus not generally suitable for an individual but it has taken over the largest part of the market for custom application.

Tru-Spread system

The Tru-Spread system uses a screw conveyor to deliver granular fertilizer across the width of a boom and drop it through openings on 17.5 cm spacing. These machines are also quite accurate and unaffected by wind.

Spraying equipment

Most broadcast fertilizer is in granular form but a sizeable quantity of liquid N solution is sprayed onto the soil, which is another form of broadcasting. This allows for the use of spraying equipment to apply fertilizer as well as herbicides. Nitrogen solutions can also be used as the carrier for herbicides, getting two jobs done with one application.

The spread with this equipment is usually even, although there is the chance of drift in windy conditions. Some field sprayers do not perform well with liquid fertilizers because they are not designed to handle large volumes or are not protected against corrosive fertilizer materials.

Variable rate fertilizer

The simplest variable rate applicators are conventional spreaders of any type fitted with a global positioning system (GPS) receiver and a link to the controller. This allows the unit to variably apply one material or blend. This system may require multiple passes over the field to meet the fertilizer requirements. However, the equipment is less expensive than the multi-bin variable rate unit. Having to do a number of passes slows application and may lead to increased soil compaction.

Multi-material variable rate applicator units have several bins and the discharge from each can be controlled individually. This allows the application rate of up to nine materials to be varied in a single pass over the field. The bins could include granular chemicals as well as fertilizer material.

Variable rate application of lime can be done using a lime applicator equipped with a GPS receiver and a variable rate controller or application zones within the field can be mapped and flagged and specific rates applied to each with a conventional lime spreader.

Banding

Banding is the application of fertilizer in a band beside and below the seed in the case of row crops or with the seed of cereals. It requires fertilizer boxes and metering systems on the planter or drill and an extra opener on planters to place the fertilizer into the soil. This can require extra power to pull the planter and the time to fill the fertilizer boxes slows the planting.

The advantage is the fertilizer is located at a high concentration where the roots of the seedlings will intercept it. This is particularly important for P, which is required early in the growth of many crops.

You must take care with banded fertilizer, since the high concentration also increases the risk of fertilizer burn. The rates of N and K must be limited, particularly where urea or diammonium phosphate is the N source. Band pH may also influence availability of other nutrients in the soil. See *Soil pH and starter fertilizer bands* in Chapter 4, page 85.

Planting equipment must also be set properly to place the fertilizer the right distance from the seed. If the fertilizer openers shift too close to the seed row, the risk of burn increases. If the openers shift away from the row, the seedlings may not be able to intercept the fertilizer early enough.

Metering equipment for banded fertilizer is fairly simple with a delivery auger in the bottom of the fertilizer boxes dropping the fertilizer through an adjustable gate. The rate can be varied with the speed of the auger, the size of the gate opening or the pitch of the auger flighting. The alignment of the delivery auger must be checked carefully. If the auger is shifted to one side, it can be delivering 50% more fertilizer to one side of the box than to the other.

Pop-up

Pop-up is the term for fertilizer applied with the seed of row crops, even though it actually delays germination slightly. This method has the advantage of producing relatively large yield responses in corn (up to 8 bu/ac in one study) with low rates of fertilizer, even at high soil tests where response from banded or broadcast fertilizer would not be expected. This method also gives a consistent increase in seedling vigour.

Because of the close proximity of the fertilizer to the seed, this method has a higher risk of injury than any other. You must adhere to the maximum safe rates and the equipment must be calibrated to apply the fertilizer evenly. Pulses in fertilizer application can easily result in wavy crop growth as some areas receive toxic concentrations of fertilizer while others don't get enough.

Liquid fertilizers are most commonly used for seed application because they can be metered precisely and handled easily. To avoid pulses, the fertilizer should be delivered to the seed openers under pressure and metered through an orifice. Care must be taken that the fertilizer delivery tube is centred in the seed opener. Liquid fertilizer dribbling onto the opener disks will result in mud build-up and plugging.

Some farmers are experimenting with converting their insecticide boxes to apply granular fertilizer to get the advantages of seed applied fertilizer without the high cost of liquids. This involves replacing the plastic roller in the insecticide box with a steel roller and running the delivery tube into the seed opener. Initial results have been encouraging but there are concerns about evenness and how well the insecticide boxes will stand up to handling fertilizer, which is much denser than insecticides.

Side-dressing

Side-dressing is the application of fertilizer, primarily N, between the rows of growing crops. This applies the N closer to the time when the crop needs it, which can increase the efficiency of N use. It also minimizes the risk of nitrate leaching on sandy soils or of denitrification on poorly drained soils.

In corn, the most common forms of side-dressed fertilizer are anhydrous ammonia and UAN solution.

Anhydrous is attractive because of its low cost per unit of N and on the clay soils of southwestern Ontario it has also provided a yield advantage over other forms of N. It must be injected deep enough into the soil so that the injection slot seals over or the losses to the atmosphere will be too high. The power requirements and application costs are higher for anhydrous and it must be handled carefully to be safe.

UAN solutions do not need to be injected deep into the soil, making the power requirements for application modest. In high residue situations, the solution must be placed below the surface residue layer to prevent volatilization losses of ammonia. The cost for UAN solution is relatively high but safety and ease of handling are making this a popular choice.

In high residue situations, injector knives can catch on and drag residue. To prevent this, no-till applicators are equipped with coulters to cut the residue and improve penetration into firm ground. Another approach is the spoke-wheel injector, which pokes the N solution into the soil with minimal disturbance of the residue. These work quite well but the initial cost is higher than for other side-dress equipment.

Granular fertilizers are used for side-dressing vegetable crops and tobacco but are not commonly used in corn. These fertilizers are as available as the liquid or gas forms.

Deep banding

Some farmers have experimented with banding P and K fertilizers 15–20 cm below the row, especially in no-till and ridge-till situations where the soil is firm. This may increase the availability of fertilizers under dry conditions and protect them from immobilization reactions but limited Ontario trials have not shown a yield response to deep banding. It may be useful in some situations.

Transplant starters

Transplanted stock will benefit from readily available nutrients to encourage new root growth and overcome transplanting shock. Otherwise, young plants will need time for roots to grow and forage for soil nutrients. Transplants receive the starter fertilizer via the transplant water or are fed a starter before going to the field.

Starter solutions are water soluble or liquid fertilizers that provide a source of fertilizer surrounding the root ball. These solutions always include P, which is important for root development and may also include N and K. Examples of starters are 10-52-10, 6-24-6 and 10-34-0.

Starter solutions are especially important when the soil is cold. Cold soils inhibit root growth and therefore the uptake of soil nutrients.

Foliar

Foliar fertilizer can be an excellent supplement to soil-applied nutrients. It can correct deficiencies quickly and is not susceptible to tie-up in the soil. There is a chance the nutrient will be washed off or the carrier will dry up before the nutrient is absorbed. The use of a spreader-sticker may increase absorption of the fertilizer through the cuticle.

Limited quantities can be applied to the leaf before the tissue is damaged. Therefore, deficiencies of micronutrients, where plants only require a few grams per hectare, are corrected more easily than those of macronutrients.

Even though urea is the nutrient most rapidly absorbed by leaves, it often takes many applications to get enough N into the plant to make a difference. For this reason, foliar application of macronutrients tends to be economical more often in high-value horticultural crops than in common field crops.

For micronutrients, on the other hand, foliar spray is often the most economical method for all crops. It is the most effective way to correct manganese deficiencies. Be sure to check pesticide labels before mixing foliar nutrients with any pesticide spray. In particular, manganese and glyphosate are known to antagonize each other's effectiveness.

Foliar application of urea has been successful in many crops. Urea-N can be applied to leaves at much higher concentrations than P or K. The grade chosen should be for feed or foliar uses, since it is lower in biuret, a by-product that can harm plant tissue. There is little research that supports maximum safe rates but results from some experiments suggest that a single foliar urea application should not exceed 20 lb/A of N and the concentration in the spray should be less than 2%.

Fertigation

Fertigation is a specialized form of broadcast fertilization in which the fertilizer is injected into the irrigation water. This allows a farmer to "spoon-feed" the crop, providing nutrients in small doses as the crop needs them. The cost for the metering and injection equipment is small relative to the cost of the irrigation system and the equipment is fairly simple and reliable.

The fertilizers may be fairly expensive, however, since they must be in liquid form to be metered into the irrigation water. Another drawback is that the nutrients are distributed to the same areas as the water and the pattern may not be even. If fertigation is used with drip irrigation, care must be taken to ensure the emitters don't plug up.

Combining methods

The choice of starter fertilizer will depend on the crop to be grown, the mineral fertilizer requirements and the equipment available. It is often as efficient to apply part of the fertilizer as a starter and broadcast the rest as it is to apply all the fertilizer through the planter or drill. The advantages to splitting the fertilizer application are savings in time and labour and less risk of fertilizer injury to the seedling.

Deduct applications of starter fertilizer and side-dressed fertilizer from the total mineral requirement. Any balance remaining should be broadcast. If only tiny numbers remain, you may want to consider adjusting the rates of one of the other nutrient sources, ignoring the small residuals or planning a fertilizer application that will meet multi-year requirements (for P and K only).

Fertilizer worksheet

Once you have established the crop requirements, you need to determine how the required nutrients are to be supplied. Economics and environmental concerns dictate that we make the best possible use of all sources of nutrients. This includes organic forms of nutrients, either already on the farm or imported, as well as mineral fertilizers.

Maximum safe rates of nutrients

Maximum safe rates of any nutrient source should be observed to avoid injury to the crop. The rates listed in Table 7-4 may cause symptoms of injury or retardation of growth in up to 10% of all cases. Use lower rates where possible. Since fertilizer injury can occur when the concentration of fertilizer is too high, uneven application can cause intermittent problems even though the average rate is low enough to be safe.

Dilution has a large influence on what rates are safe. Injury is most common when the weather is dry and in coarse textured soils with low organic matter.

Narrower rows will increase the safe rate per hectare, because the same amount of fertilizer is spread over a greater length of row.

Proper equipment maintenance is important to prevent fertilizer injury. If the fertilizer opener moves closer to the seed, fertilizer burn will occur at rates that would have been safe otherwise.

Fertilizer source and placement

Use on-farm nutrient sources first as they will be applied to farm fields anyway. Base application rates on meeting crop N or P requirements.

Many farmers find it beneficial to split nutrient requirements between organic and mineral sources, providing some insurance against variability in manure applications while taking advantage of an economical source of nutrients. Off-farm organic nutrient sources such as sewage biosolids can be considered.

Commercial fertilizers are used to supply the crop requirements not available from other nutrient sources. Apply commercial fertilizers as close as possible to when the crop requires the nutrients and as close to the plant as possible.

Fertilizer recommendations and application rate calculation

Figure 7-4 is an example of a worksheet used to calculate the rate of fertilizer application. See Appendix C for a blank version to copy.

Enter the N, P_2O_5 and K_2O requirements on the top line. Deduct the available nutrients from legumes, manure or other organic sources to determine the amount of mineral fertilizer needed to meet the total requirements.

Either metric or imperial units can be used in this worksheet.

FIGURE 7-4. Fertilizer application calculations worksheet			
Crop to be grown	corn		
Previous crop	barley with red clover		
Manure applied (type, amount)	solid dairy manure (10 tons/ac), spring incorporated		
Other organic nutrient sources	none		
Starter fertilizer (rate, analysis)	(140 lb/ac) 8-32-16		
Supplemental N (rate, analysis)	none		
	N	P_2O_5	K_2O
Requirements (lb/ac)[1]	140	45	72
less legumes	40	0	0
less manure	30	30	140
less sewage biosolids	0	0	0
Total mineral fertilizer requirements	70	15	0
less starter fertilizer	11	44	22
less side-dressed fertilizer	0	0	0
Total broadcast fertilizer requirements	59	0	0

In this example, the total broadcast fertilizer required is 59 lb N/ac, or 128 lb/ac of urea. The starter fertilizer application could also have been reduced.

If a more complex blend is required, it could be calculated using *Fertilizer blend worksheet*, page 166.

[1] Requirements as total crop need. Check whether recommendations are already adjusted for legumes and manure credits.

Other resources

California Plant Health Association. 2002. *Western Fertilizer Handbook*, 9th ed. Upper Saddle River, N.J.: Prentice Hall.

California Fertilizer Association. 1998. *Western Fertilizer Handbook, 2nd Horticulture Edition*. Upper Saddle River, N.J.: Prentice Hall.

Canadian General Standards Board. Hull, Canada K1A 1G6. *www.pwgsc.gc.ca/cgsb/032_310/standard-e.html*.

Follet, R. H., Murphy, L. S., and Donohue, R. L. 1981. *Fertilizers and Soil Amendments*. Englewood Cliffs, N. J.: Prentice-Hall.

Follet et al. *Farm Chemicals Handbook*. Willoughby, Ohio. Meister Publishing Company.

Frye, W. 2005. Nitrification Inhibition For Nitrogen Efficiency And Environment Protection. IFA International Workshop on Enhanced-Efficiency Fertilizers, Frankfurt, Germany, 28-30 June 2005.

Garcia, M.C., J.A. Diez, A. Vallejo, L. Garcia, M.C. Cartagena. 1997. Effect of applying soluble and coated phosphate fertilizers on phosphate availability in calcareous soils and on P absorption by a rye-grass crop. J. Agric. Food Chem. 45 (5) 1931-1936.

Grant, Cynthia, 2005. Policy aspects related to the use of enhanced efficiency fertilizers: Viewpoint of the scientific community. IFA International Workshop on Enhanced-Efficiency Fertilizers, Frankfurt, Germany, 28-30 June 2005.

Hall, William. 2005. Benefits of enhanced-efficiency fertilizers for the environment. IFA International Workshop on Enhanced-Efficiency Fertilizers, Frankfurt, Germany, 28-30 June 2005.

Havlin, J. L, J. D. Beaton, S. L. Tisdale and W. L. Nelson, 2005. *Soil Fertility and Fertilizers: An Introduction to Nutrient Management*. 7th ed. Pearson Education Inc., Upper Saddle River, New Jersey 07458.

Hoeft, Robert G., Emerson D. Nafziger, Richard R. Johnson, and Samuel R. Aldrich. 2000. *Modern Corn and Soybean Production, First Edition*. MCSP Publications, P.O. Box 248, Savoy, IL 61874-0248. *www.mcsp-pubs.com*.

Ontario Ministry of Agriculture, Food and Rural Affairs.

Agronomy Guide for Field Crops, Publication 811.

Flue-Cured Tobacco Production Recommendations, Publication 298.

Fruit Production Recommendations, Publication 360.

Ginseng Production Recommendations, Publication 610.

Nursery & Landscape Production and IPM Recommendations, Publication 383.

Turfgrass Management Recommendations, Publication 384.

Vegetable Production Recommendations, Publication 363.

Stevenson, C.K. 1994. Peniccillium bilaii phosphorus research with corn. Ridgetown College of Agricultural Technology report. 38 pp. Ridgetown, Ontario.

UNIDO and IFDC. 1998. *Fertilizer Manual (3rd edition).* 615 pages. ISBN 0-7923-5032-4. Kluwer Academic Publishers. *www.unido.org/en/doc/3551.*

APPENDICES

APPENDIX A. Fertilizer blend worksheet: Sample for N-K or P-K blend

1. List materials on hand and grades.

Ingredient   **Grade**

2. Obtain nutrient requirement (or desired ratio or grade).

3. Calculate ingredient required for each nutrient. Repeat for each nutrient.

$$\frac{\text{nutrient requirement}}{\text{proportion of nutrient}} \quad \underline{\hspace{2cm}} = \text{ingredient amount}$$

$$\frac{\text{nutrient requirement}}{\text{proportion of nutrient}} \quad \underline{\hspace{2cm}} = \text{ingredient amount}$$

$$\frac{\text{nutrient requirement}}{\text{proportion of nutrient}} \quad \underline{\hspace{2cm}} = \text{ingredient amount}$$

4. Add weights of materials and calculate nutrients provided.

Material   **Weight**   **N**   **P_2O_5**   **K_2O**

The total weight of the blend at this point is the application rate. The units will be the same as the initial nutrient requirements.

5. Calculate the total amount of fertilizer required.

application rate × size of field   = total weight of fertilizer

6. Adjust material weights to give formula in kilograms per tonne.

Divide the weights of the individual materials by the total weight and multiplying by 1,000.

Material   **Weight**   **N**   **P_2O_5**   **K_2O**

Total

Grade (divide total NPK by 10)

APPENDIX B. Fertilizer blend worksheet: Sample of NPK blend

1. List materials on hand and grades.

Ingredient   **Grade**

2. Obtain nutrient requirement (or desired ratio or grade).

3. Calculate ingredient (DAP or MAP) required for either N (for high P ratios)
   or P (for high N ratios).

$$\frac{\text{nutrient requirement}}{\text{proportion of nutrient}} \quad\underline{\hspace{4cm}}\quad = \text{ingredient amount}$$

4. Calculate contribution of ingredient to other nutrient.

   ingredient required × proportion of nutrient = contribution

5. Deduct contribution from requirement to determine the residual nutrient requirement.
   (Note: if contribution is greater than requirement, you calculated the wrong nutrient first.
   Return to step 3.)

   Requirement − contribution = residual requirement

6. Determine amount of ingredient to provide residual requirement (N source or P source).

$$\frac{\text{residual requirement}}{\text{proportion of nutrient}} \quad\underline{\hspace{4cm}}\quad = \text{ingredient amount}$$

7. Determine amount of potash to meet K requirement.

$$\frac{\text{K nutrient requirement}}{\text{proportion of nutrient}} \quad\underline{\hspace{4cm}}\quad = \text{ingredient amount}$$

8. Calculate any ingredients needed for any other micronutrients in the same way.

APPENDIX B. Fertilizer blend worksheet: Sample of NPK blend

9. Add weights of materials and calculate nutrients provided.

Material	Weight	N	P_2O_5	K_2O
MAP				
urea				
potash				
Total				

The total weight of the blend at this point is the application rate. The units will be the same as the initial nutrient requirements.

10. Calculate the total amount of fertilizer required.

application rate × size of field   = total weight of fertilizer

11. Adjust material weights to give formula in kilograms per tonne.

Divide the weights of the individual materials by the total weight and multiply by 1,000.

Material	Weight	N	P_2O_5	K_2O
MAP				
urea				
potash				
Total				
Grade (divide total NPK by 10)				
Now you can calculate the price of the fertilizer.				

APPENDIX C. Fertilizer application calculations worksheet			
Crop to be grown			
Previous crop			
Manure applied (type, amount)			
Other organic nutrient sources			
Starter fertilizer (rate, analysis)			
Supplemental N (rate, analysis)			
	N	P₂O₅	K₂O
Requirements (lb/ac)[1]			
less legumes			
less manure			
less sewage biosolids			0
Total mineral fertilizer requirements			
less starter fertilizer			
less side-dressed fertilizer			
Total broadcast fertilizer requirements			
[1] Requirements as total crop need. Check whether recommendations are already adjusted for legumes and manure credits.			

APPENDIX D. Conversions and equivalents

Metric to imperial
litres per hectare × 0.09 = gallons per acre
litres per hectare × 0.36 = quarts per acre
litres per hectare × 0.71 = pints per acre
millilitres per hectare × 0.015 = fluid ounces per acre
grams per hectare × 0.015 = ounces per acre
kilograms per hectare × 0.89 = pounds per acre
tonnes per hectare × 0.45 = tons per acre

Imperial to metric
gallons per acre × 11.23 = litres per hectare (L/ha)
quarts per acre × 2.8 = litres per hectare (L/ha)
pints per acre × 1.4 = litres per hectare (L/ha)
fluid ounces per acre × 70 = millilitres per hectare (mL/ha)
tons per acre × 2.24 = tonnes per hectare (t/ha)
pounds per acre × 1.12 = kilograms per hectare (kg/ha)
ounces per acre × 70 = grams per hectare (g/ha)

Liquid equivalents

litres/hectare		gallons/acre
50	=	5
100	=	10
150	=	15
200	=	20
250	=	25
300	=	30

Dry weight equivalents

kilograms/hectare		pounds/acre
1.1	=	1
1.5	=	1¼
2.0	=	1¾
2.5	=	2¼
3.25	=	3
4.0	=	3½
5.0	=	4½
6.0	=	5¼
7.5	=	6¾
9.0	=	8
11.0	=	10
13.0	=	11½
15.0	=	13½

Dry weight equivalents

grams/hectare		ounces/acre
100	=	1½
200	=	3
300	=	4½
500	=	7
700	=	10

Imperial to metric (approximate)

Length
inch = 2.54 cm
foot = 0.30 m
yard = 0.91 m
mile = 1.61 km

Area
square foot = 0.09 m^2
square yard = 0.84m^2
acre = 0.40 ha

Volume (dry)
cubic yard = 0.76 m^3
bushel = 36.37 L

Volume (liquid)
fluid ounce (Imp.) = 28.41mL
pint (Imp.) = 0.57 L
gallon (Imp.) = 4.54 L
gallon (U.S.) = 3.79 L

Pressure
pound per square inch = 6.90 kPa

Weight
ounce = 28.35 g
pound = 453.6 g
ton = 0.91 tonne

Temperature
$°C = (°F - 32) \times 5/9$
$°F = (°C \times 9/5) + 32$

Metric to imperial (approximate)

Length
millimetre (mm) = 0.04 inch
centimetre (cm) = 0.40 inch
metre (m) = 39.40 inches
metre (m) = 3.28 feet
metre (m) = 1.09 yards
kilometre (km) = 0.62 mile

Area
square centimetre (cm^2) = 0.61 cubic inch
square metre (m^2) = 10.77 square feet
square metre (m^2) = 1.20 square yards
square kilometre (km^2) = 0.39 square mile
hectare (ha) = 107,636 square feet
hectare (ha) = 2.5 acres

Volume (liquid)
millilitre (mL) = 0.035 fluid ounce
litre (L) = 1.76 pints
litre (L) = 0.88 quart
litre (L) = 0.22 gallon (Imp.)
litre (L) = 0.26 gallon (U.S.)

Volume (dry)
cubic centimetre (cm^3) = 0.061 cubic inch
cubic metre (m^3) = 1.031 cubic yards
cubic metre (m^3) = 35.31 cubic feet
1000 cubic metre (m^3) = 0.81 acre-foot
hectolitre (hL) = 2.8 bushels

Weight
gram (g) = 0.035 ounce
kilogram (kg) = 2.21 pounds
tonne (t) = 1.10 short tons
tonne (t) = 2,205 pounds

Speed
metre per second = 3.28 feet per second
metre per second = 2.24 miles per hour
kilometre per hour = 0.62 mile per hour

Pressure
kilopascal (kPa) = 0.15 pounds/square inch

GLOSSARY

Acid: A solution with an excess of hydrogen ions (H^+). This solution will have a pH reading below 7.

Acre furrow-slice: The amount of topsoil contained in an area of one acre to a depth of 6 inches. The weight of this volume of soil is about 2,000,000 pounds.

Adsorb: To stick to the surface of something, as opposed to being absorbed into something. Nutrient ions are generally adsorbed on the surface of clay particles.

Aerobic: In the presence of oxygen (air).

Alkaline: A solution with an excess of hydroxyl ions (OH^-). This solution will have a pH reading above 7.

Allelopathic: The negative effect of some crop residues on the growth or vigour of the following crop.

Anaerobic: In the absence of oxygen. In soils, generally occurs when the soil is waterlogged.

Anion (AN-eye-on): A negatively charged ion, produced by the dissociation of an acid or a salt when dissolved in water (eg. $KCl \rightarrow K^+$, a cation, $+ Cl^-$, an anion). Common anions in the soil of importance for crop production include nitrate (NO_3^-), phosphate (PO_4^{3-}), sulphate (SO_4^{2-}), and chloride (Cl^-).

Apparent specific gravity: See bulk density.

Atomic absorption spectrometry: An analytical technique where an extract is broken down to individual elements in a flame, and then a light beam passing through the flame measures the concentration of each element by determining the absorption of specific wavelengths.

Auto analyzer: A machine that automates the repetitive tasks of chemical analysis. In most soil and plant tissue analysis, the concentration of an element is determined from the intensity of a colour formed when mixed with specific compounds.

Available phosphate: In a fertilizer, the sum of the water soluble and the citrate soluble phosphate, expressed as phosphorus pentoxide. (P_2O_5).

Biosolids: Organic materials from industrial or municipal sources that are suitable for application to agricultural land. This includes a wide range of materials, from sewage sludge to paper waste.

Buffer pH: A measure of how much lime is required to neutralize the acidity in a particular soil.

Bulk density: Sometimes referred to as apparent specific gravity. A measure of the weight of a material in a given volume. In soil, bulk density is an indication of how compact the soil is. In fertilizer application, bulk density is important for setting application rates, since spreaders meter the fertilizer by volume rather than weight.

Calcareous: A soil containing calcium carbonate in the mineral form. These soils have a high pH and are very well buffered against changes in soil pH.

Calibration: The process of determining the most economic fertilizer application rates for a particular soil test value with a specific soil extraction.

Cation (CAT-eye-on): A positively charged ion, produced by the dissociation of an acid or a salt when dissolved in water (eg. $KCl \rightarrow K^+$, a cation, $+ Cl^-$, an anion). Cations are commonly held in the soil by electrostatic attraction to negative charges on soil particles and organic matter. Common cations in the soil of importance for crop production are calcium (Ca^{2+}), magnesium (Mg^{2+}), potassium (K^+), hydrogen (H^+) iron ($Fe^{2+ \text{ or } 3+}$) and ammonium (NH_4^+).

Cation exchange: The continuous movement of positively charged ions (cations) between the soil solution and the surfaces of clay minerals and organic matter. This process results in an equilibrium between ions in solution and adsorbed ions. Adding to or taking ions away from the solution upsets this equilibrium, causing an exchange of ions until a new equilibrium is established.

Chelate (KEY-late): A complex organic molecule that can surround a metal ion and bind to it in several places, keeping the ion in solution and protecting it from reactions that could precipitate it as an insoluble compound. Chelates are used as carriers for some micronutrient fertilizers and as extractants for determining the amount of available micronutrient in the soil.

Chelating: The process of combining a metal ion with a chelate.

Chlorosis: Discolouration of plant tissue caused by a loss of chlorophyll. It typically shows as a yellow colour, but may range from pale green to almost white.

Coefficient: A number describing the relation between two other numbers or objects.

Colloids: Very small particles (less than 0.002 mm diameter) of clay or organic matter. Colloids carry a negative charge and are responsible for most of the nutrient-holding capacity of the soil.

Complex: To combine with a single metal ion at several different places, as with a chelate.

Correlated: Related to one another. For example, an increase in crop yield could be correlated to the amount of fertilizer added.

Denitrification: The conversion of nitrate (NO_3^-) to nitrogen gas (N_2) or nitrogen oxides (NO_x) by bacteria. This occurs under conditions of low oxygen and can result in considerable loss of available nitrogen to the atmosphere.

Desorb: To remove an ion from the surface it was adsorbed to. Usually accomplished by adding an excess of ions, which desorb the others from the clay surfaces.

DTPA: A chelate used as a soil test extractant for zinc and other micronutrients and as a carrier for micronutrient fertilizers (diethylenetriaminepentaacetic acid).

EDTA: A chelate used as a soil test extractant for zinc and other micronutrients and as a carrier for micronutrient fertilizers (ethylenediaminetetraacetic acid).

Equilibrium: Many chemical reactions can operate in both directions, so that in the end there is a mixture of the initial reactants and the final products in balance. The most common example of this type of reaction in soil is the adsorption of cations onto negatively charged soil particles. Some cations always remain in solution, and these are in balance, or equilibrium, with the cations held on the soil particles. There is a constant movement of cations between the solution and the soil particles, but the average concentrations do not change.

Extractant: A solution used in soil fertility testing to extract nutrients from the soil in proportion to the amount available to plants growing in that soil. No single extractant is appropriate for all nutrients or for all soil types.

Fixation: 1. The reduction of atmospheric nitrogen, which is not available to plants, to ammonium by microbial action. 2. The tie-up of potassium between the layers of some clay minerals (vermiculite and smectite), rendering it unavailable or slowly available to plants.

Grade: The percentage content of total nitrogen (N), available phosphate (P_2O_5) and soluble potash (K_2O) stated in that sequence as hyphenated numbers arranged horizontally and including zero if applicable. The grade of urea 46% nitrogen is 46-0-0. The grade represents minimum guarantees in whole numbers for materials and mixes. But the grade of a custom blend (customer formula fertilizers) can be stated in percentage to the second decimal (e.g. 19.25-19.21-19.27).

Guaranteed analysis: Also referred to as guarantees, should be described as guaranteed minimum analysis, except for chlorine (in tobacco fertilizers) where the maximum percentage must be guaranteed. Guarantees are expressed in terms of the chemical element, except for available phosphate (P_2O_5) and soluble potash (K_2O).

Hygroscopic: Attracting and absorbing water out of the atmosphere. Many fertilizer ingredients are hygroscopic and will cake because of the moisture they absorb when exposed to the atmosphere.

ICP: Inductively Coupled Plasma Emission Spectrometry.

Immobilization: The incorporation of nutrients into microbial tissue and organic matter, rendering it temporarily or permanently unavailable for plant uptake. Temporary immobilization of nitrogen can occur if organic materials with a high carbon content are added to the soil.

Ion: An atom or molecule carrying an electrical charge, either positive (cation) or negative (anion). Most are formed by the dissociation of acids or salts when dissolved in water (eg. $KCl \rightarrow K^+$, a cation, + Cl^-, an anion).

Leaching: The movement of ions down through the soil and eventually into groundwater, with the movement of water through the soil. Leaching occurs only when there is a net downward movement of water (usually late fall to spring) and ions present in the soil solution. Nitrates, sulphates and chlorides are the ions most susceptible to leaching.

Lodging: Crops that lean over or lie flat on the ground because of stalk breakage or inadequate roots. Cereals may lodge because of excess nitrogen.

M: Abbreviation for mole. One mole is the number of molecules with a weight in grams equivalent to their atomic weights. In other words, one mole of hydrogen (atomic weight = 1) weighs one gram. A one molar solution (1M) contains one mole of a compound dissolved in one litre of water.

Mineralization: The release of nutrients from organic matter as it is broken down by microbial action.

Mitscherlich equation: One form of equation that is used to describe the response of crop yield to added fertilizer or to soil test. It never reaches a maximum value.

Mycorrhizae: Symbiotic fungi that colonize roots of many crop species, effectively extending the root system and increasing the absorption of nutrients, especially phosphorus. Word comes from Latin mycos for fungus and rhizae for root.

N-P-K: Denotes the grade guarantees. In formulation calculations it is common usage to use the phosphorus symbol (P) to mean available phosphate (P_2O_5) and the potassium symbol (K) to mean soluble potash (K_2O).

pH: A measurement of the acidity or alkalinity of a solution. The pH scale is from 0 to 14. A pH of 7 is neutral. Values below 7 are acid and values above 7 are alkaline. Most soils fall in a range from pH 5 to 8.

Phosphorus index: An indicator of the risk of surface water enrichment with P from runoff from agricultural land. It takes into account proximity to water, land management and erosion potential as well as P soil test and fertilization to assess risk.

Phloem: Interconnected hollow cells (vascular tissue) extending from the leaves through the stems to the roots and fruits. Water and dissolved nutrients can move in both directions in the phloem. This is the pathway for redistributing sugars and proteins within the plant, as well as mobile nutrients.

Potash: In the fertilizer industry, the word potash is used to mean either K_2O (potassium oxide), to measure the potassium content, or KCl (muriate of potash), to identify the fertilizer material.

Prill: A small granule of urea or ammonium nitrate. The name is derived from the method of producing the granule.

Quadratic equation: A form of equation used to describe the response of crop yield to added fertilizer. It reaches a maximum value and then begins to drop off as the fertilizer rate is increased.

Salt index: An index of the relative solubilities of different fertilizer ingredients, by total weight. There is no critical level, but the higher the salt index, the more risk of injury to seeds or roots when the fertilizer is in contact with these plant parts. The index is expressed in relation to sodium nitrate, which is given a value of 100.

Sodic: A soil with the majority of the cation exchange complex occupied by sodium. These soils are characterized by large shrinking and swelling and very poor structural stability when wet.

Soluble potash: That portion of the potash, expressed as potassium oxide (K_2O), that is soluble in aqueous ammonium oxalate, aqueous ammonium citrate, or water, according to an applicable AOAC international method.

Suspension: A mixture of finely ground solid material and water or a solution, which is agitated to keep the solid material suspended in the liquid. Higher concentrations of fertilizer materials can be carried in a suspension than in a true solution.

Tilth: The structure and friability of the soil; the ease of producing a desirable seedbed from the soil.

Volatilization: The loss of a vapour, usually ammonia, to the air from a solid material that has been applied to the soil surface.

Xylem: Hollow tubes extending from the roots to the leaves and fruiting bodies of a plant. Water and dissolved nutrients flow only up the xylem. Most nutrients entering plants travel through the xylem.

INDEX